Social Media Marketing
Affiliate Marketing
Passive Income Ideas
2020

3 Books in 1

Build a Brand, Become an Influencer, and Explode Your Business with Facebook, Twitter, YouTube & Instagram

Table of Contents

Your Free Gift

As a way of saying thanks for your purchase, I wanted to offer you two free bonuses - *"The Fastest Way to Make Money with Affiliate Marketing"* and *"Top 10 Affiliate Offers to Promote"* cheat sheets, exclusive to the readers of this book.

To get instant access just, go to:

https://theartofmastery.com/chandler-free-gift

Inside the cheat sheets, you will discover:

- The fastest way to start generating income with affiliate marketing

- My top 10 favorite affiliate offers to promote for high recurring commissions
- Access to a FREE live training where you will learn:
- how one affiliate marketer built a $500,000 a month business all while traveling the world...
- The 3-step system to eliminate risk and instability in your online business
- The 7 biggest mistakes affiliates make in making money online
- How tech companies are giving away <u>FREE MONEY</u> to help you start
- And much more...

Social Media Marketing 2019

How to Reach Millions of Customers without Wasting Time and Money – Proven Ways to Grow Your Business on Instagram, YouTube, Twitter, and Facebook

Introduction

At the time of writing this book, 40% of the world's population has access to the Internet, 1.9 billion websites have been created, 43 million photos were uploaded on Instagram, 3.7 billion videos watched on YouTube, and 2.4 billion people are active Facebook users. In essence, social media, with the combined power of the Internet, has immense capabilities to influence, change, and spark ideas all around the world.

To benefit from the wonderful realm of social media, a marketer needs to build a clear strategy, thus taking into account the targets you want to achieve, the goals, who your customer base is, and what your competitors are doing. There are plenty of social media platforms out there: all of it comes free and warrants easy registration- it doesn't take much nowadays, except for your email address and a relevant password.

But with all the options available to you, which one is the right one for you? Understanding the fundamentals of social media marketing is extremely important. Just because they are free and easy to register does not mean you need to jump on the bandwagon of every available account out there.

In this book, you will learn the very basics of the most accepted social media platforms in the world. You will also read about prominent case studies that have shaped businesses today, and you will also acquire how to create a social media marketing strategy among other essentials.

Before we begin, a few fundamentals are vital, so you understand what it is that social media specifically entails. These fundamentals will help build a strong foundation in your social media marketing strategy, which will serve to create a strong brand, relate to your customers, and ultimately, yield the profits you are seeking!

10 Fundamentals of Social Media Marketing

- **Listening to Your Audience**

One of the most important foundations of any marketing strategy, be it social media or conventional marketing techniques, involves listening to your target market. How do you listen? Many social media platforms nowadays provide 'Insights,' which give you statistics of where they are from, their interests, who they are, what do they identify with, and so on. Once you have gathered these details, you can create content that is tailored to their interests and needs and then spark conversations that better lead to sales.

- **Focusing on specialized content**

Too much of fluff from any brand will cause people to unfollow you or unsubscribe. Specialized content is what you need here because it builds a strong brand. So, instead of saying things like 'a one-stop solution for printing,' craft your message clearly and cleverly with something like 'exclusive purveyor of premium letterpress invitations and bespoke printing services.' Sounds classy, doesn't it**?**

- **You want quality, not quantity**

Sure, having 10,000 followers is a big deal, but what if only

1,000 of them read, share, like, and talk about your content? When you craft quality content, you'll attract quality readership and followers to your accounts and these connections will not disappear.

- **Patience is Virtue**

When you open a social media account, be ready to commit to the long haul to achieve quality followers. Sure, you can pay for sponsored content, but when you first start your accounts, having generic views, likes, and followers will help you understand who your targeted audience is, what sites they frequently visit, what hashtags they use, and what their spending habits are.

- **Work to Build**

Building an audience online is essential, and you'd get free publicity! If they like what they read, they'll likely share it with their own audiences whether it's through their own social media accounts or blogs and website. Sharing and discussing content enables you to reach new entry points and give Google more ways to find you. For example, if you type in natural skin care, the least likely brand to pop would be Sephora, but there it is, among the top 10 Google searches. You'd have thought that maybe Aesop or Kiehl's or even Origins would make the list. The reason why Sephora is up there is because of the many entry points their customer base choose to associate the brand by their postings, comments, and images.

- **Social Media Influencers**

Social Media Influencers, formerly known as bloggers, are the people you want to associate with your brand. They already have the quality audiences, and they are most likely already interested in your product, business, or service. Connect with them- don't shun them like what the Vogue editors did. Build relationships with your influencers- they will share your content with their followers, multiplying your reach, and making your brand more down-to-earth and accessible.

- **Adding Value to your Conversation**

If all you do is promote and promote your products and services, talk about your flash salespeople will probably stop listening. Part of social media marketing is also sharing, liking, and being involved in topics related to your brand as well as jumping on the bandwagon of viral trends, political, or social events that are happening in your country and in the world as well as corresponding to your audiences. You must add value to your online conversations and activities because value will further develop and sustain relationships with your online audience.

- **Acknowledging your audience**

Building online relationships reflect one of the surest ways of online marketing success. Of course, there is no point reaching out to every person that tags you or comments- you might just create a storm! But once in a while, where valid (and really use your discretion on this tip), it is proper to respond to your audience, especially when they've asked questions or have constructive suggestions.

- **Be Accessible**

Publishing your content on the first week of the month and then not posting anything for the next three months will not do you any favors. To be relevant and accessible, you need to post content at a good pace. Be consistent but do not over-share (this tactic can also cause you to lose your fan base). If followers see too little or too much from you, they will not hesitate to unfollow you. It only takes one click.

- **Create Reciprocity**

In order to ensure your content is shared, you need to do the same for your influencers as well. A portion of the time you spend on social media should be given to sharing and talking about what other content, that is being published on the World Wide Web, your influencers' sites as well as your audiences.

- **Up and coming Social Media Platforms to Watch in 2019**

As a 21st century marketer, spotting new trends and identifying the next big social media platform is paramount. You need to know what is out there in the digital world, how you can utilize these tools, what your competition is doing, and how you can reach your prospects and customers using these new tools. Here are three platforms that are set to flourish in 2019:

1- VERO

Instagram's main contender where digital photo sharing is concerned is VERO. This app allows users to share TV, movies, books, music, places, links, and photos. It also helps you open up 'collections' to build a better individual profile. Vero is an excellent tool for designers and artists who want to share their own art with a fanbase. For now, there are no ads on Vero, only content. You can also set who you can share your content with using these four options: 1) friends 2) close friends 3) acquaintances and 4) followers. Superb ways to offer you better privacy!

Vero has incredible potential to become like the greats of Instagram, with more added values. This app is divided at the top beginning with a 'search' function that users can use to look up content within Vero. It also has a next button on the dashboard which shows your connections, photos, followers, and also has links to your requests, posts, and other settings. Vero's 'Collection' feature enables you to divide your content into links, music, photos, videos, books, and places. You also have a tab for notifications as well as a chat section. You can decide who gets to see what posts with just a swipe of your finger. This unique feature of Vero enables you to create and share in different ways and reflects what gives it the potential to be the next big thing in social media!

What's in it for Marketers?

Since no ads are shown on Vero, this would mean that this tool could be used as a research and discovery platform. Marketers can employ it to uncover what matters to their wider customer base or even gain inspiration for new ad campaigns.

2- MUSICAL.LY

Musical.ly is seen as an alternative to Snapchat/Vine. Built in China, Musical.ly sets itself apart from Snapchat by focusing on 15 seconds to 1-minute videos. Users choose soundtracks to accompany their videos, apply speed effects, as well as filters to enhance the content. With Musical.ly, users can create short 'live moments' and interact with other users through the 'Ask a Question' feature, 'Duet,' and 'Best Fan Forever.'

When you get on the app, you'd see a host of videos which you can swipe on to the next to continue viewing and tap on the heart to like it. You can also click on the chat button to leave comments or click the arrow button to share it on other social media channels, via text messaging as well as email.

What's in it for Marketers?

Musical.ly is a great alternative to Snapchat and Vine because it offers the best of both apps. It also has a more connected community and additional features to edit videos. For marketers, these 'snackable' videos offer a new and exciting opportunity to engage with an audience who prefer short snippets via video content.

3- STEEMIT

Many touts it as an alternative to Reddit. Steemit is run on the Steem blockchain using STEEM cryptocurrency, enabling Steemit to store content in an immutable blockchain ledger. It also enables the platform to reward users for their contribution using Steem digital tokens. Steem tokens can be integrated for posting, voting and curating, purchasing, and interest.

Through posting, users gain upvotes from community members. Depending on how many upvotes you get, you receive a portion of the rewards pool.

While voting and curating content, if you discover a post and upvote it before anyone else does or before it becomes popular, you earn yourself a curation reward. This amount depends on the Steem Power you have.

In purchasing, users can also purchase Steem dollar tokens using Ether, BitShares tokens, or Bitcoins.

In Interest, STEEM tokens that are upgraded to Steem Power (SP) will be considered vested interest in the company, and it earns the user a small amount of interest in the form of additional Steem Power. For users to unlock this SP, they need to go through a power down process.

This platform looks at a different way to make money and may be a little ahead of its time. However, the idea of gaining money from posts and upvotes is definitely a lucrative deal.

What's in it for Marketers?

While limiting in customer base, this platform could gain some help in getting a robust marketing system. This opens up a brand-new era for a content competition where cryptocurrency is used to purchase things. Would it mean that marketers need to buy ad space with Steemit?

Bottom Line

For marketers, it is definitely an exciting time with ever-evolving technological advancements coming our way, and with each passing year, opening up increased opportunities to get people and extend your brand reach and engage with audiences in exciting ways. Being open to what's new and what's the latest will help you in your digital marketing endeavors and make marketing an exciting field to serve and innovate!

Chapter 1- Social Media and Its Prevalence in the 21st Century

According to recent research conducted by HubSpot, 90% of marketers confirm that using social media for marketing purposes has exponentially increased both business and brand exposure. Another research heralds that 66% of marketers who spend a total of 6 hours on social media each week achieve more leads.

Do these stats fascinate you? No matter what your product is and who you sell it to, social media used in marketing in today's 21st-century world can help you grow your brand in both depth and breath. You probably already have a Facebook page for your brand, and you're here because you want to continue expanding your social media presence.

If you're planning to convince your business associate to open a Twitter account or give a presentation to your board of directors to increase marketing budget for social media or you're simply wanting to explore other social media opportunities, this chapter will give you the necessary stats need to understand and convince yourself and your business on why social media is important.

Driving the right kind of Web traffic to your sites

1. An effective tool to get traffic

No matter what your industry, or audience, or segment you are trying to reach, a large chunk of these leads and customers come from social media engagement. Social media gives you access to all these customers. It boosts your traffic each time you have new content on your site. Most users know of new content on your website or blog not through Google but through social engagement. Customers only know of new content if they are in search of your product or service. Social media posts give marketers the opportunity to 'speak' to the public and get them to discover your new web content and click on your site. These posts show up primarily on your followers' feeds and those interested in your product, so the kind of traffic that you receive is extremely targeted.

2. Boosting your site's SEO

Pages that are consistently receiving traffic will be identified quickly by search engine spiders; whereas pages that do not receive traffic are forgotten, ignored, and lose their rankings on search engines. Social media helps by diverting traffic to your optimized pages, which will help push your SEO rankings much faster. Activity on social media can be as simple as re-sharing your content, liking it, or even tagging someone else on the comments section. Creating fresh, new content is vital but you can also re-share other evergreen content at least once a month. With applications such as Hootsuite, scheduling posts are not as tiresome as you think it is. You can schedule posts for an entire month!

3. The best way to use quotes from experts

Using quoted experts in your content can help drive a killer social media presence. You can email the link of your blog post to them or post it on your social accounts and the tag said expert, which in turn, encourages them to share it on their paces. This tactic creates higher visibility and ensures that fans and followers of the expert see your post, which in turn, makes them retweet or reshare your content. Some of these new found audience users will end up bring your followers, which then drive traffic back to your website.

4. You understand your customers better

Twitter and Instagram make for an effective marketing tool partly based on the channels of interaction provided to its customer base. Brands that want to engage with their fans and followers need to read tweets and status updates, especially the ones with tags. You gain immense insight into the daily lives of your consumers and their behaviors. You also receive answers to these following:

- *What products are purchased and why?*
- *What do they like doing in their free time?*
- *What posts do they share and why?*
- *What kind of websites do they frequently visit?*

As a marketer, you gain plenty of marketing benefits in understanding your customers. This strategy will help you write better content, more compelling posts, and more engaging information. These benefits, however, extend beyond marketing. You create brand loyalty and credibility, so it helps you identify customer pain points, generate a loyal following, refine product strategies, and improve sales conversions.

5. Build a relationship with your audience

When you start embarking on developing your social media marketing strategy, you may be up against a few challenges. Plenty of companies starts hard selling to their consumers, which inundates their followers with discount offer codes and new product announcements, even before consumers could even warm up to the brand. When their accounts do not bring the desired traffic, these brands assume that these networks aren't a good fit for them or social media isn't the place to focus their efforts.

Customers of the 21st century do not want to hear constant sales pitches; instead, they want authentic engagement. As marketers, you need to stop seeing social networks as just another channel to pitch your sales. You need to look at it as a way of connecting to your audience and transforming the story behind your brand.

Apart from connecting with your audience, you can also use social media to connect with experts, influencers, and industry leaders, thus enhancing your status as an authoritative expert and credible source of information for your industry. Over time, you are more than just a brand- you are part of a community.

This change of perception also leads towards higher ROI, which means you'll also get plenty of exposure. With higher ROI, you obtain more exposure and with more exposure, come leads and new leads turn into followers. These followers turn into potential customers.

6. You can target and retarget

Social media offers marketers highly targeted ad opportunities which you can customize based on your customer's needs. Facebook ads, for instance, enable you to target customers based on age, location, industry, education level, and user behavior.

7. You amplify your presence at events and get big-time media coverage

No matter what metric you employ to measure an event success, it all boils down to effective promotion, and this promotion always benefits from a social media presence that is active.

If you want to get more signups for your seminar, you can post it on Facebook and Linkedin. What if you want to get donations for your fundraiser? When you target your posts, you can attract the right kind of donors looking to put their money where it's worth. Do you want high-quality leads? Leverage for social media presence by using the right influencers to spread your message.

8. Social media is the key to customer service

If there is a problem or issue with your service or product, your customers are going to contact you via your social media channels, and they expect you to solve it immediately. Quick response time is not good enough. A study conducted by Sprout Social found that customers expect a response from companies within four hours. However, the average response time is 10 hours.

When this happens, you are not only causing a minor irritant to your customers, it will also affect your profits in the long run. Another study conducted via Twitter showed that customers are much more willing to pay more when airlines respond to their tweets within an average time of 5 minutes.

This preference is not an isolated case study. Various study and research have shown that consumers show better brand appreciation and loyalty and are more willing to spend when their requests and complaints are swiftly handled. An engaging social media presence is vital in this day and age, as it will help keep your customers happy and loyal, so you can retain a positive public image.

9. Create and build on a strong brand loyalty

A continuous and active social media presence has a more loyal following of customers. When you engage with the public on social media, you not only increase your brand presence but you also build on your rapport and spare enough time connection. You provide your followers with useful and engaging information without requesting them to do anything in return. This indirectly tells your customers that you value them and you care about them. You see them as humans, not just as customers. When this happens, customers will see you as a brand that cares, one that champions values, has personality, and clear vision. In a world with plenty of advertising noise, strong brand loyalty makes a huge difference.

10. Your competition is already social

Depending on how big the company is, smaller brands have at least one social media presence, whereas, bigger brands have multiple presences on social media. Likewise, a study by AdWeek reiterated that ninety-one percent of retail brands have at least two social media platforms to engage with customers. What hope do you have if you have no social media presence at all? Don't be intimidated by going social because half the time, most brands aren't doing social media right anyway. Big brands usually have a more mature and thought-out process, but SMEs usually don't. In contrast, they start with a few social channels simply because it's cheap and also because everyone else is doing it- which is not wrong.

It's best to be really engaging in one social media rather than to randomly post anywhere. If you take the time to develop your brand presence and voice, respond to messages and post regularly- you can build a following that your competitors cannot match even if they've got the most sophisticated software or if they have been in it longer than you have.

11. Competing at an almost level-playing field
Opening a social media account of any kind is free- we all know that. Marketers can dedicate either the time to manage a fleet of accounts or outsource them. For example, big brands have advantages such as better name recognition, increased budgets, and of course, a team to post across multiple channels, create and curate beautifully designed posts, and generally have more influencers who would want to be connected to the brand.

But where smaller brand names are concerned, one thing that these brands do have is authenticity. If you are an SME with local ties to your community or even an entrepreneur looking to create social changes, a work-at-home parent with an inspiring story- all of this offers a new and exciting brand presence for consumers looking for authenticity. You do not need to beat your competitors at the social media game; rather, you want to find a niche in your connection to build your brand.

12. You can also ride on what's trending

Riding on current trends and engaging with a story that fits perfectly with your brand while everyone is paying attention can lead to viral posts. Viral posts lead to traffic boosts, press coverage on your company, and greater visibility for your brand. This concept is called newsjacking, where you ride on what is trending while it's still considered breaking news. Newsjacking at the right time means that your voice is one of the first few heads. In sum, to be always at the forefront to get the relevant posts and designs that relate to what is trending, you need an active social media team.

Not only do you need to post something that relates to trending news, you need the team to track and react quickly to other current events. Your current followers, news reporters, blog writers, online news outlets, and influencers will see you.

Increasing your Sales and ROI through Strategic Social Media Marketing

13. Getting more sales

Social media marketing increases your sales and ROI. Period. In fact, any form of communication to the masses helps in increasing sales and ROI, but with social media, you get more than that. Here are some stats- 70% of B2C businesses mention that they have acquired new customers via Facebook and at least 84% of VPs and CEOs use social media to help them make purchasing decisions.

When you're always popping up at your customer's newsfeed, the prevalent of sales is much greater and more often to take place. Apart from increasing brand presence, it also influences a customer's choices of purchasing products or services.

14. You can work on becoming an authoritative expert and make your mark as an industry expert

Answering questions on social media such as on Quora as well as on Facebook or interacting on Reddit even- all of these provide perfect opportunities to showcase your expertise in the subject as well as show your leadership in the industry. This strategy will regularly result in your answers showing up on Google searches and on other social platforms, which means other users will retweet and reshare your posts, or refer it to friends and colleagues. These new leads will create better traction to your site and increase sales. All of this success just by answering a few questions online!

15. Getting your ROI skyrocket through social media

When you boost the right posts on your social media, you attract better and more traffic at the fraction of what it would cost you to run Google ads. Google Adwords, as of 2018, costs $1.20 per click for travel and tourism and up to $5.27 for employment and education. You could be paying up to $50 or more depending on the keywords you target. This cost per acquisition, the number of money brands spend on ads just to get one single customer, is huge.

Using boosted posts, you have better control over how and when your messages can be promoted. In turn, you receive the opportunity to use your marketing budget wisely and strategically on the content that matters. Posts that are targeted efficiently can send the right kind of target to your retail or service website, through Facebook or Pinterest or any social media platforms for that matter. What is your spend? It's $0.12 for each click, and you get 20 times more traffic than you ever would with AdWords.

This also means you can spend your marketing budget strategically by focusing on posts that matter the most to your followers. Targeted boosted posts on social media can definitely send traffic to Pinterest and Facebook for as little as $0.12 per click, and you get ten times more traffic than you would from AdWords.

16. It's always fun with social media!
Don't worry and get overwhelmed with all the information you are receiving in this chapter and even in this book. Social media is fun. Just like everything else in life, you need to know the ground rules and the basic necessities of what works and what doesn't.

Social media is a great place to create a new, vibrant ambiance for your customers- a place where your customers can get a friendlier, personal connection with you. Use social media as a form of brand expression, of a means of interacting with them, and also to build real connections. These connections are incredibly rewarding.

Remember that your audience on social media knows what social media should be. They interact with other brands too and expect more or less from you, or even better. Nobody wants to keep being bombarded with continuous sales pitches and only talk about how wonderful your company is and why your brand is the next best thing.

By showing them a more human side of you, interacting genuinely, responding to them when there are issues and concerns- all of these suggestions help you to market your brand without even knowing.

Chapter 2- 12 Social Media Marketing Trends to Follow in 2019

You kick-started your social media onslaught in 2018, used whatever resources you had, and now you're looking into having another successful year in marketing your company. What can you do in 2019? What are social media users seeking in this New Year?

Part of creating your marketing goals and crafting new content for 2019 involves understanding the trends that pick up every year to ensure that whatever strategy you create, it is a successful and fresh one, not an outdated approach. Now is the perfect time to review your existing strategy and see what can be improved, what can be introduced, and what worked the past year. Here is a closer look at the trends of the year and how they will affect 2019 to help you craft better tactics and engagement for your users.

Engagement is more important than ever

Earlier on in 2018, Facebook clarified that their focus for the upcoming year would be on more meaningful interactions and this emphasis is reflected in their updated algorithm. The algorithm is programmed to look for content that is genuine and meaningful. All of this transformation came about by Page Managers themselves, who want to create better and more insightful content that inspires, appeals, and engages.

Algorithms are becoming even more sophisticated: there's no shortcut to genuine engagement. You can't get away with getting people to just like, share, and comment on your post. You need to cut down on engagement baiting techniques in 2019 or you will risk losing your existing social media clientele. To win the right kind of engagement, as marketers, you need to start thinking of an engagement strategy that is improved on every channel to continue reaching your followers.

Influencer marketing and the rise of micro-influencers

Will influencers still comprise a big chunk of social media engagement? Yes, influencer marketing will continue growing because brands will continue seeking them for their campaigns. So long as consumers look towards them for inspiration, reviews, motivation- influencer marketing will continue. However, as big-time influencers become increasingly expensive, especially for small and medium-sized brands, companies are looking at micro-influencers to bridge this gap between having the right budget and being interested in influencer marketing.

Micro-influencers may not have the same outreach as celebrities and other influencers, but they have a tighter and bigger influence on their existing followers. For a brand, a micro-influencer with even 40k followers is already an audience.

Sometimes, it also depends on what kind of product you're trying to get engagement for. For instance, a rising makeup artist with 40k followers would have a bigger impact and deeper influence on their followers compared to a well-known celebrity makeup artist who's asking price to speak about a product could be above a 20k budget. Micro influencers or even nano-influencers (those with a following of 10k) may have a more passionate and loyal audience who listens to what their influencer says and has a higher probability of influencing a purchase.

Both Nano and micro influencers do not need a huge budget; however, in order for you to use these types of influencers, you need to spend a little more time on research to find the right kind of influencer for your brand. These types of influencers would also be seeking out a partnership that matches their needs and values and this could also lead to a longer partnership. Nano and micro influencers are easier to reach and interact with because they don't need to deal with thousands and thousands of messages each day- unless they end up becoming an overnight sensation.

Social media for sales enablement

We know that social media is already helping customers in the product discovery phase. Brands can continue promoting their services and products using social media channels and customers will continue finding of them through organic or paid posts and proceed with making purchases. Social media was first used as engagement and awareness is now transitioning towards sales enablement and consideration of products via the business funnel.

Based on the 2018 Internet Trends report by Mary Meeker, 55% of respondents have discovered a product via their social media browsing and consistent reviews later, purchased said product. Facebook is one of the fastest growing channels that enable this product discovery, followed by Instagram and Pinterest.

In 2019, brands will continue this streak of wholesome opportunity to continue benefiting from this trend. But in order to maintain the benefits and success, they need to improve their social strategy. Sales pitches are not necessary all the time in your messaging. What you want to do is to tell a story and increase this consideration of purchasing. When someone discovers you online, it's up to you to give them a smooth experience to make purchasing easier.

AI and customer service

Another emerging trend for social media in 2019 reflects the oncoming bots and automated messaging that have been creeping into people's current digital sphere as of 2018. Social media has made it extremely easy for customers to get in touch with a brand, but this access also means that response or feedback is crucial to be fast. Chatbots and automated messaging are extremely popular through Facebook's Messenger when brands realize the potential of additional customer support.

However, not all customers are on board with reaching a brand via social media, but the adoption rate is improving all thanks to the programming of the latest bot experiences as well as enhanced intelligence. In 2019, brands will invest in programming bots in ways that make them seem as authentic as possible, from giving them their own personalities or even predicting customers" questions.

AI can also come in handy when provisioning messaging to frequently asked questions by customers. Messaging can be set up by brands to keep their customers satisfied while also saving plenty of time in having to answer the same questions all the time. AI will become part of the high adoption of marketing essentials by brands in 2019 mostly to enhance customer service and also to give customers the answers to what they are looking for as quickly as possible.

Stories, stories, stories

No matter where you look, you will find content in vertical formats popularly known in the 21st century as Stories. They are on Instagram, Snapchat, Facebook, and WhatsApp and off late- YouTube and LinkedIn. This visual content, which usually lasts 24 hours, is a global trend for people of all ages, wanting to show their life in a day, even for a short while.

To date, there are about 400 million people consuming Stories on Instagram alone, on a day-to-day basis. Advertisers are aware of how prevalent Instagram Stories are among social media users and Instagram Stories ads are extremely effective. Snapchat and Facebook are runner ups to this kind of hype and demand.

The end of fake followers

In the social media arena, Instagram is currently the most popular of apps. Many influencers currently begin on

Instagram and have benefited from the app's success. However, as time passed, it became no secret that some Instagram accounts have increased their followers' rate artificially just to boost their popularity. Plenty of services provide fake followers for a certain fee, and Instagram knew they just needed to stop this.

Recently, Instagram made the announcement of removing inauthentic follows, likes, and comments from accounts that use third-party apps to boost their popularity. Specific machines and algorithms have been built to identify these activities in order to prevent them from happening again in the future. This effort is undoubtedly a huge step for Instagram in maintaining their reputation as a popular and authentic social networking site for brands and people to mingle in a growing community based on genuine interest and like-minded engagement.

In 2019, having a huge number of followers will not be the only denominator to measure actual influence and engagement that you have with your community. As a brand, you don't need to keep wanting to increase your followers; instead, engage with existing ones. Instead of focusing on driving users to like and follow you, focus your efforts on spending time in growing your community organically.

Messaging will grow even more

In 2019, messaging apps will continue to dominate the year as they have already surpassed social media in terms of usage back in 2018. Users are moving beyond posting their entire lives on social media and instead prefer more private means of engagement, to connect to their friends and also to stay in touch with their most favored brands.

This private messaging platform is something marketing need to take note of, as it helps you with the much-desired engagement and to understand how users use messaging apps. For now, WeChat, WhatsApp, Viber, and Messenger take up a big portion of the private messaging market.

Data breaches make trust more important than ever

Remember the data breach of Facebook in 2018? There is a growing lack of trust for social media networks and people are moving towards messaging apps as it makes them feel more secure. Privacy concerns continue to rise and social media platforms are waking up to the truth that trust is extremely crucial among users and platforms needs to be more mindful about how data is used.

For brands, this also means that you need to be part of the discussion on privacy and build on it to ensure that your audience continues trusting you. Brands that make the effort to be transparent with their audience have a higher opportunity to retain existing clients and attract new ones. This transparency concerns admitting when mistakes are made or updating audiences for any changes with your systems or updates on Privacy Policies.

Narrowing down the focus on specific channels

As social media marketing becomes much more competitive, marketers have come to the realization that instead of opening every available social platform to connect, you instead focus on the platforms that are best-performing for your brand. Brands these days choose where they want to start off with, instead of choosing to open a Facebook page just because everyone else is doing it.

Some brands start with Pinterest or even Medium while some just focus on Instagram. It's more important to stick to where your audiences prefer interacting with you. Kayla Itsines, for example, only uses Instagram. How To Cake It started off with only YouTube. The point is you do not need to broadcast the same messages on all platforms when you don't see the success in it. If you are using a variety of platforms, then you need to place the right messages on its specific platforms.

There's no need to worry about limiting your platforms to only two channels and worry about losing audiences. The best way to see which platform brings you the needed ROI is to test it out and see which is worth your time and effort. Just spend your time and money on channels that are worth your attention. The more distractions you have, the less time you will have to focus. Analyzing your audience will help you decide which platforms and channels work best towards your business goals. This New Year, you still have time to review your performance on social media and set your goals with the right platforms.

The ad spend is increasing but you'll need to consider ad saturation

In 2019, social media advertising will continue to rise as it has in the last few years. However, with the multiple channels to advertise on, marketers have to decide on which objectives can be focused on the right channels and use paid ads for the specific channels to increase success.

For instance, Instagram has become a favorite for advertising since Facebook has become saturated with existing competition. Brands are more inclined to advertise on Instagram stories and feeds as they seem to bring in better ROI, but as soon as other brands keep advertising on Instagram, it may start increasing the costs to promote your business on this same app.

2019 will continue to see marketers increase their social ad spend and Instagram will continue to be the crowd favorite in 2019. That said, you cannot rely too much on just one platform whether on paid or organic growth. Your marketing strategy must be in line with your goals and objectives so your ads will be placed on the right platforms to hit the right targets with the right type of audience.

Videos, podcasts, and live streaming

Before social media blew up on the Internet, blogs were the main go-to Internet space for updates, for news, and for information. Some blogs are still popular based on their contents such as lifestyle blogs, recipe blogs, and blogs catered to politics and government issues. Long-form posts specific to certain types of content still bring in readers so long as they are properly formatted to facilitate the reading experiences on a variety of devices.

The consumption of content will continue to rise but not just in written text. Videos and photos and podcasts will gain rapid rise, especially with the incoming IGTV and crowd-favorite YouTube. Even Facebook has adjusted its algorithm to encourage the use of video posts and GIFs to show up on our feeds. Video marketing, especially those under 1 minute, is becoming more attractive and appealing for brands. Eventually, videos will take over the social media world as people have more access to watch videos on all their various devices. 2019 will enable brands to continue experimenting with different video formats and expanding on these various versions:

- **Short videos** are the favored type of video content at this point. Plenty of brands use them now for ads, and they sell even better if the videos come with captions. Short videos are those made in less than 1 minute. Consumers want to know what it is and why they should get your product or service in less than 1 minute.
- **Vertical videos** as seen on Instagram Stories as well as on Snapchat. These types of videos are extremely popular for many different types of content such as recipes, how to videos, and even makeup or workouts. This format will continue growing simply because you can skip to the next storyboard, and it improves viewing experiences because it gives viewers the flexibility to skip or continue viewing the story.

- **Long videos** have the capability of powerful storytelling. This feature is an especially tricky format because you need to hook your audience's attention immediately in the first few seconds to keep and retain their engagement. These video formats, whether it's YouTube, Facebook, or even IGTV needs to be interesting enough to convince viewers to watch till the end of the video and view the call to action.
- **Live streaming** is a popular trend for events as users themselves turn into publishers and broadcasters, thus bringing audience viewership much closer. It works great if you can bring in influencers to your event and get them to live stream their experience of the event at a real time.

Apart from videos, podcasts are also a growing success especially combined with music apps such as Spotify. Audio content brings back the good ole' days of radio. Podcasts work effective for motivational speeches, talks, learning languages, and also catching up with stories and brands while you are on the go.

In 2019, marketers will be spending more time experimenting with podcasts to build their own personal brand or to offer more content to promote their services and products. Podcasts are special in the marketing and consumer sphere because their main focus is still on content rather than promotion. People subscribe to a podcast because they're interested in the content offered, not because of the promotions delivered by a person or product.

AR to become more mainstreamed

In 2019, you will see AR making a comeback together with social media. This will become more common in other channels as marketers continue to experiment with the use of this trend to offer more immersive content experiences and content consumption.

AR, or Augmented Reality, can provide brands with an even more engaging experience while making it fun for consumers. AR also presents an opportunity for brands to show off their personality and create content that leads to more actionable end results. If consumers are given a different way to experience a product or service, this choice will lead to better conversions and sales. Facebook is already at the forefront to dominate the field in AR, which means marketers can also look forward to experimenting with this potential.

Facebook has already announced the introduction of AR specific ads to make the social commerce sphere more immersive and appealing. With AR camera effects already being built in devices, customer experiences in the AR fields will continue improving, and it will be another way for brands to keep users on a specific platform.

Bottom Line

Social media in 2018 was the driving force in many of the world's changes from influencing politics, consumer purchasing behaviors, crowdfunding, and crowdsourcing and it will affect our futures even more than what we can predict now. Social media marketing will continue to focus on new technologies and also building a better relationship between brands and their customers.

So what do all these trends mean? As a marketer, do you have to jump in all these trends and spend money on them? The only way to navigate your way in between emerging tech, data breaches that nobody likes, and new and upcoming platforms, you need to:

- Understand your audience and put your money where it's worth
- Always review your social media marketing strategy
- Allocate budget and time to discovering new tools and tech
- Keep your focus on what works
- Continue building trust with your users at every campaign milestone

Chapter 3- Which Platforms Best Fit your Business in 2019?

So your company has been on Facebook and Instagram since the time it formed and now you're looking into other platforms to attract new audiences to your brand. Or maybe, you want to close one or two platforms which you feel is not getting the kind of traction you want and venture into something new. Whatever the case, you need to continue your social media presence, but in 2019, it's a matter of understanding which of these platforms are still lucrative and worth your time and money and which are not.

Plenty of social media strategies fail because companies prioritize the wrong platforms. If you open an account simply because other people are doing it, but if it is not pulling in the traction you want, you are wasting your time. Social media is fickle, so staying on top of the best practices and platforms takes time, a good strategy, as well as dedication.

So which platforms do you continue your efforts in and which should you call quits? Before you list on your social media platforms, you should ask yourself three key questions:

- Are you a B2C company, a B2B, or do you do both?
- Who is your target audience?
- What is your overall objective?

The answers to these questions are your main focus. When you have the answers to these questions, it will be a lot easier to flesh things out, so you can decide a minimum of two to a maximum of three platforms that you can dedicate to reaching out to your customers.

A solid two or three is ideal but if you have the support of a strong and active social media team, then by all means, go ahead and branch out to other platforms. But if you don't have this kind of luxury, better just stick to a maximum of 3 channels. Each chosen channel will take time to grow and develop. Think of it as a plant that you need to nurture, water, and fertilize to see fruitful results.

In this chapter, we'll examine at the best five social media platforms of 2019, their main audiences as well as the top industries for each of these channels.

1. Facebook

2. Twitter

3. Instagram

4. LinkedIn

5. Pinterest

Once you have the answers to the questions above, you're on your way towards crafting a successful social media strategy. If, however, you're still not sure or if you want a definite answer to your social media concerns, then you should get a social media audit done. Most of it is free, and it gives you a more personalized and immersive idea on data and recommendations.

1. Which one are you- B2C or B2B?

Identifying your company focus will impact the way you position your social media. The way social media is used in today's world is primarily for engagement. Where products and services are concerned, social media is used mainly to check out reviews, tutorials, finding out what's being talked about a certain product or service, how-tos, and so on. Those opting for social media are at the very top of the sales funnel, which means for marketing, you could be targeting your ads at the wrong stage in the buying process. Unless your product is in the impulse buy category, the possibility of users traveling down the sales funnel instead of going to the next post is next to none.

Identifying if you are B2C or B2B will help you aim your social media strategies. For instance, B2B strategies are usually geared towards increasing leads and generating interest in a brand.

2. Do you know who your target audience is? Answer these 10 questions:

Have you ever seen an ad that is so irrelevant to you? You probably would have if you are on social media. You get ads for pregnant moms when you are not pregnant; you get ads for herbal remedies for men when you aren't male. Whatever the ad may be, you can bet that there were times when you were the receiver of an ill-targeted ad. You're probably thinking i) these businesses just wasted money on me and ii) whoever is in charge of these ads needs to get a social media targeting lesson.

And you're right- these businesses are wasting their money. If they wrongly targeted you, they could have wrongly targeted many other users. So, how do you know who to target when you create your own strategies? Take out a piece of paper and answer these following questions:

- Where does your audience live?
- What is their age?
- Are they mostly females or males?
- How much do they usually earn?
- Do they own a house?
- What do they like to do?
- What are their jobs and where do they work?
- Do they have kids?
- What kind of problems do they face?
- What are their main sources of information?
- Who are the top paying customers and who are the most loyal?

From answering these questions, guess what- you've just created a profile of your average buyer. To help you a little bit more, you can use this simple tool by Facebook to profile your target audience: Facebook Audience Insights.

1. What is your main goal?

Are your goals aligned with your company's goals? When you talk about goals, do both teams and departments have the same idea of these goals?

When crafting your goals for social media specifically, you need to remind yourself that social media is an extremely visual platform. People go to these platforms to SEE things and not DO things. Just like how you purchase this book not to read it but to LEARN something.

The Top 6 Social Media Sites Best for Businesses in 2019

The table below gives you a brief idea of what each social media is about and who should post what kind of content.

These are some of the most popular social media, but there are plenty more out there such as Tumblr, Snapchat, Periscope, and so on.

It is always a good idea to explore each of these platforms because each is unique in one way or another. However, for more traction, audience reach, and access, Facebook, Twitter, and Instagram should be your top priority.

Platforms	Who Should Use It?	What is it great for?
Facebook	Everyone, of course! Even baby-boomers are at it.	All types of online content, events, ads

Platforms	Who Should Use It?	What is it great for?
Twitter	Everyone – from individuals, small businesses to large multinational corporations	Start, join, and lead conversations; converse directly with consumers, brands, and celebrities
Instagram	Food, Fashion, Fitness, Lifestyle, food, personalities, advocates, and luxury brands	Share visual content from images to gifs and short videos (less than 15 seconds)
LinkedIn	Businesses, influencers, Recruiters, and Job-Seekers	Company descriptions, Job ads, survey data, and research
YouTube	Brands with video content and ads, anyone giving explanations or sharing expertise	Short (1.5 minutes or less) video content
Pinterest	Fashion, Travel, food, design, home décor, makeup, and DIY- audience ratio is female 4: 1	Creative, visual content, Infographics

FACEBOOKGreat for: B2C as well as some B2B

Age and Gender: Between 25 – 55+, both men and women

At the end of 2018, at least 1.5 billion Facebook users logged on to Facebook on a daily basis with the most common age being 25 to 34-year-olds. Whether you despise Facebook for your personal profile, you still need one for your company even if it is not the main platform you choose to market on. You need a Facebook account simply because Facebook provides the local SEO signal. In other words, search engines look for your Facebook business profile to put out other local searches. The Facebook business profile pings your business to SEO.

TWITTER

Great for: B2C as well as for some B2B

Age and Gender:18 – 29, both men and women

Plenty of people thought Twitter was dying and heading in the same direction as MySpace. But thanks to plenty of events such as the US presidential elections , the solar eclipse of 2017, the Royal Weddings, the World Cup, and natural disasters, Twitter has proven time and again that it is an invaluable tool, especially for news and information and political rants all in 280 characters or less. Twitter is also proving itself to be an invaluable tool for brands to be used for customer service. Nike, Wendy's, Virgin Airlines, and even the British Royal Museum use Twitter to tweet their businesses and respond to customer service issues.

Twitter is an excellent tool to connect with the movers and shakers of your industry, thought leaders, politicians, and business owners at a more elegant scale and to give your brand a unique personality that reflects your products, your brand, and your creativity.

INSTAGRAM

Great for: Works extremely well for B2C, so you can try it on B2B, provided you have the right angle

Age and Gender: 18 – 35, mostly men and women

If you have a visual product, then Instagram is your best friend. Instagram is everything you like on Facebook but without the fluff.

Instagram is in its very essence, a photo app. When it first began, Instagram users randomly uploaded images to share but as Instagram becomes more sophisticated, so did its users. Now, you see curated, high-res photos, carefully timed and placed on the grid. With high-impact images, brand captures the imagination, the personality, and the spirit of their target audience through stunning visuals, hashtags, and stories. Facebook, as we all know, owns Instagram and you're required to have a Facebook account to open an Instagram account. This also means Instagram shares the same features and ad targeting options that you would find on Facebook which makes it an incredibly excellent option for brand engagement and awareness. To tell a story, you want high-quality images-nothing less, and please, stay away from stock photos. Nobody in 2019 is going to buy that. If you're going to post on Instagram, you'd better have access to high-quality photos that showcase your company and your brand and its people.

PINTEREST

Great for: B2C**Age and Gender:** 18 – 45, mostly women, but men are increasingly becoming part.

Pinterest begins as a hobbyist's platform to 'pin' inspiration from all over the internet. Whether you are planning a wedding, remodeling your car, starting out on your hydroponic garden, or learning to cook, there is a pinboard for you to explore. Most people have a Pinterest account even when they aren't planning anything or learning something- it's just a great place to have all your internet clippings nicely organized in virtual boards, which you can access anytime! Again, Pinterest is very much a visual platform: so if you a visual product or you offer services that involve visual planning- such as remodeling a car or even run a health and fitness business, this platform can inspire inspire, and vice versa! It is the beehive of social media.

So which social media platform should you choose for your business in 2019?

The answers to the three questions posed to you at the beginning of this chapter should already give you a direction of which platform to open up and concentrate your efforts in. However, sometimes, the most unconventional of platforms seem to work for some business provided they've found a niche content they'd like to target. For example, Instagram can be used to showcase a company's culture. Pinterest is mainly for motivational quotes and inspiration.

If you've found an angle for your content, then, by all means, go ahead and experiment with the social platforms you choose. However, if you don't see it bring in the kind of traction you want, end it.

You need to monitor, post, and respond on your platforms, so using platforms such as HootSuite and Sprout will make this easier.

On the other hand, you can also employ a large enough social media team to curate, create, post, monitor, and respond for your company's brand or you could also outsource this task to a social media marketing agency to do help you.

In sum, remember that social media platforms are exactly that- to be social. Keep this in mind when you strategize or you'll just cause a social media suicide for your brand.

Chapter 4- Instagram Marketing

Instagram opened up its new ad feature in 2015, utilizing Facebook advertising's system. With this, marketers now have the ability to reach a niche segment of the population, which is currently at 800 million users and growing. Instagram ads have become an avenue for brands looking to increase their engagement, and by extension, their profits, to the 500 million active users who use Instagram every day.

In this chapter, we will focus mostly on Instagram Ads. We will examine what and the whys of Instagram ads, so you gain a firm foundation to get you started on creating ads, measuring performance, and improving your ad results.

So, you've got your Instagram business account all set up and you're ready to get your marketing going. Excited to get started on all those Instagram campaigns which you're hoping are going to turn into sales numbers for your business? More than a million businesses and advertisers are already getting things done using Instagram, and it is evident because their campaigns are hard to miss. Here's the thing though, how do you know when you're spending far too much on your Instagram campaigns? The platform may be free, but the advertising isn't necessarily.

Advertising on Instagram has become such an indispensable marketing tool because it is among the simplest and most effective ways of reaching your target audience. Getting started on the platform, however, is an entirely different story, and it can be overwhelming if this is something you've never done before. There's a ton of information and things which you need to remember. It seems almost impossible to know whether you're covering all your bases. Not to worry though, because we will break it all down for you in this book as we sift through the information chapter by chapter.

Running a successful Instagram ad or marketing campaign can sometimes be a hit-or-miss process. There is an immense amount of pressure to ensure that the content you're creating is awesome enough that people want to share it, spread the word, and get involved. The content you created may seem perfect to you, but that doesn't necessarily mean that your audience will feel that, too. They may have a completely different view of it.

How Much Does It Cost to Advertise Anyway?

The cost of your Instagram advertising would depend on several factors. The demographics which you're targeting, the mobile device you're aiming to advertise on, whether you're targeting your ads to be on display during a major televised event or something, and even what day of the week you're planning on running your ad. All these factors will contribute to determining how much you end up spending on your advertising campaign. In turn, every marketer should know his or her Instagram demographics.

According to Sprout Social, for example, Instagram grew its everyday user numbers to 100 million users back in 2016 within a 6-month period. Given that there are more than 600 million users who are active daily on the platform, it's no wonder this social media platform just seems to be booming in popularity. When you know your demographics, you'll have much better insight into how you can apply your best marketing strategies and take advantage of its growing popularity.

Why use Instagram ads?

Since launching its ad platform in 2015, Instagram has driven more than one billion user actions to date. Just last year alone, advertising dollars have doubled and its advertiser base, which began at just a few thousands, is now at 500,000 advertisers.

In 2016, a survey by Strata found that 63 percent of US-based ad agencies included Instagram advertising into their marketing budget for both their own companies and that of their clients as well. This outcome is a significant jump from the year before, which showed only 34 percent of advertisers chose to include Instagram advertising into their marketing arsenal. Accordingly, it makes Instagram the most popular choices for advertising.

Not only that, 60 percent of users on Instagram are under 30, and by 2019, agencies estimate that Instagram will pull in $6.74 billion through global mobile ad revenue, thus increasing the profit share of their parent company, Facebook's global ad revenues.

Managing Your Instagram Ads

If you're new to creating Instagram ads, the process can seem rather overwhelming. With so much information to filter and sift through, how do you know what's going to work best and what isn't? Believe it or not, Instagram ads are far easier to make than you think, especially with the availability of tools like AdEspresso (a third-party tool), Ads Manager, and even a tool called Power Editor to help you through the process.

Reading the Right Audience

For your ads to count, they need to reach the right audience. After all, that's the whole point, isn't it? Draw in new potential customers and retain the existing ones you have by keeping them interested. To ensure that your ads are reaching all the right people that you care about making an impression, keep these targeting options in mind during your ad preparation process:

- Which location are you targeting? (Country, city, region)
- Who are the demographics involved? (Age, language, gender, race)
- What patterns to behavior have you observed? (How does your audience behave in and outside of Instagram)
- What are the interests of your audience? (Apps they use, ad links they have clicked in the past, what Instagram accounts they currently follow)

- Are you targeting a custom audience group? (Showing ads to selected customers depending on their phone number or email address)
- Are your new target potentials similar to your existing client base?

Getting Started with the Process

Instagram's advertising works on the same premise as Facebook, using similar advertising tools, so it's much easier for you to track, run, and even set up campaigns for your Instagram platform the same way you would for your Facebook ads. This is especially helpful if you're new to the whole Instagram advertising game. Now, let's get started with the process:

Step 1: Creating Your Instagram Ads

You could use Facebook's Ad Manager to get started. Once you've selected that option, you will then be directed to the Ad Campaign, Ad Set, and Ad Levels section, which is where you will be able to create multiple ads. These multiple ads can be used to fit into a single ad set, which can then be employed to fit under a single ad campaign.

Ad Campaign is where you will begin by choosing your objectives for your ad. There is a list of objectives where you can choose from, and these include building brand awareness, increasing traffic and reaching, boosting engagement, enhancing lead generation, prioritizing video views, or app installs, messages, conversions, catalog sales, and more. Your objective would be based upon your advertising goals, which was discussed in Chapter 2, so use those goals as a guiding point to help you make a decision. As long as your objective aligns directly with your ad campaign goals, you're good to go!

Once you're done with that, you'll move onto the Ad Set portion, which is where you will be choosing your target audience, setting your budget, scheduling your content, deciding on your ad placements, and bidding on the platform. This is the decision-making phase of the process. If you decide that you would like to send traffic to a secondary location through your ad, you will start by choosing where to send the ad. For example, you could choose to send your ad to your website, messenger, or even your app. The great thing about Instagram advertising is that you're given full access to Facebook's existing incredible range of targeting choices at your disposal.

You'll be able to target your audience based on users' job title, language, gender, age, parental status, relationship status, diet, whether they are engaged online shoppers or not, where they shop (high-end or budget retail), and more. These targeting options will be advantageous to you if you're not relying on custom audience advertising. You'll be able to even target audiences exclusively who may not be connected to your app yet, too.

If you're going with the custom audience target, an example of how you would connect with them through your ad would be targeting those who have visited your website within a certain time frame. Or you could aim to target these custom audiences based on the customer's email addresses if you're looking to create ads which are highly targeted. You could even choose to custom target these audiences based on who has interacted with the content on your site, whether it is your friends, Instagram profile, or even those who watched some of your video content.

The third step is the Ad Level step, which is where you'll decide on what your creative content should be. Basically, this step denotes the phase where you shape what your ad content is going to look like, what it says, and ultimately, determine how successful your ad will be.

Step 2: Choosing Your Ad Placements

Facebook's Ad Manager usually already has most of its placements selected automatically. You can opt to change these placements, of course, by simply clicking the "Edit" button. With Instagram Ads, you can opt to run other ad placements options simultaneously, even if you're running other ads on your Instagram newsfeed. Unless you're running Instagram Story Ads, then you won't be able to choose any other ad placement options. Another important tip to remember with ad placements is that while you can choose to run mobile-only ads, you'll be unable to run your Instagram ads if your settings are "desktop-only" enabled.

Now, with your Instagram newsfeed ad content, you will be able to choose the option of enabling other ad placements. This includes Facebook's newsfeed and the ads which appear on the side column, messenger ads, and even audience network ads while you're at it. A common mistake that many marketers tend to make is to only run their ad campaigns with Instagram Ad feature enabled because it seems much easier to create. However, this may not always prove to be the best decision, because, sometimes, it can affect your business's budget, and not in a good way either, since Instagram Ads tend to cost more than other placements on Facebook.

Step 3: Budgeting and Scheduling Your Ads

Budgeting is a big consideration for all businesses, both big and small. It is all about the numbers, and it has to be if your business is going to survive. A business that is running at a loss is not going to make it very long. With budgeting for Instagram ads, there are two options which you get to choose from - a daily or lifetime budget.

A lifetime budget could prove to be your best bet if you're keen on letting Facebook automatically distribute your ad spend for you for a fixed amount of time. With this option, there's one guarantee which you get - you will never be over your advertising budget if you happen to schedule incorrectly, for example. You could also choose to have your ad set run continuously, or if you would prefer to schedule a start and end date, that works too. Having a start and end date will guarantee that you never forget a campaign. The date can always be extended later, if needed.

Step 4: Bidding

Next, we move onto the bidding process. If you're not already familiar with the system, both Facebook and Instagram ads work on a bidding system. What this means is that whoever is willing to bid more will be the one who wins the ad placement for one's target audience. Think of it as an auction. Your bid would depend on what you're optimizing for. For example, what you could be bidding for could include bids for impressions, daily unique reach, landing page views, clicks, and more.

The manual bidding option will give you the most control over how much you're spending per result for your Instagram ads. You have the option of putting a cap on your bid amount, safeguarding yourself against overspending. The cost of Instagram ads is much higher than average, compared to that of other social media platforms, which means that you could benefit from having an average bid using the bidding system. An average bid would allow for lower-priced placements to help balance out the more expensive placement options. Even though the option is called manual bidding, you're not actually "doing anything" per se because Facebook still automatically bids on your behalf. Not to worry though, since their bids are usually pretty good.

Step 5: Choosing Your Ad Formats

Instagram gives you four different types of formats to choose from - carousel ads, single ad images, Stories ads, and video ads. The single image ads are the most straightforward, simple type of ads there is. Straight to the point, clear, concise, and they work brilliantly for ads which only want to feature single products or something with high visual appeal. You can't go wrong with this ad option.

Carousel ads are also known as multiple ad images. If you're planning to showcase several different products, it gives you more space to elaborate your content and the point that you're trying to make with your audience. Videos can also be slipped into your carousel ad selection to "spice things up" a little and create even more engaging content.

Video ads on Instagram work similar to Facebook, whereby, they run on auto-play. They also start automatically playing without sound, although this is easily fixed by adding closed captions into your videos. The best video ads are kept at 60 seconds or less, and a minimum of 15 seconds at least to start.

Boosting Your Instagram Posts

Instagram's Ad system can be intimidating, especially when you're just starting out and trying to figure out how things work. If you're looking to promote one of your posts quickly while still not entirely sure you're confident enough in your Instagram ad abilities, there's one option you could use to save the day - Boost Posts. With this option, you'll only be paying to promote one specific post (so make it your best one!). As long as you have an established business profile on the social media platform, you can boost any post you have on your Instagram.

In your Instagram business profile, simply by clicking on a selected post, you will be able to see the option "Promote," which should be placed directly below the image. Clicking on this option will prompt you to select your focus objective, and you will only have two options to choose from. The first option could be to increase your website and profile visits, and the second option is to reach your target audience based on their location. When you've selected the objective of your choosing, you'll then be prompted to choose your call to action, determine how long you want to run your campaign, and set your budget. Voila! All set! Be sure to preview your ad before you submit it, though (very important!).

How to Monitor Your Ads

Ads Manager on Facebook is the easiest way to monitor your Instagram ads. The dashboard has everything that you need, especially at a quick glance. The data that you'll be presented with includes what your cost per action is, how many results you're getting, relevance score, and more. Monitoring your ad campaigns closely will help you see what's working and what's not, pull the plug on ineffective ad campaigns, and determine how you can reallocate your ad spend the budget on more successful ones. Keep a close eye on your campaigns by checking on them regularly.

Instagram Story Ads

Instagram Story Ads get their own chapter because they're in a league of their own. When they were introduced onto the Instagram scene, they brought with it an exciting new range of possibilities for businesses and advertisers to capitalize on.

With over 400 million accounts and counting currently using Instagram Stories, it has easily become one of the ways businesses can quickly generate a high volume of views for their contents.

But first, let's get to know this feature a little bit better.

What Is an Instagram Story Ad Anyway?

If you're a frequent user of Instagram, you would already be familiar with their Instagram Stories feature, available to every app user who is on the platform. Instagram Story ads exist within this same space. Meaning these ads are going to appear on top of your newsfeed, shot in full-screen vertical video formats and optimized for mobile viewing. Just like Instagram Stories. When one of your ad stories ends (either on its own or by swiping away), the next story begins automatically. When that story ends, the next one begins and so on, creating a continuous stream of content which, when used correctly, can end up telling a very engaging story that keeps your audience coming back for more.

Now, for the regular user, these Story ads would appear in between the other stories in their newsfeed, sort of like dividers. You've probably experienced this yourself when you're watching a story that a Friend A has uploaded, and before stories move on to what Friend B has uploaded, there's a random ad which appears in between. That's Instagram Story Ad. What's captivating about the ad stories is that they look like your ordinary organic posts, with the only dead giveaway being the "sponsored" word that accompanies the ad.

One of the story ads most intriguing features is that enables your brand to link within your posts, and to access this link, the viewers would only need to swipe on your call-to-action button (usually "swipe up to shop" for example, which appears at the bottom of the video) and they'll quickly be directed to your website's landing page. Using this story ads feature could help you achieve the following advertising objectives:

- Help to increase brand awareness
- Boost your reach, so that your video is viewed by as many people as possible
- Increase conversions by driving people to your website
- Encourage more viewers to install your app after watching your video content
- Allow your video content to reach even more viewers
- Drive sales through lead generation (for example, through phone numbers and email addresses)
- Enhance traffic to your website using the call-to-action button and link

Instagram story ads can be created quickly using your Ads Manager or via the Creative Hub function. They are still part of the overall Facebook ad system, except that they work slightly differently than the regular Instagram newsfeed ads that you see. As mentioned in the previous chapter, for example, Story Ads can only be run on its own, and it cannot be run simultaneously with another ad set at the same time. This is because there are no equivalent platforms since Story Ads tend to work on their own creative platform and require a different technical approach to it. The only similarities Story Ads has to the conventional Instagram Ads encompass the ability to choose a detailed budget, scheduling, bidding, and even targeting system, but that is where their similarities end.

Instagram Stories have a whole different kind of aesthetic appeal, which is apparent if you compare them to the regular newsfeed ads side by side. When it comes to Instagram Story Ads, the content should be kept fun. Filters and stickers, for example, are acceptable with Story Ads, but the only catch is that you need to add these features in yourself using video editing tools (Photoshop is a good choice), and then upload the completed file to your Ads Manager platform.

Creating a Story Ad

You can either choose to start creating your Story Ad using either an existing ad campaign or even a new one if you prefer. Don't forget to select a clear marketing objective beforehand. Once you've done then, you can begin by first naming your ad set (similar to what you could do when you create your Facebook Ad). After that, you would work on refining your audience, selecting a budget, and choosing your targeting options. See? That wasn't so bad, was it? It's actually pretty simple to create an engaging Story Ad once you've got the hang of the process. It's just a matter of familiarizing yourself with the tools and features after a couple of practice sessions.

Now, the only snag here would, again, be the fact that you can't run these stories together with any other ad placements. In fact, you'll probably need to make a couple of granular adjustments. For example, if you were thinking of running a single image ad campaign, you might have to upload the images separately to your Instagram Stories and your Facebook news feed. Facebook will let you know if this needs to be done.

How to Get the Most Out of Your Instagram Story Ads

Every advertiser wants to get the most from the time, money, and effort invested in their ads. They want to see returns, and they want to know ads are working. How do you get the most from your stories? Utilize the following best practice strategies and tips:

- **Do Something Demanding:** You need to command your viewers' attention. The minute they choose to swipe away from your story, that's it. It's over and gone. To combat this, what you need is to have a story that grabs the attention of the viewers and make it so interesting and riveting that they watch the entire 15 seconds and even like it enough to respond to your call to action.

- **Video Power:** Videos are a lot more powerful than a single image, especially when it comes to stories. The key word here being *stories*. A story isn't still; a story is alive, moving, and exciting.

- **Don't Forget Your Logo:** You only have a short time to make a significant impression on your viewer. You need to remind them of who you are, and your logo is the best way to do it. Place your logo clearly and definitively in your story, so your viewers will be hard pressed to miss it.

- **Own Your Ads:** The first few seconds is all you get, so make it work! Time is of the essence, and every single second is precious. Use it wisely, use it well. Create a story which has volume, tells your viewer what your business is about, be powerful, be impactful, and believe in the power of what you're trying to sell.

- **Keep It Short:** Viewers don't have the time to read through a long essay because your story is only going to last 15 seconds before it moves onto the next. Think about what your story message is going to be and keep it short, concise, and to the point. Every word should carry meaning; make it punchy and easy to read.

- **Stay True to Your Brand:** Instagram Story Ads are still an extension and a part of your business. While it involves its own creative approach, it is still important to remember that your stories should stay true to what your brand represents, and be consistent with the rest of your brand's aesthetics. Staying true to your style makes it easier for your audience to be able to immediately identify you, thus increasing brand awareness while you're at it.

A Strong Call to Action Makes a Difference: Nothing pumps up the adrenaline quite like a limited time offer. Or a special, one-time deal that's not to be missed. Creating that sense of urgency with a strong call to action encourages your audience to swipe up for more information or head directly to your website, which hopefully translates into a sale for your business.

- **Get Some Music in There:** According to Instagram themselves, 60% of the Story Ads which were viewed by audiences were viewed with their sound on. So, put some music in there and pump up the beats, because it makes for a much more engaging story with even more power to draw in your audience.

Are Instagram Story Ads the Way of the Future?

It certainly seems like the case, especially with the introduction of Instagram TV into the mix. Story Ads are on the rise, with more audiences interacting and engaging in a way that is a lot more meaningful with the brand. Viewers seek to engage with their favorite brands in a way that is convenient, effortless, and easy, while at the same time, still be engrossing enough to keep them hooked. Instagram Story Ads do just that. It doesn't take up too much of their time, it's fast-moving, easy to interact with, and requires little to no effort to get the results that they want. The vertical format makes it ideal for mobile viewing on the go, which is how most of the viewership is taking place these days anyway. There is already a trend which indicates that viewers are transitioning from newsfeed ads and unto story ads because of its more vibrant and engaging nature. It's almost impossible to go a day without seeing at least two to three ads pop up in our stories feed, and this trend is only going to increase in the future. For marketers, now is the time to start tapping into the full potential of Instagram Story Ads.

Hashtag Strategies for Better Instagram Success

Start learning to love hashtags, because it is the best way for audiences who are outside your existing group of followers to find you, connect with you, and even make a purchase from you. Hashtags can be incredible tools which can help your business skyrocket to new heights. However, if used incorrectly or without a concrete strategy in mind, hashtags could become pointless, and worse, ineffective. You'd have wasted all that time, effort, and energy on nothing.

Want to maximize the potential of your posts being discovered across Instagram? Here are a couple of strategies to keep up your sleeve:

- **Use Your Hashtags Strategically.** Before every post is sent out, ask yourself how many hashtags do you think would be best? And which of these hashtags is going to benefit your ad the most? Having a quick think about these questions will save you a lot of time and prevent you from blindly hashtagging every word which you may *think* is going to help your post. Go with popular hashtags, but not the ones which are *too popular* where you run the risk of being lost in the tsunami of other content. 65,000 Instagram posts were analyzed by TrackMaven, and it was discovered that if you want your post to receive the highest possible engagement rate, then having 9 hashtags was the way to go.

- **Researching Your Hashtags.** A simple yet effective method is to simply do a quick search by typing in a few keywords on Instagram's search function. Then make a note of all hashtags which get auto-generated. It is also a great way to check up on the kind of hashtags your competitors are using. What sort of hashtags are your competitors or followers using at the moment? What are your influencers using?

- **Organizing Your Hashtags.** Keeping your hashtags in an organized system is the best way to keep track of which ones you're using, how often you're using them, and which ones have proven to get the highest number of engagement and traffic. You could keep track of them using your own organizing system, keep them on an Excel sheet, or simply use Instagram's analytics tool to help you out. Using Excel sheets or your own filing system would mean you need to manually keep track of them consistently, which can be rather time-consuming, but necessary. This method is the only way to see which hashtags are working best for your brand, so you can eliminate the ones that don't.

- **Narrowing It Down.** Hashtags which are on a smaller scale could prove to be much better for your brand. Take HubSpot, for example, who avoid using the hashtag #marketing because it is simply far too broad. Whenever possible, you should look at narrowing down your hashtags to more specific keywords, while still remaining relevant to what your brand is about.

- **Follow Yourself.** What better way to determine when people are talking about your brand than to follow your own hashtag? This way, you'll be the first to know when an Instagrammer is talking about you, and you'll have the opportunity to connect with them and build a relationship.

- **Have a Hashtag Related to Your Brand Campaign.** This can be tricky, but if you manage to pull it off, it can pay off in a big way. There have been businesses which have successfully attracted followers in droves because of the brand campaign hashtag that they devised. For this to work though, your hashtag has got to be memorable. These sorts of hashtags are especially useful if you're looking to promote a new product launch, an upcoming campaign, or even if you're just looking to inspire your audience. One such successful example is a campaign which was done by LuluLemon, where they encouraged their audience to post pictures of themselves being active and using the hashtag #sweatlife instead of utilizing the traditional advertising campaign methods.

Creating Your Own Hashtag

Thinking about coming up with your own hashtag that's unique to your business? Use your brand name as a hashtag to start with. Or it could be something relevant and related to your brands, like a value that you stand for, or a slogan that you use. Keeping it catchy and short so it's easily remembered will make it more likely that your audience will reuse it.

Using your own unique brand of the hashtag can be beneficial because it helps your audience access and connects with your business easily when they know specifically what to look for. It makes things a lot easier for them (which are what they want!). It also helps to facilitate word of mouth for your business and makes it easy for Instagrammers to track down your business or products by simply using the hashtag. Plus, if your content goes viral, having a unique hashtag that is special to your business can earn you major bonus points!

Tagging Your Instagram Stories

Instagram Stories deliver another great place to make full use of your hashtags. Stories were introduced back in August 2016, and it has been growing in popularity ever since. It only took Instagram a year and a half to bring in 300 million users daily, all thanks to the introduction of Instagram Stories. With the introduction of more interactive features filters, stickers, and more. In May 2017, Stories just got even better.

Instagram Stories are a little better than Snapchat's similar feature because even though they disappear from your profile after 24 hours, Instagram Stories still get saved in your archive (unlike Snapchat, where they evaporate into cyberspace once time runs out).

Stories which contain certain hashtags will get compiled together and show up in search results depending on the popularity and engagement. Once your brand gains enough popularity on the social media platform, and your hashtags get used often enough, Instagram will compile a set of stories for that particular hashtag. This might take a while to happen, though.

Still, despite that, we know that video content tends to get a lot more views than images do, so even if your stories with your hashtags are only seen by your loyal followers, it's still great for interacting with them. Plus, it reminds them to keep using your hashtag.

Chapter 5- Facebook Marketing

It's 2019, and by now, you know that everywhere you look on the online, you're bombarded with ads. One of the biggest ways the Internet knows what you like, what your last search was on your browser, who you are friends with, what articles you clicked on, and what was your last online purchase was through Facebook. One of the most prevalent ads popping up everywhere you look is Facebook ads. So what are they? We see them all the time, but do we know anything about them?

Here's a little info about Facebook Ads:

1. With Facebook ads, you are generally in control of your creative elements as you are the advertiser. This includes the title of the ad to the images used, the design as well as the text.

2. Facebook ads use an auction type method whereby those wanting to use Facebook ads are charged based on the clicks they receive, the impressions the ad gets, and the actions it results in. There are different formats of ads that Facebook offers which users can use.

3. You can even craft and create all the different types of ads on your own or use Facebook's interface which enables you to self-service. You can also use certified API ads developer like Qwaya if you require a more wide-ranging tool for working your ads on Facebook.

4. Facebook ads can be categorized according to i) Ads and ii) Sponsored stories. Here are the different types of ads that you can create with Facebook ads. There are a total of 10 different types that fall into the ad category:

- Mobile App ad
- Page post photo ad
- App ad
- Domain ad
- Page Like ad
- Page Post video ad
- Event ad
- Page Post ads
- Page Post Link ad
- Page Post Text ad
- Offer ad

Where these ads appear on Facebook is entirely dependent on the type you choose to use.

Facebook Usage Statistics

Believe it or not, not every business is on Facebook simply because they feel it's better for interacting and engaging with their customers or target market on other social media channels and that is not a crime whatsoever. On the other hand, if you're planning to reach a wider audience, you might want to rethink and focus your marketing efforts to include Facebook as well. Here are some stats to enlighten you on the power of Facebook:

Usage Statistics

- Active users- On June 30, 2017, Facebook reached a total of 2.09 billion active monthly users.
- An average of 79% of Americans uses Facebook.
- There are 50 million businesses using Facebook Pages.
- A total of 22% of the world's population uses Facebook.
- Every minute, there are at least 400 new users signing up for a Facebook Account.
- There are at least 1.2 billion monthly active users engaging and communicating via Facebook Messenger.
- At least 83% of parents with children aged 13 to 17 years old are friends with their child on Facebook.
- Facebook is currently available in 101 languages.

Marketing Statistics

- 1 pm and 3 pm on Thursdays and Fridays are the most active times of usage for Facebook.
- Facebook Page contents reach an average of 2.6 percent of organic reach.
- Pages with smaller followings have a higher reach and higher engagement rates.

- Facebook is currently ranked as the most important platform for marketers

- On average, brands post 8 times each day.

- 57% of consumers say that Facebook has influenced their shopping.

- User-generated content has more traction compared to brand-generated content, often creating a 6.9 times engagement rate.

- Finance and the Insurance industries have the highest cost-per-click on Facebook at $3.77.

- The apparel industry has the lowest cost per click at $0.45.

- 93 percent of advertisers use Facebook ads.

- 4 to 15 words for a link description is the most effective length for ad titles on Facebook.

- Images make up for a 75 percent to 90 percent performance for Facebook ads.

- $9.16 billion is the number of Facebook's advertising revenue for 2017.

- 26% of Facebook users reported that they made a purchase after clicking on ads.

Google AdWords vs. Facebook Ads: Which should you be spending on?

Facebook Ads and Google AdWords are extremely powerful platforms for advertising and also suitable for almost every type of business in our 21st-century world. All platforms should be seen as complementing each other in your advertising arsenal, as opposed to adversarial when an advertiser wants to evaluate the strengths and potential applications of each platform.

The good old days of PPC advertising was simple- you needed to get clicks on your ads to get money. For early adopters, AdWords was a game changer in online advertising. The traffic was good, the cost was even better. But over the past 10 years, the cost per click on AdWords has increased. In essence, AdWords can make you tons of money, but it also makes you squander loads of cash, too.

But as we know today, AdWords is not the only available and viable PPC solution. You have plenty of options where PPC advertising is concerned. So, which one should you choose? Of the available options out there- Twitter, LinkedIn, Facebook and AdWords - you should start with both AdWords and Facebook.

But which one is the right one for your business?

- B2B Marketing

Let's begin with B2B marketing. Using this solution, your product is in the niche category so, in this sense, it's best to work with a target lower funnel traffic that searches for your service. For B2B companies, AdWords works fantastically. B2B searches also incur high cost-per-clicks or CPC but the customer lifetime value or LTV is also pretty high. You could pay $15- $25 for each click, but if the sale is $10,000, then that is the CPC you can handle. Another beneficial acquisition channel is LinkedIn Ads but for now, the main brands we are looking at are Google and Facebook.

Facebook has also entered the Business-2-Business domain because it now also lets you create ads that can be refined to Job Title, Industry, Company Size, Job Role, Seniority, and Office Type. As an added benefit, you can also create lead ads which Facebook auto-populates with the user's contact information and allows you add at least three more additional fields to further identify the lead for your sales team.

For some companies though, these features also enable Facebook ads to become a better fit for their B2B efforts in advertising since these companies are mostly interested in generating top-of-funnel leads. While you can exert a big portion of your marketing budget focusing on AdWords, it's also ideal to test out Facebook. The quality of B2B traffic and leads you get through Facebook, however, will be significantly lower than what you would receive from AdWords.

- Retargeting

Despite how much advertising focus you place on Google or Facebook for your B2B, you must always remember to retarget on these platforms. You've already generated a significant amount of traffic to your site. You can continue this position of staying at the top of your user's mind during the sales process by simply retargeting. For both these platforms, you are always best to use different ads so you do not end up with ad fatigue. With Facebook, in particular, it's also wise to use a range of ad types such as video, single image, GIFs, and carousel, so that your ads are always entertaining and fresh.

Facebook vs. AdWords

The use of Facebook or AdWords for B2B is straightforward. You can start by investing 90% of your advertising budget on AdWords and the balance 10% on Facebook Ads. Allow the cost per lead and also ultimately cost per sale data decide on what that ratio woud be.

- B2C Marketing

When it comes to B2C, Facebook offers the better option because of the cost-per-click. InB2B marketing, your LTV can easily absorb a substantially high CPC. However, with business-to-consumer (B2C) advertising, it's much more cost sensitive.

The cost-per-click for a B2C business on average would be $0.90. On the other hand, clients do pay around $8.00 for clicks on AdWords. Advertising on Facebook for B2C business is the same as going back to the days when Google was just clicks and cost pennies.

However, with Facebook traffic being higher-funnel-traffic compared to the AdWords one, your Facebook conversion rate is also typically lower than you AdWords conversion rate. Despite that, your CPC is significantly lower on Facebook as your cost-per-conversion is also still very much low with Facebook than AdWords

Facebook vs. AdWords, which is right for your business?

There are plenty of factors that lead to which pay-per-click platform is the most suitable for your business and brand, but if you want to have some considerations, there are factors that you can also explore:

- B2B Businesses: Good to begin with AdWords and start to retarget on both Facebook and the AdWords Display Network. Also, test Facebook for your business by investing at least 10-20% of your monthly ad budget.

- B2C Businesses: Good to begin with Facebook, unless your product is expensive or it is a niche. In this case, start with AdWords and progress to Facebook. You also need to spend at least 10-20% of your ad budget to test on your non-primary market.

Paid Ads vs. Creating Free content on Facebook

Facebook Ads vs. Boosted Posts: Which Should You Choose?

This question is extremely common among the admins of Facebook pages. Even if you're new to a page, you're bound to see Facebook's prompt to 'boost a post' and this usually comes in when Facebook detects high activity on a certain post or if its algorithms have found other pages with similar content boosting a certain type of content that matches yours. The ability to boost your post is a very simplified addition to

Facebook Ads' system. This system is designed to be simple and easy to use even for a non-marketer or advertiser.

However, simple doesn't always mean better. Boosted posts come at the cost of significant customization the complete ad system provides. In this chapter, let's look at the difference between boosted posts of Facebook campaign ads, so you can decide which is best for your business and when to use paid ads.

What have boosted posts on Facebook?

With boosted posts, advertisers have the choice to use a post that has already been posted at any time and promote it. When boosting a post, page admins can choose their target audience, decide on a budget, and how long the boosted post should run. This can be done on any post on your Page's timeline.

Facebook Ads vs.Boosted Posts

A post that is boosted focuses on increased visibility for that particular post and more engagement as possible. Boosted posts are great for brand awareness and an increase in engagement can be value added for social proof. An increase in engagement can also mean a lower CPC (cost-per-click) or CPA (cost-per-acquisition). You also could yield more results with the same value of the investment.

With Facebook's recent update, you not only can increase engagement for that particular post, but you can also choose the outcome of it- whether you want people to visit your profile more or visit your site. If this is your option, compared to increasing engagement on the post in terms of likes or comments, your ad will be visible to people who will most likely end up clicking. This selection is available only if your boosted post has a link to it.

Changing the Objective of the Ad

Boosting posts right now is much simpler and Facebook admins do not have or need to make many choices. For smaller businesses, which comprise a big percentage of Facebook pages, this method is preferable. With a few simple clicks, you already have a boosted post.

Boost Posts Interface

Boosted posts are much more limited than the full Facebook Ads system. There are some other things that you need to do on Facebook Ads compared to boosted posts. These choices include:

- Having plenty of objective options

it's vital to define what your ad objective is at the start as this will help you determine what your campaign should be about. Posts that are boosted will allow you to focus on whether you want to increase engagement or increase website clicks. On the other hand, full systems will allow you to determine a specific objective whether it is conversions, store visits, or lead generation. Boosted posts do not allow for these types of campaign objectives.

- Campaign types

Identifying your campaign types is imperative because Facebook will use this info to focus your ads on users who have a higher likelihood of taking the kind of action you're optimizing your ad for. This is determined based on the user's history of activity.

- Choosing detailed placement options

When you decide on boosted posts, you can uncheck or check an Instagram placement whether on desktop or mobile and this includes Facebook's side ads and news feeds, Instagram stories and feeds, articles, messenger ads as well as audience network ads. You can determine if you want your campaign to be shown whether for desktop users or mobile users only.

- Allowing for more targeting customization

As far as boosted posts, you cannot use multiple audience types. For example, you cannot custom your audience and also add interest targeting. You can achieve this goal and so much more useful Facebook ads. With Facebook Ads, you can customize by doing the below:

- Enabling manual bidding

You can conduct manual bidding through Facebook Ads. You can choose either a maximum per-bid rate or a maximum average bid. You can also choose what you want to pay for, whether clicks or impressions. Since you're able to select these methods to scale your Facebook Ads, this choice is a significant but small feature to know if you ever opt to use it.

- Bid settings

You can create carousel ads, even add descriptions and add headlines as well as choose the call-to-action button that would work best for your ads. These are the different creative and formatting options that you can do through Facebook ads but not through boost posts.

- Gaining additional creative control

You can also add in your own headlines and targeted descriptions and choose a CTA that will work efficiently with your ads. These formatting options are unavailable when it comes to boosted posts.

When to use the full Facebook Ads vs. boosted posts?

Facebook Ads, about 99% of the time, are the most obvious choice for most marketers as they offer much more flexibility in crafting the right ad to hit the right audience. You can even customize the exact objective you want your ad to achieve, and it can be optimized to give you the desired results.

You can also create video awareness campaigns via Facebook Ads. You can also do retargeting towards the 75% of people who have watched the video and target them with a lead ad that is automatically filled out with their information. Once they become conversions, you can then focus on retargeting users who have visited your site and show them similar items to what they are interested in buying with a carousel ad that has high-conversions.

When should I use boosted posts?

Boosted posts work amazingly in very specific conditions. Here are the circumstances in which boosted posts excel:

- When you want to maximize visibility on a specific post
- When you want to build social proof
- When you want to create brand awareness
- When you want to create profile awareness

Examples of when boosted posts work amazingly well:

- When announcing a specific event and you want to increase attendance for that event as well as do social proofing simultaneously
- When you have a major announcement such as launch or a release of a product or service or even a grand opening and you want more engagement and visibility

- When you have shared a user-generated content and you want to win over customer trust and gain new followers

- When you need a quick engagement boost to help with your social proofing or if there is a specific message you want users to see, your best bet is Boosted Posts.

However, if you want a full-fledged ad campaign that gives you better customization to reach a specific and wider group of users and match with your campaign goals, then Facebook Ads is the way to go. There's no right or wrong with using either boosted content or Facebook ads. The only consideration is what your goals and objectives are and matching the right method with the objective you want to achieve.

Pros and Cons of creating Paid ads vs. creating Free content to encourage more organic growth and traffic

Let's be honest: it's difficult to get people to your business whether you are doing this virtually or physically. If only it was that easy to just push a button and the right customers just show up. But alas, life is not that way. It takes effort, intelligence, and pairing the right tools to attract your customers.

Whether you're seeking to drive traffic to your site with Google Ads or Facebook Ads, or reaping traffic through social media, blogging, or email marketing, you're paying for your traffic either with money or with time or both.

The question here is not necessary if you want to pay for Organic traffic vs. Paid Traffic - either way, you'll be paying but the ultimate question here is, which is more worth the effort, time and money.

1- Pay-Per-Click vs. Organic Traffic

• Organic Traffic

Organic Traffic really just means traffic coming in via organic search. Organic search is only from search engine results. This concept literally means a user goes on a browser of their choice, looks for whatever product and service they want and when the search results come in, then click on whatever links they want, which will direct them to a specific site.

While this type is organic, advertisers and marketers can still influence this decision. But most often than not, organic traffic already knows what they want and have made a decision the split second they click on search. It's only a matter of deciding which link to align with as well.

• Pay-Per-Click Traffic

Also known as PPC, this traffic is a result of users clicking on an ad that you paid to be placed at a specific location on the internet. Almost every platform or search engine allows you to set up advertising campaigns that you only pay based on the number of times people have clicked on your ad. You decide how much you want to pay and the ad service you use will charge you until the funds you have stipulated run out. You can also set up an ad runtime, which charges you based on the clicks that happen during a time period.

The location of the ads or placement is entirely dependent on several factors such as the ad relevance, bidding process, as well as desired audience response. The position your ad takes on a page is directly dependent on the performance of the ad or the bids. Where PPC is concerned, you're simply utilizing a middle person, and in this case, the ad platform to link your website with to people who wouldn't other accesses your site.

2- Organic Traffic Benefits Vs. PPC Traffic Benefits

Most of the time when people use a search engine to look for certain products and services, they don't intend to click on ads. 70% of link searches are usually organic and hat is consistent with organic traffic anyway.

- Organic Traffic Pros

Positive Bias

The biggest benefit of organic traffic is that they will click on links that they already trust to find what they need. If you rank high on a search engine result, that status means the user already has a positive perception on your site and trust that you're an expert in the industry.

However, you really need to be at the top for this perception to take place. This ranking is where organizations and businesses use SEO to ensure that they remain at the top 10 of a search engine result, specifically Google. Google is the gold standard simply because they have a large share of the search engine market. Google creates the SEO rules, and other search engines follow suit.

What Google does is to weed out spam and give users who use their engine the best content there is. When doing so, Google has consistently improved and changed their filtering systems in order to provide the best quality content on the World Wide Web.

The SEO game is built on the quality of a site, their relationships with other websites as well as the traffic flow to that site. Of course, it involves much more than that when it comes to Google algorithms such as quality images and a responsive site, but the main focus is quality content.

- Encouraging Improvement

Before you begin an organic traffic campaign, you must already have built a site with great content. No content, no traffic, and no search engine result ranking. Your ultimate goal is quality that keeps bringing people to your site, especially if your marketing objective is to be ranked higher in search engine results. SEO enables you to stay high on the ranking list and with better content; you can always be at the top. Great content needs to be on all pages on your site. This visibility will not only optimize your site for search engines but also improve your customer's user experience, satisfaction, and also increase brand awareness and favorability.

- Organic Traffic Cons

Time

The cost of organic traffic is, of course, time. You'll need to spend a decent amount of time to wait for organic traffic to pick up. People need to know that you exist in order to want to find you and depending on your strategy for search engine optimization, this can take a few months or even years if you want to be on the first page of search results.

You may not have that kind of time to boost your website traffic.

Resources

Organic traffic also requires an immense amount of resources, but the good thing is there are also plenty of free tools on the Internet to help you optimize your site to attract organic traffic. Yet knowing what kind of tools and how to use them are essential in your marketing arsenal.

PPC Traffic Pros

PPC traffic is an excellent source of traffic and if you create excellently paid ads, you'll see the kind of traffic build up. Plus, that appears at selected top positions which will get an average click-through rate of 7 percent. Those looking for brand specific or product specific searches will also see your ad and increase this click-through rate compared to organic traffic.

- Time

You can definitely pay an agency to search engine optimize your site. There are plenty of services that do this and while this does not necessarily take out the time from your hands, it certainly does not eliminate the fact that it does indeed take time to see results. However, PPC traffic is faster than unpaid organic traffic. Once you have paid and secured your spot at the topmost ranking, that spot is yours until some other site comes up and has a powerful SEO that pushes you down. Whatever it is, the likelihood of you being at the top 3 or even the top 10 will still be there, unless you stop optimizing your site or doing any other marketing or advertising initiatives.

- Tailored fit

The ads that you pay for will also be tailored to meet your objectives and hit the specific audiences. Through PPC ads, you can target your customers as well as potential customers in ways that organic traffic cannot do.

If you do not measure the intent of the user when you pick your keywords for SEO, you probably may not get the kind of customers you want. PPC advertising disseminates to segments that you may not have covered through your organic SEO methods. With PPC, you can target audiences by age, marital status, income even, education level, and even hobbies.

PPC Traffic Cons

- Money

The problem with many things in this world reflects the lack of money. Without enough budget, your best option to increase traffic is by sticking to organic traffic. If you want to generate tons of leads in a short amount of time, then PPC is the way to go and you need to put in a serious amount of cash for this to happen effectively. However, the great thing with paid ads is that you can turn them off whenever you have what you need.

Both paid and organic is essential to your site. There really isn't the perfect way. Both methods bring in traffic in different ways, and usually, a good ad campaign takes advantage of both organic as well as paid traffic to create brand awareness and visibility as well as drive traffic to your site.

Chapter 6- YouTube Marketing

How many videos have you watched today? Perhaps an average of 5? Or maybe 3?

Regardless of the number, you know that video content makes the arsenal of content marketing. It facilitates the success of many campaigns in 2018, and it'll surely continue in 2019. Again, here are some stats to entertain you concerning   YouTube:

- <u>8 out of 10</u> web users watch YouTube videos.
- YouTube is the <u>second largest search engine after Google</u>.
- The total length of YouTube each month is now <u>3.25 billion hours</u>

YouTube is an essential tool for plenty of industries. Even before YouTube, brands and companies have been creating videos to showcase their products and services, and now with YouTube, it makes it much easier for both brands and individuals to create and upload videos.

1. Developing a YouTube marketing strategy

The first step in creating a marketing strategy on YouTube is just like any other social platforms and it begins with defining your goals. With YouTube, you want to write down specific targets that you want to achieve such as clicks and traffic, engagement as well as reach and subscriber numbers.

You can use the SMART model to help you create objectives- Specific, Measurable, Attainable, Relevant, and Time-Based. You also need to be able to measure your videos to see if they are performing according to the objectives you've set. At this period of strategizing, you also need to establish what your KPIs are to be able to measure these results.

2. Commit to a schedule

On YouTube, consistency is crucial if your main aim is to grow your channel. Much like blogging, the more consistent you are at posting content on your channel, the higher the probability of reaching a wider audience.

A strict publishing schedule is what most YouTubers stick with- they post at least one video each week on a specific day. How To Cake It posts videos every Tuesday, for example. Subscribers to this channel look forward to watching these videos and since they are scheduled for each Tuesday, so videos views tend to spike immediately upon release.

Other social media platforms are used by these YouTubers to promote these videos to their audience, so even if they are not subscribers, these users can still view these videos on Facebook or Instagram and share it to their pages.

When you set up your YouTube marketing strategy, you need to factor in the time needed to make these videos as well as commit to posting new content on your channel. When you make this commitment, you'll need to stick to it. Once you've determined how often you'd be posting, you should also factor in when you would be releasing your videos.

According to research done by Oberlo, viewers watch YouTube videos mostly during the weekends but also in the evenings, mostly right after work. So, the best time to post your content is in the afternoons on weekdays or early on weekend mornings. When you do so, your videos will be indexed by the time your targeted audience looks for it or watches it. You also need to make a note of all upcoming events and holidays, so that you can add this as part of special content and make it relevant to your audience.

Types of marketing videos

Once you have decided and determined your goals and your publishing schedule, the question is what are the kinds of videos you can make?

Your focus on content can be the same but the type of videos can differ. You need to do so to keep your audience entertained and coming back for more. Experimenting with the different types of videos can also help you understand which ones appeal more to your audience and which ones don't.

Here are some video types that you can focus on creating:

- **How-to videos**: These are among the high-performing videos on YouTube because they provide plenty of value to users. Since YouTube is the second most used search engine, people go to YouTube because they want to see something done or learn how to make something or cook something or build something. How-To videos are great for plenty of business, no matter what industry you are in. If you are using this format, you need to look at what aspect of your business can be turned into a 'How-To'. For instance, you sell car engine oil. You can do a how-to tutorial on how to use this oil, how to change your car engine oil, and the benefits of good oil. Look up blog posts online for materials you can use to create your video. Make this video entertaining!

- **Behind-the-scenes videos**: Remember that YouTube is also another social media platform. You can use YouTube to humanize your brand and show a different side of your product or service. Behind-the-scenes work great to showcase product development and event development in stages, brainstorming sessions, your work culture as well as your team.

- **Product videos**: Videos are definitely the way to go if you want your users to see your products and services. Viewers need to see the highlights of your new product or the new offerings in your service, so the best way to show this diversity is via videos. These videos do not have to be long; instead, they must be short and succinct.

- **Case studies**: Case studies can be a little longer in its format. You don't need to produce a case study to showcase the exclusivity of your product. That's for your product videos to do. With your case study videos, you focus on the client and their stories and how your product or service helped with their pain points. These videos also need to showcase achievements and also plans for the future.

- **Interviews**: Who doesn't love a good interview? Featuring videos of well-known experts in your industry as well as influencers is another way to attract viewers, similar to how you use influencers and experts in your blog posts and also tag them in your Twitter posts. These people can help drive traffic to your YouTube channel.

- **Listicles**: This type of content is another popular format. Listicles can be created to highlight your products or services. People love clicking on listicles, so you can start your videos with '10 most popular destinations of 2019' or '15 Ways to use X product'. As much as you want it to be informational and entertaining, you must also remember that these lists should always be relevant to your audience, your business niche, as well as the brand.

YouTube Video SEO: What You Need to Know

Imagine the potential you can accomplish with YouTube videos with almost two billion users watching YouTube videos for a variety of reasons. As we know, YouTube is among the popularly used platform to search for things. So, if you take the time to optimize your videos, use the proper tags as well as churn out good quality videos on a consistent basis, you'll reap in your targeted viewers dramatically.

How can you optimize your YouTube videos?

There are plenty of important factors that you need to look into to increase your search results ranking. Some of these elements are within your control but others are not. Keywords that you use and how you use them are completely in your control. However, elements like how many people subscribe immediately after viewing your videos are not exactly things that you can control or regulate. Here are some crucial ranking elements that you need to know:

- The keywords you use: Using the right tags is essential to ensure that YouTube knows what your channel features.

- Video descriptions and headings: You need to determine what exactly your audience is looking for in your industry and use these keywords in places such as the descriptions as well as headlines. Make sure to use at least one keyword in your headline.

- Video tags: Apart from the videos you use, you also need to make use of the right video tags so your videos are discoverable. Again, doing a bit of research will help you identify which are the ones that perform best.

- Transcripts: Another wonderful way of making your videos discoverable by YouTube bots are by including the video transcript. Viewers can look at the transcript for spelling or for words they don't know or they can read the transcript if they can't turn the volume.

- Watch time: Watch time equates to how many minutes and hours your video is watched as well as how many people watched your videos. Your total watch time also contributes to your search ranking. The bigger the watch depth, the better! Thumbnail image: Your thumbnail image is extremely important because what you show will affect how users click on your video to watch. These images should be relevant to your video and compelling.

- Engagement: Another ranking element would be your channel's engagement. YouTube looks at the likes or dislikes you get and the comments and shares your videos get.

- Subscriber numbers: YouTube does not only look at the number of subscribers of your channel but also the number of people who subscribe after viewing your videos. This distinction matters as well because it shows that your video was relevant, and it also provides value for your viewers.

If you're considering expanding your presence on YouTube, then look at this SEO tool called TubeBuddy that has plenty of SEO features specifically for video content. These features include:

- Keyword research tools that you can use to find the specific long-tail keywords to target

- Tag explorer which you can apply to find relevant and popular tags for your channel and your videos

- Keyword rank tracking, so you can track videos' ranking easily

- A/B testing for videos

- View and copy video tags

The last feature which allows you to see other video tags is extremely useful as you can look at popular videos that are ranked high and see what kind of hashtags are used that are also relevant to your niche or your videos and integrate them to help increase your rankings.

To use your YouTube content on other channels, make sure that you make it a feature either on your website or on other platforms to increase its chances of ranking. Search bots will not search high and low for a hidden video ranked low on a page. It usually indexes the first video.

You also have to optimize your video content in order to establish your YouTube marketing strategy. This step is imperative because it helps while you're getting started. Using any keyword research tool is also a good route to go for finding ideas for your videos. Before you get started on creating videos, take the time to do your research on keywords as well as video content, so you can create a video that fits these keywords for the audience you want to target.

Next step: YouTube marketing success

Used in the right way, YouTube is extremely powerful in promoting your brand, increasing its awareness as well as reaching the right kind of customers. What's strategy that is bound for success? Here are some key steps that you need to make:

- Planning is everything. Create a strategy well ahead of time to craft the content you want, have enough time to create these videos, and have a few of them lined up so that you can establish a consistent publishing content strategy.

- Your first few videos will help you understand what your audience likes. Stick to what is favored by also creating different types like how-to, listicles, and so on so your content is always fresh, and you give your audience much more than what they were seeking.

- Engagement is everything because YouTube is still a social media channel. Comment, like, and read what your commentators are saying on your videos.

- Optimize your channel as well as your videos so your videos are boosted on search engine rankings.

What else can you do to make attractive, high-ranking videos?

The devil is in the details. Having a high-quality, well-crafted video is a good start but without the rest of the elements that make a good video stand out, your well-crafted video will never be found. Here are other crucial elements to consider in your YouTube marketing strategy:

1. Make Compelling Titles

Your video can be so awesome but without a title to hook a viewer, nobody is going to click on it. Having a killer title is so important because this hook is the first time a viewer will see. Here are some tips to write a compelling title for greater reach as well as for clicks:

- Use the right keywords. The keyword in the title will tell your users what your video is about and it will also make it easier for search bots to discover your video.

- Keep your titles short and sweet. The ideal length that you're aiming for video titles is within the 60-character limit. You must keep it short enough so that viewers can see it at a glance, without having to click on your video.

- Craft descriptive and clear titles and do not let your viewers try to interpret it. They must already explicitly know what the video is about just by looking at your title.

- Your titles should also tell viewers WHY they need to watch your video. You do not need to write it down for them, but the title alone should reason enough for them to spend their time to view your content. Your title should tell them how they can directly benefit from watching your video.

Here is a handy formula that you can use:

1. What is your video about? Identify the main focus or idea of your video.
2. Search for short and descriptive keyword phrases that are relevant to this theme.
3. Choose a title which answers the most important question for viewers.

Useful resources which you can use:

- For keyword research: <u>SE Ranking keyword suggestion tool</u>
- To analyze your titles: <u>CoSchedule Headline Analyzer</u>
- To check what is trending and other titles: <u>Trending on YouTube</u>

2. Create Perfect YouTube Thumbnails

The second most important factor viewers look at is your thumbnail. The right kind of thumbnail will attract a reader to click on it, making your video trend as well as make your channel recognizable. Just like the title, your thumbnail should be relevant to the content as well as correspond with your video title. Attractive thumbnails result in higher clicks. Also, include short descriptions in your thumbnail so viewers can understand what your video is all about.

You want to immediately catch the interest of your viewers by telling them a quick story just by your thumbnails and your title. Not only should these elements tell viewers what your video is all about, but they should also make them wonder- what happens next?

Here are some tips to help you choose the right thumbnail:

1. Always opt for standard video sizes – 1280×720 or 1920×1080. Smaller sizes can end up looking blurry.

2. Opt for only high-quality images.

3. Image formats should be JPG, PNG, GIF, BMP, or TIF.

4. Include the video title on your thumbnail as it helps attract more views.

5. Use emotion. Include excited faces and focus on the eyes.

6. Apply the 16:9 aspect ratios that work best for YouTube players.

7. Keep a consistent look and adhere to this style to all your thumbnails.

Useful resources to use:

- Use editing software to customize your thumbnails such as Photoshop or Illustrator.

- Test your thumbnails with AdWords to see how well they work.

3. Limit Videos to Less than 5 Minutes

The total time watch time of your videos is also crucial. According to this Comscore survey, the majority of YouTube videos are about 5 minutes.

Long videos that have content repeating itself will not help. So, if your videos are longer than 5 minutes, you need to ensure that it gives a good enough reason for your viewers to want to continue being interested in your videos. Recipe videos, how-to videos are generally longer but the content needs to be interesting and not too draggy. You can, of course, experiment to see what works for your audience, but generally, 5 minutes should be your goal.

Here are a few tips you should follow:

- Always use high-quality content for your video
- Ensure they're under 5 minutes
- Optimize them to make it interesting, short, and informative

Useful resources to have:

- To view what's working for your channel, you can use YouTube Analytics to gain deeper insights into views, subscribers, watch time, and more.

4. Brand Your YouTube Channel

Let's face it. YouTube viewers and channels are so sophisticated now that there is no way you can get away with not having a consistent image for your channel. If YouTube is going to make a big part of your marketing arsenal, then you better brand it, so it is consistent with your other platforms and digital spaces. You need to make it visually attractive to not only encourage your visitors to take your brand seriously but also to brand it cohesively and deliver the same consistent marketing message across all platforms- both online and offline. Branding also increases brand recall and awareness.

If you're a company, use your company logo. If you're an independent vlogger, use a logo if you have one or just your headshot. Use an image that's consistent with the ones you use on your Facebook Business Page as well as your Instagram and Pinterest.

Keep your titles and descriptions somewhat similar to how you sound on other platforms. You can tweak it, of course, to cater to the content you are posting and the audience that you want but do not stray too far away from how you want to sound and look like virtually. Brand presence does not only relate to the visual identity but also your voice.

Your bio should be informative and relevant to your brand personality and company. Let people know what inspires you and what interests you. Make it engaging and sweet.

Useful resources you can use:

- Use <u>Bannersnack</u> to create creative and optimized online banner covers for your YouTube channel.

5. Include Calls-to-Action (CTAs)

Adding calls to action to your videos will help you create more engagement on YouTube. They can also be irritating, so try to use them in the right way. No matter what goals you have, to get more likes or more subscribers, be clear and concise about key actions people need to take. You can add your website link or ask for subscribers to your channel within the video or at the end to help people understand the next step. If your goal is to attract many subscribers, try to do it smartly. Your efforts will be rewarded in the long run.

6. Share Videos via Social Media

To grow your channel, sharing is important, whether you share on your social channels or people share your videos. You need to publish your latest videos on your other platforms as well as engage and stay active on your social communities and groups. Each social platform has its own distinctive culture- as a savvy marketer, it's your job to find out what this distinction is and use it to your advantage.

Here are some savvy tips to promote your videos:

- When making presentations using SlideShare, add in your YouTube.
- Share your videos on Twitter and Pinterest.
- Make 1-minute videos as promos and link it back to the full video on YouTube.

- Integrate your blog content with your YouTube Videos.

- Use Scoop.it to publish your videos.

- Share and promote your videos on Google+, LinkedIn, and Facebook.

- Add your YouTube channel to your social media platform iOS.

- Use Reddit or Quora to attract viewers.

Useful resources

- To upload, schedule, or share your videos, use <u>SE Ranking social management</u>

- Create YouTube badges using <u>YouTube APIs</u> for your website to increase visibility and enable link backs to your channel.

- <u>Boosterberg</u> allows you to evaluate automatically and promote your videos that create much value on Facebook.

7. Work with Other YouTubers

If you read the comments on other YouTubers channels, you'll see that viewers or fans will comment hoping that this YouTuber collaborates with another YouTuber. This is part of your engagement- understanding what your viewers want and working to enable it. Video collaboration is popular among YouTubers and it is a great way to gain a new audience as well as increase your subscriber base. It's a win-win situation for both YouTubers as well as the target audience- to see their favorite YouTube stars together working on something or creating something.

This is also a fantastic social proof for your audience. Working with other well-known YouTube stars cements your reputation and makes you look good just by association.

Here are some ways on how you can do that:

1. Interact with your audience and ask what else they want to watch in the comments. Man About Cake's Joshua John Russell always asks his viewers what else they want to see next.

2. Find YouTube influencers and other brands within your niche and make videos together.

3. Collaborate with like-minded brands and YouTubers that are more powerful than yours. Popular YouTubers will only work with those they know well or can help their brand.

4. Connect with several brands and YouTubers and work with them on a seasonal content.

Collaboration has so many obvious advantages so long as you do it with the right people and brands. Sometimes, these brands or people don't necessarily have to be in your industry- try looking for complimenting brands and influencers to work with, as this will grow your audience exponentially.

Chapter 7- LinkedIn Marketing

LinkedIn, the professional equivalent of Facebook with 380 million members and at least 4 million company pages, has grown leaps and bounds over the last 14 years since its inception in 2002.

By now, every professional who's got a page or account with LinkedIn knows that it is not just a social media platform to engage and connect. LinkedIn offers so much more. LinkedIn's unique approach to content marketing made it noticeable with influencers who want to share and engage via content distribution.

Content marketing advantage for social media has shown that influencers aren't just going to LinkedIn to look for jobs. Nope, they are there to share and engage with other professionals, job seekers, and influencers.

In this chapter, we'll examine more closely into LinkedIn Marketing and what you can do to optimize your page and use it to marketing your products and services.

Optimizing your LinkedIn Page

1: Optimizing for Users and Search Purposes

This is your LinkedIn profile just as you would your company website. Your LinkedIn Page represents your brand. In optimizing your LinkedIn page, there are three fundamentals that you need to consider:

Consistency

Consistency is essential when it comes to how you present yourself online and offline. Your branding collateral regarding your message, voice, personality, and corporate design need to be in sync across all profiles.

Accuracy

Whatever figures or stats, links or facts that you post on LinkedIn must be accurate because your LinkedIn audience is not just any audience. LinkedIn is full of highly educated and influential groups of people.

Semantics

Anything that you post up your social media accounts, especially on LinkedIn shows up in search results, so apart from being careful of what you post up, you should also optimize your LinkedIn Page with identifying keywords that you've used on your website as well your social media pages. You can also use industry-specific keywords to target your LinkedIn audience; bearing in mind that their users are much more sophisticated than the audiences on other social media sites.

2: Optimizing your LinkedIn Profile

There are several sections that you want to use targeted keywords to optimize your LinkedIn profile such as the 'Products and Services' section as well as the 'Careers' section.

At these sections, you want to pay more attention to the words for the titles, subtitles, of course, as well as the copy of the page. Each of these elements, as a whole, must be consistent, accurate, consistent, and project your brand personality. Authentic and high-quality content is what will give you organic reach, and this is what ultimately matters. When you get visitors via organic search and reach- whether through a LinkedIn search or a direct visit, your content must be compelling and targeted to continue engaging users. The real results on your content will be measured by the clicks you receive from your audience on the content on your page and what actions they take as your content directs them to as well.

3: Expand Your Social Reach

As much as it's easy to use ads to build your social network reach fast, without knowing where you stand in keyword research and compelling content is no use. Growing your reach in LinkedIn is the same with building your reach with Twitter, Facebook, or Instagram.

So, what do you need to do to add followers to your LinkedIn page? According to a survey done at BrightEdge, there was a positive connection between the numbers of employees to the number of LinkedIn followers. Every company that was among the top 100 brands had a greater percentage of its staff on LinkedIn than the number of followers. The top 10 brands had at least 60% of their employees on LinkedIn.

What does this mean for marketers?

Here's where you invest in your employees. Get them to set up their LinkedIn profiles, identifying themselves as your company's employees. Step back and wait to see if this strategy has an impact on your network—if it's working, then reinforce or double your efforts. More people will be attracted to your organization when they see your employees identifying with your company. This will also increase your messages and updates.

4: Create and Share Your Page's content

Search engines will search for the keywords that are connected to you, and awesome content will show up in search results and on other sites. Your content should be engaging with its targeted audience. So, how do you continue to maintain your audience's interest and engagement in your brand?

- **Share Updates Often**

To constantly maintain an ongoing interest in your company, you need to continue posting up relevant content on a timely basis to connect and engage with your followers and influencers. Updates can be anything related directly or indirectly with your company, best practices, leadership material, and industry news and job openings. Remember to always stick to what users will care about most and try to share as much relevant and useful content as possible.

Relevance and uniqueness of content are much more important than the number of postings.

- **Create Inspiring, Relevant, and Creative Content**

Create content based on what's happening at the time. When Kim Kardashian achieved a cover picture with *Time Magazine*, LinkedIn published a post on how to successfully market you just the way Kim does.

- **What does this mean for you?**

Every time you feel an international event has a direct relationship to your company, write something about it. It doesn't have to be industry-related news all the time. It can be related to something such as 'How Hurricane Matthew will impact sustainable travel,' for instance, or even "10 things I learned as an intern.'

- **Link Social Profiles**

It's an obvious best practice to connect your social media profiles with your LinkedIn ones. Cross-platform linking will help the sharing of content across multiple interest ranges, thus reaching a wider audience.

5: Encourage Recommendations

The number of recommendations seen on a page is similar to the number of likes a Facebook page gets. Recommendations are like the word-of-mouth of the online version. When you are selecting a partner company to work with, many marketers look to LinkedIn for social proof. Recommendations on Linkedin tell your visitors what products and services you have to offer, but it also tells you how amazing you describe yourself in your products and services section. Try to gain as many recommendations as you can from customers, associates, and business partners- these strategies build trust.

Using LinkedIn for Your Marketing Strategy

Once you're done optimizing your page, do not let the page idle away without having some form of business strategy to uncover new opportunities for growth. Depending on the answers you gave in the questions in Chapter 3, LinkedIn may or may not the right platform for your business. However, if you already have a page and you've optimized it- time to look at a business strategy.

As mentioned in previous chapters, you need to start with the SMART goals for your Linkedin. What do you want to achieve from your LinkedIn Page? These goals can be very basic but as complex as you want it to be because LinkedIn can support your brand in many ways. Do you want to only connect with your employees and other partners? Do you want to get reviews? Do you want to build a network for social selling? Do you want to recruit talent? Do you want to see yourself as a thought leader?

Whatever your goals are, you need to create a plan. Here is how you can use LinkedIn in your Marketing Strategy:

1. Encourage employee connection on your LinkedIn page

Your employees and your colleagues are your best resources and your best advocates. Adding them as your followers also taps into their networks and increases your reach. Encourage your employees to add their positions on your page and link them with their own profiles.

2. Publish value-centric content

Part of becoming a thought leader is to publish articles and company updates on a regular basis, at least once a week. Not only will your post appear on your company page, but it will also appear on your follower's newsfeeds. Share blog posts and news articles from external sources that are relevant and beneficial for your followers, even if this content does not originate from your team. It shows that you have your eyes and ears in understanding and keeping abreast of your industry news. Add in your thoughts as status updates when you share these posts because you can provide value and context when you post and also help to foster connections with other thought leaders.

3. Include variety rich-media

Having variety is similar to YouTube videos. You need variety to make your content stand out. Posts with images have 98% more comments than posts that only have texts. Link your

YouTube channel to your LinkedIn page as this can generate more interest and viewers.

4. Join relevant LinkedIn Groups

Joining groups can help you network with other businesses and professionals in your field, both in your immediate circle of interest as well as second or third tiered ones. Use LinkedIn's search feature to discover groups that align with your business goals and interests. You can even start your own group based on your industry and the topics that you like.

The point here is, when you belong to an association online, it can be a valuable source of professional networking and development. It's similar to joining groups and associations in the real-world, except this is on a virtual scale.

5. Understanding LinkedIn's algorithm

So, we generally know how Facebook and Instagram's algorithms work. Now, it's time to understand LinkedIn's version. Here it is in a nutshell:

- Their bots evaluate content based on Clear, Low-Quality, or Spam. Knowing this, your content needs to be of value and clear. You want to aim for a clear ranking.

- Their algorithms measure initial user engagement which refers to the likes and shares that you get per posting. Are users marking your post as spam? Are they hiding it from their newsfeed? Quality is the key but so is relevance. Your posts need to be relevant to your followers so give them a reason to engage with you.

- LinkedIn's algorithm also checks for spam and credibility based on the quality of your account and your network.

- LinkedIn has human editors who review content which means they determine the posts that should continue being displayed or even boosted.

6. Using LinkedIn Ads

Members of LinkedIn add information on the network about their associations, professional interests as well as skills. This means that LinkedIn has exceptional and specific targeting capabilities which allow you, as a user, to laser-focus your strategies so that it aligns with LinkedIn's goals as well. LinkedIn offers various self-service advertising solutions such as:

- **Sponsored content**: This can be used to amplify your content so it reaches a wider, targeted audience.

- **Text Ads:** These are CPM or pay-per-click ads that appear on the various elements of a LinkedIn profile such as the homepage, profile pages, Groups pages, search results pages, and more.

- **Sponsored InMail:** It's LinkedIn's version of email marketing, which uses its built-in ecosystem. With sponsored InMail, you can send personalized ads directly to LinkedIn member's inboxes.

Chapter 8- Twitter Marketing

Twitter offers another powerful social media tool to help achieve your social media marketing goals. In this chapter, we'll review the fundamentals of Twitter marketing strategies as well as tips to use Twitter marketing for your business.

As we already know, whether you are using Twitter, Instagram, Facebook, or Snapchat, a well-crafted social media marketing strategy is the foundation for success. Without a plan, you'll never be able to hit your goals and objectives, so you'll never know if you're performing well and you'd just be wasting time and money.

1.   Start by defining your goals

Again, you can use the SMART method in defining your goals. What is it that you want to achieve with your Twitter account? Generate leads and sales? Build brand awareness? Increase customer loyalty? Defining and measuring your goals will enable you to see whether your strategy is producing real, measurable results.

2.   Get to know your competition

Knowing what your competition does helps you identify their weaknesses and strengths. Hootsuite has created a really good competitive analysis template, which you can use to identify points of interest between your company and your competitors.

3.   Identify your audience

The audience for Twitter varies differently than that of Facebook and Instagram. You want to release content that the Twitter verse would appeal to positively and proactively. Long winded texts are a no-go. Visuals sometimes work and sometimes doesn't. Knowing who you are targeting can help you focus on creating real value content.

4. Integrate Twitter with the overall strategy

Working in silos is never good especially where social media is concerned. You want a team of people working collectively to ensure messages are consistent throughout all social media channels. You can have different teams working for specific platforms but they all need to stay connected.

5. Keep your account unique

While you can post the same content across all your social media networks, you need to fine-tune this content to fit the specific publication platform. While it may seem like a nice shortcut, it'll cost your engagement and authenticity.

Optimizing your Twitter Marketing

Yes, creating great content, posting at the right time, and optimizing your Twitter profile are all the fundamental things you need to do for your Twitter profile. So, you've done it already. What else can you do?

In this section, we will focus on other details to help your Twitter account stay at the top of search rankings as well as get you the publicity it needs.

1. Use valuable Twitter tools

There are plenty of tools out there which help you manage Twitter marketing at a scale. Hootsuite has a 40-strong list of tools to use for various purposes from generating leads, finding the right influencers as well as managing your followers. You can opt for the free or paid versions depending on which part of the Twitter funnel you are at and the goals you want to achieve through your Twitter account.

2. Using a variety of multimedia to drive engagement

According to a survey conducted by Twitter, 82 percent of users prefer watching video content on Twitter. If this statistic is any indication that multimedia will continue to dominate user viewing preferences, then you better get a team to create good and high-quality multimedia content from videos to GIFs. GIFs, for example, have garnered over 100 million shares on Twitter alone. They're the go-to option to add some fun into your brand.

3. Engage with your audience

Of course, this cardinal rule governs social media. Engagement, engagement, engagement is what social media targets and cultivates. Twitter and other social platforms are all designed to connect and engage so do not forget this in the midst of your marketing plans. Follow your networks because your followers' tweets provide a wealth of information. Respond to queries quickly, retweet, follow, and link because it keeps your followers happy. Use @mentions and tag people where it is appropriate. You want to maintain an interactive presence on Twitter.

4. Monitor your brand and your business

Monitoring your social presence is vital to keep an eye out of the on ground and online sentiment towards your brand as well as mitigate any issues that may arise. Monitoring also means looking at your competitor's Twitter accounts to see what they're sharing and also what people are saying about them.

5. Develop a crisis communication plan

This LinkedIn article referring to 'tone-deaf' brands are the reason why you need a crisis communication plan and it doesn't matter whether you're a big brand or an SME. Learning from brands that don't listen to their audience and end up in PR disasters will help your brand and company avert any communication crises. Remember that this era denotes the age of camera phones and fast-instant messaging- anything that seems out-of-touch with reality or faux pas made will be caught on cameras, retweeted, re-blogged, shared, and reposted.

6. Measure your results

Why would you not want to measure your results? Just like YouTube, Facebook, and Instagram and any other platform you're on, you put a lot of effort and time, not to mention money, into your accounts. The only way to know if it's' worked or not is by checking and analyzing the data you have.

For Twitter, you can use the following: Twitter Analytics which gives you an overall look at your tweet performances, who is engaging with you and when the influencers in your network as well as individual metrics.

You can also use Hootsuite's analytics tools which have real-time analytics of your performance and engagement.

7. Use various strategies

Apart from the above, you can also delve deep into advanced marketing tactics to get your Twitter reaching out to the millions. You can Advertise on Twitter, or host a Twitter chat with a specific hashtag for followers to join, you can even share live videos on Twitter.

You can also use Twitter Moments to curate your biggest and most far-reaching tweets so those visiting your site have easy access to tweets categorized by specific information.

You can also offer social customer service support by turning Twitter into a customer service platform for users to Tweet you with their concerns. For every tweet you respond to, the mileage you receive is enormous.

At the end of the day, make your Twitter a platform for meaningful engagement, not just about you, your brand, how wonderful and great you are, and only post stories about yourself. Talk, respond, like, retweet, and create a community on Twitter that your followers will love and one where you can have a sustainable following.

Chapter 9- Creating Your Social Media Marketing Plan

Social Media Marketing, or for short, SMM is a form of internet-based marketing that incorporates a variety of social media networks to achieve branding and marketing targets and goals. SMM involves the activities of sharing content, videos, and images socially, for marketing purposes. Brian Solis, a digital analyst, author, and speaker created a social media chart known as The Conversation Prism to categorize social platforms into various services and types of social media.

Social media is an essential component of a person's online life. With each new year, there are new social websites and applications that make social communication even more profound. Businesses use social media to promote brands, market products, connect with customers, expand reach, and influence and build new business ties.

The following exemplifies a variety of terms commonly associated with social media marketing and are essential, so you'll be able to use them effectively in your online marketing campaign:

Social Media Analytics- one of the primary reasons why social media marketing is an arsenal for any marketer is the fact that data can be obtained easily and quickly. Social Media analytics is all about gathering data from social media websites and blogs. This data is analyzed to enable marketers to make better decisions for their businesses and brands.

Social media analytics is commonly used to assess customer sentiment towards a product or service and how their reactions can support marketing and customer service activities. Social Media Marketing reaps the benefits of social networking to enable a company to increase its brand recognition and presence as well as expand its customer reach. Social Media Marketing's goal is also to continuously stay relevant by creating compelling content that will prompt users to share what they have to say on their own social networks.

Social Media Marketing also includes social media optimization (SMO), and it works similarly to SEO, search engine optimization, except with SMO, the main goal is to attract unique visitors to a website via social networks.

There are two main ways of handling SMO which embody:

1. Adding social media links to content such as 'Tweet it' buttons, RSS feeds, sharing buttons, and Pin It buttons

2. Promoting activities through social media via tweets, pins, blog posts, and status updates

Social CRM, also known as Social Customer Relationship Marketing, is another powerful business tool that marketers use. When a visitor to your social network 'likes' or 'follows' you, this action opens a host of communication, marketing, and networking opportunities. Social media sites enable a customer to follow conversations about your company and brand in real-time, and the company receives market data and feedback.

Social Media CRM works both ways. It further enables a customer to tell a company and everyone about their experiences with the company's products or services, both good and bad experiences. For the business perspective, it allows them to respond in real-time to both these positive and negative feedback, attend to customer problems almost immediately, as well as rebuild or regain customer confidence. How a brand reacts is imperative to the overall future and growth of a company.

Enterprise Social Networking, on the other hand, encourages a company to connect people who have similar business interests or activities. For a company's employees, it enables them to access resources and information that they would require to work together effectively and solve business issues and problems.

Public social media platforms also enable businesses to stay connected with their customers, and it makes it easier for them to conduct research where this data can be used to enhance their business process and operations.

Crowdsourcing. Of late, social media is also popularly used for crowdsourcing. Crowdsourcing is the practice of gathering information, data, ideas, and even funds as a community towards a common goal.

How to Create a Social Media Marketing Plan

Without a shadow of a doubt, we all know how crucial social media marketing is in today's world. Things keep changing and evolving- without using new media tools that come into our lives to innovate, upgrade, update, and stay relevant.

Before you embark on social media marketing, a little bit of investment in research and a plan is always a good idea. Here are the most relevant steps when creating that perfect social media marketing campaign:

1. Start with A Reason

Your plans should start with listing out your reasons for having social media accounts. What is it that you want to achieve? What are your targets? Who is your audience? Where do they hang out? Do they even use social media? What do you want to say to them? With your team, brainstorm your reasons- if you do not already have some. Your current business plans using conventional or traditional marketing tools would already give you a good sense of what you are trying to achieve. From there on, write down your reasons and connect them with your targets and goals.

2. Develop your objectives & goals

SMM can help with a variety of marketing goals such as:

- Growing your website traffic
- Building conversions across different interest groups
- Increasing brand awareness
- Creating strong brand characteristics & personality and positive brand relationship

- Improving communication and relations with major audiences and influencers

Only when you establish your goals will you be able to achieve and measure your ROI for social media.

To ensure you stay aligned with your goals when establishing your social media marketing across different types of networks, here are some essential tips for you to remember:

- Planning – Do a keyword search and brainstorm for ideas that will attract and engage your targeted audience.

- Content— Consistent content reigns supreme when it comes to SMM. Ensure that you offer valuable information that your audience will find interesting to the point where they want to share, like, link, or comment on your posts. Use images, videos, quotes, infographics, and even GIFs to compliment your text-based content.

- Consistent- While each platform has its own unique audience, environment, and voice. Use these differences to tailor your messages, but always keeping in mind that your messages need to be consistent across all platforms.

- Blog- Having a blog and a website enables you to share a wide variety of content. Blogs are relatively easier to maintain and make sharing information such faster. Your company blog is part of your social media marketing campaign because any recent social media efforts, activities, events, and promos will be highlighted in your blog.

- Links- It isn't social media marketing if there's no sharing of your unique, original content to reach out to your current followers and gaining new ones. Linking content from other parties and organizations is also part of SMM.

- Tracking Competitors- Tracing your competitor's activities can give you valuable insight into keyword research and other social marketing media stats. If your competitors are using social media and you aren't doing any of it, then it's something that you get going on as well- just do it better!

- Analytics- What would social media marketing or traditional marketing for that matter be, if it weren't giving you some form of data? The successes of your campaigns are determined by the data you get. Google Analytics, Facebook, Instagram, and Twitter Insights all have analytics that helps you measure and track your social media input so you would be able to monitor them.

Conduct an Audit on Your Social Media

You need to assess your current situation with your social media use and how it's been working out for you so far. it's always beneficial to go back to the drawing block and to revise, change, and mix things up with your social media because after all, things change quickly. What campaigns worked for you before may not work so well now.

Conducting a social media audit includes determining who is currently connecting with you on social media, which sites your primary target market uses mainly and how your presence as a brand on social media differs from that of your competitors. HootSuite has created a social media audit template that you can use to process this information.

Social Media Audit Template

This template is to help you conduct a social media audit for your business. Follow these steps to execute your next social media audit.

 ## Step 1

Create a spreadsheet and write down all the social networks you own and the owner for each.

Social Network	URL To Profile	Owner

 ## Step 2

Go on Google and search up any other social media profiles that is representing your company that you don't own (imposters). Create a separate spreadsheet.

Social Network	URL	Owner	Shutdown Y/N

 ## Step 3

Evaluate the needs for all your social media profiles and create a mission statement for each. For example: Instagram Profile—To share company culture and company achievements.

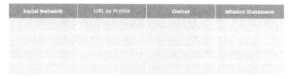

Social Network	URL to Profile	Owner	Mission Statement

 Hootsuite

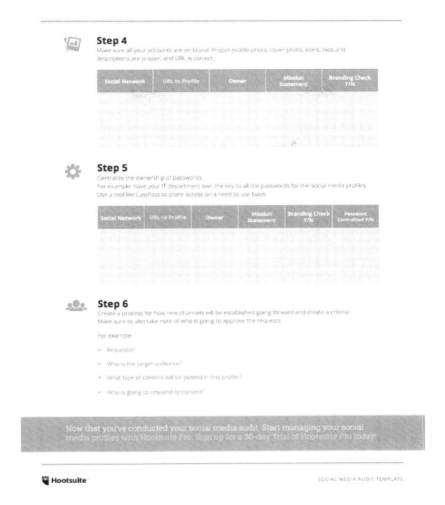

Step 4

Make sure all your accounts are on brand. Proper profile photo, cover photo, icons, bios and descriptions are proper, and URL is correct.

Social Network	URL to Profile	Owner	Mission Statement	Branding Check Y/N

Step 5

Centralize the ownership of passwords
For example, have your IT department own the key to all the passwords for the social media profiles.
Use a tool like LastPass to share access on a need to use basis

Social Network	URL to Profile	Owner	Mission Statement	Branding Check Y/N	Password Centralized Y/N

Step 6

Create a process for how new channels will be established going forward and create a criteria
Make sure to also take note of who is going to approve the requests

For example:

* Requester
* Who is the target audience?
* What type of content will be posted in this profile?
* Who is going to respond to content?

Now that you've conducted your social media audit. Start managing your social media profiles with Hootsuite Pro. Sign up for a 30-day Trial of Hootsuite Pro today!

 Hootsuite   SOCIAL MEDIA AUDIT TEMPLATE

This audit will give you a clearer picture of what each social account represents for your business, who is running it, and what each platform's purpose is. This inventory should be updated regularly as your business grows.

You'll also want to create a mission statement for each platform. Keep them one-sentenced declarations, so there is a focus on a specific goal. If you don't have a purpose for a platform, then you probably should delete it.

Here are a few mission statement examples:

- **Instagram:** We'll showcase how-to videos of how we decorate our cupcakes and connects with other fans of baking

- **Facebook:** We'll use Facebook to promote our specialty cake baking products and ingredients as well as preview videos, events that we've been invited too, and events that we are organizing.

- **Youtube:** We'll post our full-length video of cupcake baking tutorials.

- **Blog:** Most detailed explanations of our cupcake baking tutorials, events that we have been invited too and events that we're organizing.

3. Know Your Platform

In the previous chapter, you were given a deeper understanding of each social media platform and how to sign up or open a page or account. In this section, we will offer a brief overview of how each social media platform can be used for marketing purposes, deriving full benefits from each of its unique environment.

Platform	WHAT	WHY
Facebook	Facebook is obviously one of the best social media networks for brands because of it being the first one that companies joined. Companies can quickly update their pages, share photos, and content with their audience. Paid advertisement is also successful on Facebook. Facebook is used as a primary login for many other social apps.	Every type of brand can benefit immensely from using a Facebook page. Simple to update, it has an ad platform and affords a large audience base.
Twitter	With only 140 characters to publicize a message, brands can interact with their audience in real-time. Organic reach is always the best because all of your brand's followers will be able to view your Tweet in their feeds.	Your audience wants to be able to communicate with a real person, never mind, if it's on mobile or PC. This is what makes Twitter popular. People will praise your brand and interact with your Twitter handle before anything else.

Platform	WHAT	WHY
Instagram	The photo-centric and video-centric platform that makes uploading videos and photos easy. While there are paid ads, organic reach works best as people will follow what they like and want to see continuously.	Using pictures and videos to promote your brand personality can make Instagram a worthy social app. Cultivating a brand personality, giving it a humanized look and feel is what Instagram emphasizes. It's not savvy for text-based promotions.
LinkedIn	It's a necessary platform for any brand- corporate or non-corporate. It's the most professional route because it is a place where brand to brand interaction takes place.	Perfect for more professional brands looking to establish themselves as serious competitors and interact with a more professional base.
Pinterest	Extremely visual so if your brand is visually heavy, then Pinterest is a must. Pinterest also has promoted	If your brand is in the travel, fashion, food, fitness, or DIY brand, Pinterest is for you. Take note

	pins which are an avenue for advertising your brand. Pinterest is a very easy way to feature your products and curate your boards.	that is has a vast female audience that you would need to cater to.
YouTube	It's all about video content. YouTube is the place if you want to host videos whether it is DIY projects, How-Tos, and branded commercials. Vlogging, the video equivalent of blogging, is an excellent way to get your brand out there.	Youtube gives the opportunity for brands to reach their audiences via videos on all devices, at all times. People who watch video content have a higher chance of purchasing your products and services.

4.   Using location-Based Social Media Tools

Networks such as Yelp, FourSquare, and Level Up are ideal for brick and mortar businesses, especially car service centers, food outlets, and salons. Use these sites to claim to your location spot and then increase your presence by adding in extra incentives such as check-in rewards or exclusive discounts. Be mindful of how you present your business and provide service because before you can say 'Thank you for coming,' you might find a bad review on these platforms, which could hurt your business.

5. Create an Editorial Calendar and Content Plan

An editorial calendar will help you structure your social media marketing plan and this calendar should include your strategies for content creation as well as content curation. Here's a good example of a social media calendar that you can use. Your marketing plan should address these critical elements:

- The type of content you want to post and promote
- The frequency of postings
- The target audience for each type of content
- The person in charge of content creation for the different platforms
- The promotion of content

Your calendar should also include the dates and times that you want to publish posts on your blog, photos on your Instagram, and links on your Facebook or tweets to your Twitter. These kinds of things related to your very own account should be scheduled in advance, but you also need to make room for anything that happens in the world such as catastrophes and viral moments. Sometimes, you would also need to halt your social media activity in respect of a world event such as the shootings in Paris, the King of Thailand's demise, and so on. You'll also tend to be on board with news events such as the Oscars or Emmy Awards just to maintain trends. Be spontaneous with your content, engagement, and customer service.

Conclusion

In sum, the world of social media is a constantly evolving one. As the years pass, newer trends are introduced, and competition strengthens between different platforms, each one vying for the attention of the Internet savvy Gen-X, Millennials, and Gen-Z. Competition is good though because it brings about disruptive innovation. That's why each social media platform is constantly enhancing and introducing new features to stay relevant to its audiences, giving them better tools to share their content, better ways to engage, and more interesting ways to publish content.

One of the best ways to engage in social media marketing for your business is first to use it as a personal platform for personal use. Utilize it as an experiment, play around with it, upload images, and get accustomed to it before you embark on opening up an account for your business. This way, you'll be better equipped to make a decision whether that particular social media is worth your time and effort or not, and you'll also know how audiences in different platforms react to content.

Social Media Marketing, on the other hand, has many benefits, and it does a lot to improve site traffic and help a business reach more customers. Not only that, social media marketing helps brands to gain a better understanding of their audience and learning from them- their purchasing habits, their likes, dislikes, interests, and so on.

Any business stands a chance to lose out on its potential customer base if it doesn't evolve with the current times. In brief, no business will lose by investing in social media!

Affiliate Marketing Secrets

How to Start a Profitable Affiliate Marketing Business and Generate Passive Income Online, Even as a Complete Beginner

Chapter 1- What is Affiliate Marketing?

Make money while you sleep. That is the ultimate dream, right?

If you are considering a passive income stream, one great way to do this goal is through Affiliate Marketing. The idea behind affiliate marketing is that you promote someone else's products or services using an affiliate network. In turn, you earn a commission, if any products are purchased based on your marketing.

The mechanism behind affiliate marketing is revenue sharing. For example, if you have a product or service that you want to sell more and target to a bigger audience, you can offer financial incentives to promoters using an affiliate program. If you have no product and just want to make money, then you can be the promoter of the product that you feel has substantial value and can earn income as an affiliate marketer.

In this book, we will endeavor to uncover the basic secrets of affiliate marketing, the simple strategies, and how you can get started on it. But first, let's look at the definition of affiliate marketing. To put it plainly, affiliate marketing is cycle of getting commissions or a cut for promoting a product or service that is not owned or produced by you. This person can be a company, organization, or a sole entrepreneur. You find a product that you know and like, promote it to your channels and audience, and accrue profit for every sale made.

What components are involved in affiliate marketing?

Essentially, there are 3 components to affiliate marketing. They include:

1- The Affiliate

2- The advertiser

3- The Affiliate network

Who is the Affiliate?

The affiliate is the individual who does the promoting or the website's owner. Anyone can build a website nowadays is suitable for the business; however, when building a website for marketing purposes, consideration should also go into marketing the specific website. In this website, you will find details or reviews about a product or service that is sold on the advertiser's website. The affiliate's website cross-links to the product page of the advertiser using a link known as affiliate link. This special link specifically indicates the link's source to the advertiser.

What is the advertiser?

The advertiser refers to the business that sells the product or service. It could be an individual, a company, an organization, as long as there's an online commerce site.

What is the affiliate network?

The affiliate network refers to the tracking cookie that is dropped into the buyer's browser when he or she visits an advertiser's website. This cookie is dropped when a buyer clicks on any affiliate links on the affiliate's website. This cookie is the reason that makes affiliate marketing possible because they send the payment to the affiliate.

Still unsure what affiliate marketing looks like? Let's see it in action.

Let's assume that Jane is an affiliate. She has a website that showcases products about woodworking. She even has a blog that she shares videos of her latest woodwork as well as images of her crafts and the places she visits to purchase her materials. She also provides in-depth information on the best and worst places to get resources for woodworking.

Her information provided also gives reviews with links to the advertiser's website where the recommended woodworking supplies can be purchased. The key is that the link included denotes no ordinary link.

An ordinary link would be like: janewoodworks.com/best-wood-supply-store

In actual fact, an affiliate link would like: janewoodworks.com/best-wood-supply-store/affiliateID112783

If a visitor goes to Jane's site and decides to purchase a product after reading her reviews about places to buy the best supplies, then Jane as the affiliate will be rewarded with a commission for referring a buyer to the advertiser's site.

No matter when a buyer decides to purchase a product from the advertiser's site, maybe in a week after reading the review or in two weeks, the affiliate will still be rewarded the commission simply because of the cookie used on the affiliate network that remains on the browser.

How long do these cookies stay?

A question affiliate marketers always have involves how long do these cookies stay and when will they disappear? There are ways that this would happen:

1-If the buyer decides to clear his or her cookie cache on their browsers, then this step can be done either manually or using tools such as CCleaner.

2- The cookie also can expire. Most cookies on affiliate networks have a 30-day period. However, vast majority of advertisers now opt for lifetime cookies. So even if someone opts to purchase a product one month after reading the review, the affiliate will still get paid.

The Affiliate's Advantage

The advantages are quite obvious for the affiliate marketing business model. To have the opportunity to 'sell stock' effectively, without the hassle of any of the costs or responsibilities of buying, storing or manufacturing items is a plus point that is quite liberating. Plus, when working with high-paying networks, the profits can be substantial.

Affiliate marketing, when done correctly, can turn into an extremely profitable passive income. It is most likely that you will need and also want to keep your eye on the price: and if you can get into the business to bring in substantial income, you may be able to outsource plenty of seemingly routine tasks to freelancers in the long run.

Plenty of affiliate marketers stumble at the point where they believe that success in affiliate marketing is easy and quick. Affiliate marketing takes work and hours of learning, as well as the willingness and commitment to adapt to the changing situations of things. Besides the obvious advantage of running your own business, affiliate marketing also offers the individual, you, the freedom to work online anywhere, anytime and also have the freedom to choose how hard you want to work. As affiliate marketers, you also have the probability of acquiring some freebies from advertisers who want to boost brand awareness.

A website is critical to the affiliate marketer. Depending on the topic, the marketer has the ability to give a company enough exposure to the point where he or she will ask you to trial one's products for free.

The Advertiser's Advantage

So what's in it for advertisers? The very same business model for affiliate marketing can yield huge potential for the sales of their products and services. Paying only when you see or receive the results desire is an excellent way to advertise and requires very minimal budget to begin. This is an ideal model for start-up business when they have little funding to market their brands.

Apart from this benefit, what could be better than having thousands of websites promoting your product? This is an example of online 'word-of-mouth' marketing at work. People are talking about your products online through reviews and blog posts, so what better way to get your brand out there?

How much can you earn from affiliate marketing?

Your income will depend entirely on a few massive factors such as:

1- The reliability and efficiency of the affiliate network you are working with currently.

2- The advertisers' conversion rates and commission levels.3- The level of commitment within your investment

4- The depth of willingness and knowledge to learn all you need to know about your niche to succeed

These commissions and networks vary widely. There will be new affiliates that can take over a year just to make their first sale, but with the right training, acquiring knowledge as well as persistence, you can earn a lot of money.

Through affiliate marketing, you can easily make some pretty impressive earnings. Top earners earns multiple millions of dollars a year.

This all sounds great but don't be quick to hand in your resignation letter just yet. Before you can go on full speed on affiliate marketing, laying the foundations of affiliate marketing is imperative. It will definitely take some time, but once you get the gears running, it will be easier for you to better judge whether you want to leave your day job or not.

Chapter 2- Benefits of Affiliate Marketing

When you become an affiliate marketer, you automatically become an independent proprietor of a chosen product or service from the generic to the niche, on behalf of the vendors. When you become an affiliate marketer, this also means you now have absolute freedom to create online presence. You get to call the shots on when or where your job needs to get done, how to optimize your marketing process, as well as how to reach your customers.

As discovered from chapter 1, affiliate marketing is an online business model that is great to start off if you want passive income online. It is a low-cost but high-profit industry. Affiliate marketing gives you the flexibility to earn how every much you want. It all depends on the determination you have, the approach you take as well, as the affiliate strategy applied.

Before we explore the strategies, it is worth to explore the pros and cons list so you are aware of what you're heading into, what works and what doesn't. So let's dive into it.

Advantages of Affiliate Marketing

- **It's a billion-dollar business**

There's no denying that affiliate marketing is a billion-dollar business. Plus, with the Internet, it seems that it will continue to prosper. Because it is a big industry, there's plenty of potential and it also means there's unexplored territory-products and services that have not yet been created or advertised.

- **It involves extremely low costs**

A relatively easy to join business model, affiliate marketing offers no barriers. This is one of its biggest attractions. The biggest hurdle to take is to decide to do it or not and when you say YES, the next steps are relatively easy. Your main asset is your affiliate marketing website or even becoming an affiliate marketer without a website. Next involves about choosing a familiar niche. Finally, the last step encompasses i finding the right products or services that appeal to your market. By signing up to an affiliate program, you're ready to begin!

- **You don't need excellent business prowess**

The big mantra here is practice makes perfect in affiliate marketing. You do not need to be a marketing whiz to be able to become an affiliate. This is the other great thing about affiliate marketing- you can learn along the way. Affiliate marketing is about testing both organic and paid advertising to see what works and what doesn't for your product niche. What's more, you also have plenty of options to run and manage the affiliate program. You will need to test several sequences to see which performs well or which combination of strategies perform effectively with your target market. From here on, once you've found a good formula, it's all about optimizing and repeating successful patterns to obtain the best results.

- ## It has low investment costs

When you start out, the operating expenses of affiliate marketing is next to nothing, especially when you compare it to other industries. Most of your work is online, which means you do not need office space. Your home is good enough to operate from and then you will only need basic utilities such as a good and stable internet connection, electricity and ISP subscriptions. You may also need to spend on other expenses such as web hosting capacities as well as some minor costs related to website design. This can be done once you have a better grasp of your affiliate business. Other costs related to your affiliate business only takes place later on in the growth cycle such as renting out a co-working space when you have freelancers working for you or if you have a partner. These costs can be controlled- it is up to you if you want it or not.

- ## Second source of income

You do not need to leave your current job to make it in affiliate marketing, even if you can afford it. The choice is yours. You can make affiliate marketing as a side business and accrue extra income.

- ## Convenience and Flexibility

To increase your income, you can create and conduct multiple affiliate campaigns on different affiliate websites to market your links. This way, you can abandon the ones that are performing poorly and pay more attention to the channels that are performing well. You can utilize many different affiliate programs. Selecting various products from the chosen niche is the preferred route for many affiliate marketers and it also enables them to test these niches. You can promote each one on a daily basis.

You will also know which product sells better and which one doesn't. If one is difficult to sell, the other might be easier and more profitable. If a single program is not working out for you, you are also not obligated to stay in it. In sum, this approach will help to mitigate the risks of failure and maximize the opportunity for a marketer to earn a good income. Do not put all your eggs in one basket- keeping your portfolio diverse is the best route.

- **Customer Service is not your priority**

As an affiliate, you do not need to deal with customer service. No managing customers or worrying about retaining customers for you. All you need to care about is your commission so when you do get a post-sale query, you can just pass this request to the merchant's site. Of course if you do want to deal with customer service, then you can make a mutually beneficial rate with your merchant. User-generated content for your reviews can definitely boost your SEO so you if you want do customer service, then you need to have a comprehensive system of replying to these queries as fast and as accurate as possible. Customer service is at the end of the day- YOUR CALL! No one will impose this on you or expect it from you.

- **The independence**

You have the flexibility of making your working environment the way you want it to be and according to your own wishes. You can be working anywhere, from a cafe in Hungary to an island in Thailand. All you need is internet connection. You decide where your office should be. As an affiliate marketer, there are no company regulations to follow or daily meetings to attend or weekly reports to hand in. You set the rules yourself; you decide what time you start, what time you finish, and what your dress code is.

- **Marketing kits are your disposal**

Any marketing materials are provided by vendors, so you do not need to fork out any money to produce your banners or any other promotional materials.

- **Reaping profits even while you are asleep**

Another strong feature of becoming an affiliate marketer is the idea of gaining passive income while you sleep. It is possible for you to get money while you sleep because people are still buying products after clicking on your affiliate links. But to get there, remember there is some work involved.

- **The Sky's the limit**

There are very different ways to market your affiliate programs. You can set up a website, you can set up a blog, you can create affiliate emails, you can create PPC campaigns. The options are endless. You can also use the power of social media and platforms such as Facebook and Quora to market your affiliate products. You can also do a combination of organic and paid advertising to cross-promote your campaigns.

- **Sole proprietorship**

As an affiliate marketer, you are basically a freelancer and you still need to establish your business activity. The advantage is the costs, since mobile phones or laptops can be claimed as tax write-offs.

- **It's a flexible working schedule**

Being your own boss means setting your own rules and framework as well as daily working schedule. If anything unexpected comes up, you can always change your timetable to meet or fit in unexpected activities or events. You can also decide to take a vacation anytime you want.

- **Performance based income**

Some marketers think of this as a disadvantage. The thing is, affiliate marketing will determine if you are good at online marketing. To be able to get a good stream of income, you need to be able to be good at writing reviews, writing articles, recording videos as well as marketing your site. It's hard work still but all of these just bring you more revenue which is why affiliate marketing is a performance based income. The more you do, the more money you'll get.

Persistence is the essential factor here. It takes time to amass traffic to your site before you can make money from, it but once you've struck gold, it's a yellow brick road all the way to success!

The Disadvantages of Affiliate Marketing

- **You Don't Control Affiliate Marketing Programs**

You are dependent on the program that you choose, the merchant's rules as well as the conditions set. You will not be able to adjust the terms on your own. All you can to is communicate the need for any adjustments that you see from your perspective such as giving discounts and being more visible on social media. The merchant then takes the necessary steps to implement changes.

- **You Cannot Control Your Competition**

Depending on your particular industry, the competition differs. There are strong benefits of joining an affiliate program such as the high-profit-low-cost investments and no immediate expertise required. But those that are highly talented from the same niche can give you a fierce competition and are an obvious danger to your own performance and survival. This however should not scare you. No matter what kind of business you go into, there will always be someone doing better than you are, so the key here is to be persistence and work smart!

- **You do not have control over your customer base**

Once a referral has been made, a repeating customer is highly unlikely to purchase from you again. This customer may just do it directly from the affiliate vendor to repeat their purchase again. That is the truth about affiliate businesses. While you commit to driving new leads again and again, recurring customers are unlikely to visit your site. This is why most marketers do not bother with after-sales services and leave it to the vendor itself to provide.

You can however engage with marketing affiliate programs that do provide commissions for return customers.

- **No Guarantee of Revenue**

Unfortunately, this is a major setback. The pay-per-performance can be both an amazing opportunity as well as a significant risk. No one can promise that working in the affiliate marketer will be easy and do not be fooled if you think that you will be able to earn your expected revenue immediately. It is a challenge that you have to face, and you need to put all your efforts into increasing this opportunity. It is difficult to estimate how much money you will make on affiliate marketing.

- **Freelance Jobs are not for Everyone**

Yes, freelance jobs are not for everyone. Some people prefer to have a safe and stable 9 to 5 job, but for many people, freelance opportunities present a different set of freedom. On one side, you have flexibility, no meetings, you can work anywhere and be your own boss. But this also means that you will face some form of loneliness as well as stagnation. You might feel like you do not have motivation to work. There are ways that you can prevent this though. You can start working in a co-shared space with or working in a space outside your home.

With plenty of offices now going on cloud, there are co-working spaces available, coffee shops designed for the freelancer in mind as well as buildings that enable you do rent a desk or a space just for quick meetings and for freelancers just like yourself. You can just look around to see what suits you best.

- **Quantity Approach**

Some marketers end up doing the spammy marketing approaches and while this has some kind of benefit, it is a short-sighted campaign because it only produces misleading content everywhere. Marketers may get small wins, but they are very short-lived.

Once you end up in the black hat of affiliate marketing methods and false advertising, it will crush your growth. You will lose credibility and you will also put your merchant at risk. Doing spam affiliate campaigns will also lead you to a breakup from the vendor's side and then, you will break your commission.

Quality is always better than quantity so focus on long-term, quality solutions in creating your affiliate strategy. Invest in quality leads as this gives better investment for the time and effort you put in. Plus, it will also bring you sustainable and recurring revenue. Be legit because it is the only way you can gain trust with your vendors as well as other affiliates in the business.

- **It's Possible to Hijack Affiliate Links**

Hijacking affiliate links is a method used to deprive affiliates of the commission which is that they should rightfully be earning. Hijacking is done by bypassing the full link where a person types the affiliate link in a browser instead of clicking on the links. The other way is by removing the affiliate ID in the link and adding their own. While hijacking is still pretty rare, there are a few bad apples who will resort to this method to get commission. When it happens, you cannot get your commission back unfortunately. You can report it and ensure your website has the necessary security.

Now that we know the advantages and disadvantages of affiliate marketing, it gives us a deeper understanding of the nature of this business. It will help you, the affiliate, in making objective business decisions and it will also help you build a capable business model to decide if this is the right kind of business for you. If you look at this list, there are more benefits than disadvantages which is a great thing. There will also be risks and issues with a business, but it is up to us to be aware of these things and learn from them in order to avoid making mistakes. Speaking of mistakes, let's look at the common mistakes that beginner affiliate marketers make, which you can avoid.

Rookie Mistakes in Affiliate Marketing

- **Picking the Wrong product**

There are plenty of products out there for you to choose. But choosing the right one to market and plan your affiliate marketing campaign around will ultimately be the deciding factor in your success or failure. Selecting a product wisely is an absolute must. When you hone the right product and the right niche, you will automatically be geared to create marketing activities around it. Whatever campaigns you create, they will be authentic because you know the product and you know what it takes to sell it.

A rookie mistake made when it comes to picking a product is that the affiliate picks a prominent product just because they think there is money behind it or because it is easy to sell. The product you choose must drive you on its own otherwise no matter how popular it is, you will not be able to market it because you are not invested in it. Your affiliate business will not excite you in the long run. You do not want to make yourself a slave to your money that comes from a product you have little interest in and one that you are only doing out of 'getting money.. Pick something you are passionate about and one that you know. It will prove to be worthwhile in the long run as it will be something you can sustain.

- **You are promoting too many products**

It is not wrong to promote various different products. After all, you need diversity. When you choose the products you want for your own affiliate collection, many rookies make the mistake of selecting too many of them. Being overly ambitious and over-enthusiastic is not the approach you want to go for when you start. Over time, you will be less enthusiastic to promote and market your products because you will likely be too distracted by trying to achieve too many things at one time.

Selling too many products at one go will eat up valuable time and decrease your value in the long run. When this happens, it ultimately leads to fewer affiliate sales. What you can do though is to pick selected products and to focus all your motivation and enthusiasm on them. You would be able to commit more time with a few, selected products and then turn your endorsements and reviews into the right actions-which are making sales. Over time when you have a better handle of the affiliate business, you can add more products to your portfolio and grow your business. Just ensure that you continually give each campaign the individual attention it deserves to succeed.

- **Designing and operating a poor website**

There is no excuse anymore to have a bad-quality website, especially when there are plenty of services that allow you to create beautiful websites simply by dragging and dropping elements. Making websites is easier nowadays than ever.

So what happens when you have a poor quality website? Low quality sites mean low sales volume- it's a quick reaction. While you do not need to create a high-end, high-tech website with plenty of amazing user friendly interfaces, you still need to provide a basic, accessible and friendly site that will turn visits and clicks into immediate sales. Plenty of platforms enable you to create free sites, but then again, taking the option of investing in a website with a good domain name and hosting capabilities can take your sales from zero to hero.

You will want to avoid a slow or unresponsive website. Remember that it takes only 3 seconds to make a first impression online so make it worth it. Messy templates and an unorganized site will also get your customers frustrated and lose interest in what you have to sell. They also will not be coming back because they have associated your site with all things negative.

You will want to provide a nice online shopping environment, easy navigation and an overall pleasant experience when customers browse your site-much like how you would be providing a nice space to shop if it was a regular shopping store.

When you build your site, keep these things in mind. We all like shopping on a website that provides easy access. So when designing a website, answer these questions:

- Is it easy to navigate?

- Is your website easy to find?

- Does your website enable you to quickly and easily find the section?

- Does it highlight the products?

- Are there clear calls to action?

- Is your website simple enough to find information?

- Is your website responsive?

Your site does not need to have flashy graphics to attract users. It just needs to be intuitive and simply enough to be interactive and easy to navigate. Identify what you want on your site, what products you want to display and the content you want to have on your site. Make sure that your website also personifies the kind of products you are selling.

- **Not having high-quality regular content**

High-quality and updated content is an essential part of affiliate marketing. Heck, it is an integral part of any kind of marketing. Users nowadays are very used to high-quality images and content, so having low-resolution photos and poor descriptions only damper your ability to sell.

This rookie mistake is a major problem that is very often overlooked. Content is important in marketing and no matter what your site is made out for, whether it is comparisons, product reviews, blog articles- all of these contributes to your online sales either directly or indirectly. Do not make the error of posting content that has no actionable item or is not insightful. When writing a piece of content, always make sure that there is a solution or a purpose. Put yourself in the shoes of your potential buyers and imagine what kind of content they seek. You want people to get hooked on stories and cool facts, not random ramblings.

Good content alone is not enough. You must also ensure that you churn out content on a regular frequency. When your users are interested in what you have to say, they will be expecting some form of consistency in terms of your uploads- they want to know more and you have the job of getting them consistently engaged.

- **Not tracking the performance of your website**

As someone new to the business of affiliate marketing, knowing how your website is doing with the users are coming is helpful so you know what they click on, where they click on, how long are they on your site and what buttons attract them. Part of marketing is optimizing your data and tracking it. You will want to see the cause and effects that happen when you do tracking so you know what works for you. You can use various tracking tools such as Google Analytics, Hubspot or Sprout Social. The website you choose to host your content should also be able to give you plenty of analytics for you to see.

- **Not continuously learning**

As an affiliate marketer, you must always keep abreast of the things and trends that are happening in your line of business. Changes take place rapidly in the online world and you need to keep up with the standards. It is a challenge to always stay updated but reading and subscribing to business news and marketing blogs will help stay informed. Educate yourself and read online guides to ensure that you know what is happening. Trends take place frequently and some work for your business while some don't but knowing them helps you navigate through the business of affiliate marketing as smoothly as possible.

- **Not being brave to try new things**

It is imperative to test out the various tools and versions of copy and content, media and campaigns when you want to sell your products. The online world has plenty of online marketing capacities that are easy and fast to set up. Delivering the same kinds of messages just because they worked before does not mean that you will have continued success. While some users may take the bait, most will eventually get bored and this will lead to slumped sales. You must keep things fresh in terms of content as well as campaigns to reach out to new target markets.

Never accept the status quo. Explore a variety of marketing opportunities and experiment towards perfection and when you do this, do not forget to conduct A/B testing. You can test out plain emails versus HTML emails, you can also test out different subject lines to see which one hooks your client base.

You can also try different approaches towards the same pain points for the same buyer persona.

Testing out is fun because it helps you to evaluate your campaigns effectively. Now you know the advantages and disadvantages as well as the rookie mistakes made in affiliate marketing.

Are you hungry for more? Let's examine the next chapter.

Chapter 3- Common Types of Affiliate Marketing Channels

So what are the types of affiliate marketing you can try? With affiliate marketing, it is important that you understand the fundamentals of what makes up affiliate marketing and the difference between programs and networks. Affiliate programs are individual merchants, whereas networks are a grouping of merchants under one umbrella.

Affiliate marketing, on the other hand, is basically a relationship between the affiliate, the merchant and the consumer. As we know, the affiliate is YOU- the person who promotes a product or service from the merchant in exchange for a commission. The merchant is the person you partner with - the one with a business and pays you to help them promote his or her business.

The affiliate works with the merchant on a contractual basis and provides the merchant with creative data that they can incorporate into their website in order to promote their product or service. The consumer bit is pretty straightforward. It is any individual who takes an action after seeing an advertisement. This action is clicking on affiliate links to make a purchase. This act is known as a conversion. In any affiliate channel you decide to take, having an online base- whether a website or a blog, is a good way to start. In this chapter, we will look at the different types of affiliate marketing channels available so you can make a better decision of which one works for you and is right for your needs and expertise.

Essentially, there are three types of channels:

1. **Unattached affiliate marketing**
2. **Related affiliate marketing**
3. **Involved affiliate marketing**

Unattached Affiliate Marketing

Unattached affiliate marketing is your basic pay-per-click affiliate marketing campaign. Here, you do not have any authority or need not even show presence on the product niche that you promote. You need not worry about having any connection whatsoever between the product and the consumer.

All you have to do is place an affiliate link using Google Adwords or Facebook Ads and this way, you hope that someone will click on your link, go to the merchant's site and purchase a product, thus earning you a commission. This type of affiliate marketing is extremely attractive, as it requires little to no presence. Plus, it's less of a hassle, compared to opening a blog or a website. This type of marketing is not really a business model but it is a straightforward income generating model. This model eliminates the pressure of meeting people and instead focuses more on the potential income, rather than the customers.

Related affiliate marketing

With related affiliate marketing, you have some level of presence online, meaning through a blog or a podcast, on social media or even on YouTube. You create affiliate links to the products related to your niche. Placing affiliate links on your site that are related to your niche is a more comprehensive and decent strategy to earn a little bit more income from your blog or website.

You can place this either in the sidebar or in a banner format or even text link them into your blog posts. Because you have a blog or a website, the credibility is higher, and you also get to decide where to place these ads.

If you use this type of marketing, then it is best to work on a product or service that you know and like. This is because people coming to your site, whether your blog or website, are under the impression that you know your product and you know what you are writing about and that you are in a way, an industry expert.

People will trust you and decide to purchase the products that you have linked on your site. Do not promote anything that you have not tried or loved on your own. Support a product because you really like it and you'll have a better chance of increasing your online presence because people will sense and read your honesty.

If you do not promote the right products, even if you know the owner of the product or service or you think that this product may be a great fit, you run the risk of losing the trust you have built among the online community of readers and users who flock to your website in search for credible information.

It takes a lot of work to build authority and trust, so a one bad affiliate link can potentially ruin this trust. So when you recommend a product, make sure you trust this product and the merchant selling this product.

Involved Affiliate Marketing

In this type of marketing, you really need to use a product or service and truly believe in it and you personally recommend it to your audience. This is not done in a banner format or through Google Adwords or a section on your website with the title 'Recommended Resources'. This is deeper than that. You are involved as you should be when talking about a product or service and this type of affiliate marketing produces the more sustainable of results. Your involvement and experience with the product or service is the reason why people flock to your site and why your site is at the top of Google search ranking results.

In this type of marketing, the level of responsibility is high. You also have plenty of authority and influence over your followers, which is why you need to ensure that your content is both helpful as well as honest. This marketing is the complete opposite of unattached affiliate marketing, where the affiliate is not even seen by the consumer for a transaction to take place. In unattached affiliate marketing, you use money to make money.

With involved affiliate marketing, your readers or consumers have their eyes and ears on you. You use your reputation, authority and trust to get recommendations, use it and get paid in the form of commissions. So which do you think works well for you? Either approach you take involves some form of advantage and disadvantage as well as varying degrees of responsibility and credibility. No matter which approach you take, you will see some form of success through your affiliate marketing.

Affiliate Marketing Channels based on the degree of involvement:

- ### Webmasters - Related affiliate marketing

Webmasters are individuals who own their own sites and also those who build websites. They are thousands and thousands of webmasters and they all have different levels of expertise. Most of these webmasters are signed into <u>sharesale</u> or <u>CJ</u>. These are affiliate programs that affiliates can partner.

- ### Search Affiliates- Related affiliate marketing

Search Affiliates are individuals that spend their own money to leverage search engines, Facebook advertising and other Paid advertising models to generate ROI for other affiliate offers and also for themselves. These kinds of affiliates have a strong entrepreneurial spirit and are business-minded. They love testing many different capacities of affiliate marketing. You can engage with search affiliates as long as there are rules in place and they use recommended procedures to generate the right kind of traffic as well as revenue.

- **Bloggers - Related affiliate marketing**

Blogging is another kind of affiliate marketing that is great for those who can write and want to continuously post information about a company and also reviews about new products. It is one of the most popular options for affiliate channels. For bloggers, all they need to do is get samples of products from merchants, try them out, and write a review (preferably a positive one), which will help spread information about these products. Credibility is a key issue with blogging and the more people read about your reviews or content about a merchant, the higher this content will rank on the search engine. Blogging can help increase traffic for the merchant and provide genuine number of conversions for the merchant.

- **Coupon Sites- Unattached affiliate marketing**

Coupons are always in demand no matter what the economic condition. What's not to like with saving a few extra bucks, right? Coupon sites make for really crucial and popular affiliate sites for a merchant's business. If you are planning on venturing as an affiliate here, keep in mind that coupon sites are like a double-edged sword. They have their advantages as well as disadvantages. The advantage here is that you can use these sites to direct traffic to your own website and thus channel these to the merchant's site but enabling affiliate links on the coupons.

The downside of using coupon sites is that they capitalize on organic rankings that are connected to your company's name and the coupon code. Coupon sites usually have a member base that is established, and it can be quite beneficial to you as an affiliate who wants to increase traffic to one's sites.

- **Review Sites- Involved affiliate marketing**

Review sites are another popular option for affiliate marketers. For this option, you need a website that can review different products in a specific niche. Affiliates that use this kind of channel usually deal with flower companies, dating companies, internet marketing companies and phone companies, taking up at least five to eight different advertisers and putting them on a site then running an organic search or paid search throughout all the pages that feature various reviews. The affiliate will earn commissions when a business is referred to any of these advertisers, making the review site large and converting demography of the marketing affiliates.

- **Loyalty Portals- Involved affiliate marketing**

In loyalty portals, companies usually have a very large membership base and they are able to expose your offer as an advertiser to members and these offers sometimes contain a cash-back policy. There are plenty of loyalty portals in the market and most conduct themselves on a performance-basis. A merchant can select any of these loyalty portals to improve his or her business.

- **Incentive Programs- Involved affiliate marketing**

Incentive programs have their good things as well as the bad things about them. The great thing about incentive programs is that as an affiliate, you can get loads of traffic from prospective buyers but the disadvantage here is that other affiliates can take action on your ads and can skew down the quality of leads and sales. There is also the problem with virtual currency through the use of social networking. Users can earn virtual currency using their social channels and then you also get some companies that leverage their affiliate advertisers to allow these users to redeem their virtual cash to make purchases. During the process, they also attain a good savings deal.

Most Popular Affiliate Networks of 2019

Speaking about affiliate networks, there are plenty out there online, and choosing the right one will make your road to success slightly easier. In this section, we will look at the most used or most popular affiliate networks to check out. This list is not complete because there are numerous out there, but it's good to know which networks are available for you to choose.

ShareaSale

ShareASale is among the most popular of affiliate networks and it has been in business for over 15 years. Their technology makes them an exclusive affiliate marketing network and they often receive accolades for efficiency, speed as well as accuracy. Plus, they are known as an honest and fair business within the affiliate marketing business.

PeerFly

This award-winning and international online affiliate platform removes the risks, headaches and costs usually associated with traditional forms of online advertising by channeling that burden across thousands of professional affiliates who get paid only when a measurable transaction takes place, such as a sale or a lead.

Rakuten

Formerly known as Buy.com, Rakuten has rebranded and has now transformed into an affiliate marketing giant. It ranks among the top three e-commerce sites in the world featuring over 90,000 products from 38,500 online shop owners. Rakuten also boasts over 18 million customers. It is known for its flagship B2B2C model and the e-commerce site Rakuten Ichiba has the title of largest e-commerce site in Japan. It also has the world's largest volume of sales.

ReviMedia

This online lead generation network focuses on operated campaigns for home services, insurance and financial verticals as well as exclusive advertiser's campaigns that is primarily focused in the US. They also have their very own proprietary lead management platform that is called Px.com, which gives users quality scoring for each lead and insight into performance by enabling key demographic info. ReviMedia is also flexible in running campaigns in various integrations. ReviMedia also has extreme transparency with their clients, something they are proud of as well as flexible payment terms. It also gives their advertising partners access to their huge direct publisher network of over 2,000 publishers.

RevenueWire

A global e-commerce platform, RevenueWire is specifically catered to companies that sell digital products and all of them online. It uses industry-leading services like Affiliate Wire, and their e-commerce platform is used in more than 120 countries.

Payolee Partners

This is an affiliate program that is specifically designed for online marketers that join and promote Payolee. Payolee is an online payment service that is best for small business. Relatively new to the affiliate market, Payolee empowers small businesses to accept one-time or even recurring payment options on their website. As an affiliate of Payolee, you can earn 55% of monthly commissions for every customer that   you   refer.

Clickbank

Clickbank is another huge affiliate network that has been in the game for over 17 years. It is one of the largest online retailers with a library of over 6 million unique products that reach a total of 200 million customers worldwide.

Wide Markets

This affiliate network provides unique cross-channel advertising capabilities for e-commerce businesses. This network owns Wide Markets Fashion, Wide Markets Media as well as Wide Markets eStores and Wide Markets eTickets. Using this network, advertisers can use it to sell their services, their goods and their products through native products created by Wide Markets. Publishers on the other hand benefit from a native method to monetize their online assets to find higher conversion rates. This network supports the Performance Marketing Association and is an active Champion Member.

CJ Affiliate by Conversant

CJ Affiliate was known as the Commission Junction before, but they have now reached an average of 1 million monthly customers using their site to go shopping online through their vast affiliate marketing network. CJ Affiliate also networks with companies such as the Commission Junction, Greystripe, Dotomi, ValueClick Media as well as Mediaplex.

Amazon Associates

Amazon.com, a huge name in the affiliate marketing business needs no introduction. It is an American e-commerce and cloud computing company that is headquartered in Washington. Being the largest Internet-based retailer in the US, Amazon.com's affiliate network enables you to tap into millions of products to advertise to your customers.

CPAmatica

CPAmatica, with its rather interesting name, is based in Kyiv, Ukraine. It is an affiliate network that operates throughout North and South America, Asia as well as Europe. It began as a one-person company in 2015 with its founder, Evgeniy Prima who was interested in helping others expand their business with a smarter approach. This network specializes in an innovative and simple approach, one that is deemed as more humanized.

AffiBank

AffiBank is a private affiliate network that you can use to promote a wide range of products from cryptocurrency to health products. It gives 75% commissions on each sale made using PayPal. Payment is made twice a month. AffiBank adds products on a consistent basis and it also has the 'AffiBank School' where affiliates can learn and access tutorials to learn affiliate marketing. It also helps affiliates to succeed in their promotional efforts. Joining this network is free and it also includes a $10 bonus into your account.

Leadbit

Leadbit manages thousands of digital and affiliate marketing projects. This network consists of 400 professionals in Moscow as well as others from around the world. Their ideology is monetizing at every possible niche. They are also very open to working with their publishers and also providing them with exclusive offers.

Affiliate Partners Ltd.

This is an affiliate network in the financial industry and it is known for giving among the highest payouts (CPA) up to $600 for niches such as gaming, casino, trading as well as sales funnels. Affiliate Partners makes affiliate marketing easier simply because they have a professional team that is reachable 24/7 through email and Skype.

CrakRevenue

CrakRevenue is also another long-time player in the industry. The CPA network has proved to be one of the most trustworthy platforms for affiliates throughout the world. They have 700+ quality offers that marketers to choose from and even from exclusives from MyFreeCams. CrakRevenue is a definite answer for affiliates who want to enjoy some of the industry's cutting-edge tools such as Surveys and Smartlinks as well as for those interested in joining a caring network.

eBay

Another well-known brand for e-commerce but not known as an affiliate network. eBay has now been online for over 20 years and its Partner Network also provides exceptional class tools, reporting as well as tracking.

Avangate

Another player in the digital commerce field, Avangate is backed by a cloud platform and it focuses on subscription billing and online commerce as well as global payments for Saas, Online Services and Software companies. More than 4000 digital business in over 180 countries use Avangate such as Kaspersky Lab, Spyrix, Brocade and Bitdefender as well as Absolute Software.

Flexoffers

This is a premiere affiliate network that builds profitable partnerships that are mutually beneficial between skilled, strategic as well as trustworthy online publishers. They also have a robust relationship with over 5,000 popular advertising spanning all verticals. Flexoffers have 10 over years of experience in the affiliate marketing industry and they also over excellent customer service, data delivery tools and dependable payments. Their game is flexibility when it comes to affiliate success FlexOffers is also ranked at the top 8 overall in CPS Networks 2015 Blue Book Survey.

Avantlink

Avantlink is known for its industry-leading platform for affiliate referrals. It works extremely hard to maintain its cutting edge upgrades and updates as well as introducing rapid implementation of new tools and technology. Their emphasis is on quality, rather than merely quantity.

Commission Factory

Commission Factory strives to provide performance-based marketing available to everyone without the steep learning curve. They do this to get more people involved and be successful in affiliate marketing. This platform is designed to specifically target a sense of collaboration between Affiliates, Agencies as well as Merchants to grow a substantial and beneficial partnership. Commission Factory has a fast growing user base that enables companies of various sizes to be part of the performance-based marketing.

AdCombo

Another CPA Marketing Network, AdCombo uses its own in-house technology system that enables marketers to customize their advertising campaigns to reach a targeted audience all over the world. AdCombo aims and hits their targets to encourage strategic and lucrative partnerships between publishers as well as advertisers.

Olavivo

As a boutique affiliate network, Olavivo focuses on e-commerce, beauty, health and cryptocurrency verticals. Their network promises transparency, dedication, as well as unique technological capabilities using the highest professional service.

Chapter 4- How to get Started with Affiliate Marketing

In this chapter, we will review the most basic and required steps to get started. You will go through 5 steps which embody:

- **Step 1- Finding your Niche in Affiliate Marketing**
- **Step 2: Create a Website or A Blog**
- **Step 3: Choosing and Signing up for an Affiliate Program**
- **Step 4: Creating Content and Using Social Media for Promotions**
- **Step 5- Optimizing your Content**

Keep in mind that these steps are the most basic in order to excel in affiliate marketing. Without these essentials, there is no way you can even call yourself an affiliate marketer. Essentials are important to start anything.

Step 1- Finding your Niche in Affiliate Marketing

It may sound overwhelming to find your niche in business because there are plenty of areas where you can specialize. While it does sound overwhelming, it is not hard as there are a few methods that you can employ to find that perfect niche that would give you profits. Here are some methods t for determining the right niche:

Tip #1- Brainstorming

Brainstorming is always effective for practically anything you need to work on- ideas, solutions, methods and finding the right niche. To begin brainstorming ideas for your niches, meet up with your business partner or like-minded friends who will be able to help you or someone you trust. Friends and family who know you and your business partner are the most ideal. Next, you will want to block off time to focus on your brainstorming- so set a meeting, time and date for this goal. When you meet, one of the things to think about is the items that you or your business partner or friends have bought online or recently purchased. Write these things down, even if they perplex you. There will be tons of niches that are profitable but that does not mean you should rush into picking one for your affiliate marketing business. When you have your niches, list them and filter them according to:

- Competition: Look out for other affiliate marketing business and explore the kinds of products that are oversaturated. You do not want to get into selling these.

- Loyalty: Avoid getting into niches that are dominated by national brand

- Pricing: The higher the price of the product, the higher to get the margin profits

- Weight: The winning combo is a high-priced product, but it has low shipping weights.

- Returns: Do not go for products that have different sizes and style preferences- they usually come with high return rates

Tip #2- Research, compare and evaluate trends

eBay is one of the recommended places to check whether items sell online but do not use eBay to determine the price of your products as eBay's prices are relatively low.

Once you get onto eBay, you will want to research and identify the products in the different niches in the higher-priced bracket, the ones that are expensive so it can be anything like $50 or $200 or $500 depending on the product. When you obtain your search results, allow them to show 'completed listings'. Completed lists shows items in red or green, red denotes the item did not sell and green reflects sold.

Look at the items only for the products you are considering to niche in- it is okay to go over this list a few times until you identify about 20 products within your niche that sell out almost always- at least 10 units a day. From here, request for price lists from various suppliers, get shipping quotes from customs brokers as well as storage capacities for a product.

Tip #3- Utilize Amazon

Being the world's largest retailer, Amazon sells everything imaginable. Because of this dominance, Amazon is one of the best things on the Internet to find profitable niches and other amazing possibilities that you never thought of. You can find profitable niches using Amazon and it is one way to attain this objective.

Firstly, just click on the 'All' tab which is located on the left side of the primary search toolbar. Upon clicking on it, you will see niches or a list of categories

- Click on a category that interests you and clicks on 'Go'.

- When the new page pops up, you will see on the left, a list of 'sub-niches'

- By clicking on a subcategory, you will then see more specific sub-niches

- You now have specific niches! You can go down this list if you really desire.

Amazon is also a great place to help you in a specific niche as well as the product that sells the best. You can also choose 'best sellers' from the navigation bar located just right under the search bar at the top of the page. You can see all the items that are currently selling the best.

Tip #4- Put on your Marketer Cap

One of the best things you can sell with drop shipping is to sell EXPENSIVE items.

The average affiliate marketing profit is about 20% of your total sales. You make 20% profit on an item that is $1,000 which is $200 or 20% on an item that is $10 which makes you $2. If you want to start making money, start selling the big toys. Sounds simple, but in truth, you will need to do more research. You will also need to identify potential future competition, which involve other online retailers who are selling the items you want to sell.

The roadblock here is there is no way to determine how much money a retailer makes on each and every sale at this point unless you use a MAP procedure.

Should I choose passion or money in a niche?

It really depends on you. To some people, starting a business in affiliate marketing also means that they can work on a product or be doing business that they love. Whereas to others, they find motivation the more money they see in their bank account and they don't care what they sell.

The truth is, you want to make a profit for any kind of venture or business you are in. So you will most likely look into a balancing act of pursuing your passion and creating a successful profit line.

Having said that, you still need to have some kind of interest in the product that you are selling because it will keep you motivated to explore even further on your audience needs, which will also help you to better align your content. When it comes to pursuing your passion, it doesn't necessarily mean that you'd be successful.

So how do we balance the two?

Passion does lead the way. Finding profitable niches to things, items and products that you are passionate about not only makes your bank account healthy but also it makes you have fun and love what you do. To help you discover your passion, if you already have not, let's take a look at niches that are based on your passions. Here are some questions you can ask yourself:

- What kind of blogs and websites do you interact with and visit the most?

- What kind of pages or accounts do you follow on social media that you enjoy?

- Which online stores do you usually purchase from?

- What do you think are your biggest obsessions?

- What kind of products do you usually collect or buy most frequently?

Create a shortlist of products based on the answers you give to the questions above. Next, if you want to choose a niche based on how much money you can make, then you might want to ask yourself this set of questions:

- Which niches hold the biggest audiences?

- Which online retailers have been increasing in popularity lately? And what products do they sell? (Answer these questions focusing on a few specific niche-based retailers instead of big names like Amazon)

- Which products are the most popular right now?

- Which products have huge profit margins?

Evergreen Niches vs Trending Niches

An evergreen niche is a niche that most retailers would like- it stands the test of time. Things like gaming, beauty, fashion, and weight loss are extremely evergreen niches. However, on the other hand, trending niches have instant profits and surge, but they also fall in popularity pretty fast.

Tools that you can use for finding a Niche Market

There are a variety of different tools that you can use to create shortlists of niche ideas in order to determine if you can see any niches that show signs of being highly profitable or aligned within your passions.

First, start your search with these:

- Oberlo
- Amazon
- AliExpress
- Treadhunter

On all these websites, you can easily find the trending niches. Keep your eye out for niches that keep coming up and also try to find potential sub-niches that you deem as interesting that might complement each other.

Trending Products Blog Posts

Another tip is to assess for updated product lists. Oberlo is one such company that regularly shares updated product lists to ensure that they are always at the forefront of today's most popular products. These lists can also help you determine your specific niche. Besides, keep an eye out for blog posts with lists such as:

- 20 of the best gardening tools to have in 2018

- 30 Fail-proof Business ideas to make money in 2018

- Best Buy Beauty Products for Summer 2018

- Top 10 Polishes To Get your Car Shining like Brand new

Check out the products mentioned, as well as the affiliate marketing products being sold and the business ideas related to them:

Wikipedia's List of Hobbies

Wikipedia's list of hobbies is a great way to find a niche of practically anything that you can think of from hobbies to passion, from crocheting to baton twirling, resin art to golfing, furniture restoration and terrariums- you will be surprised to find an extremely extensive list of both indoor and outdoor hobbies. Assess the lists to determine if there are any hobbies that compliment your passions or research to find profitable niches within these categories. Some are hobbies are popular enough to have a large market of followers, so you can actually build an entire store dedicated to selling these products or the items that help these hobbyists work on their passions.

The amazing thing about hobbies is that you will have like-minded people join groups and spend the money to pursue their hobbies. This itself gains you an audience you can immediately sell to. Some of the hobbies on the list that you can build e-commerce stores for include:

- Jewelry making
- Astrology
- Do it yourself
- Fashion
- Flower arranging
- Gardening
- Magic
- Pet
- Various fitness niches
- Baking

Google Trends

Yes, Google Trends is another tool you can use to discover your niche. What you want to look out for are niches that have a stable growth, no matter how slight. Here is a list you can check out- Google Trends.

Do you need to be an expert in finding your niche?

You do not necessarily need to be a niche, but some experience will help you a long way. It may be slightly harder to build a successful brand without having some kind of niche experience, although it is not entirely impossible.

Alternatively, you can also fake it till you make it. This means that you can just find the right target audience through Facebook ads as well. You can also engage influencers using the power of Instagram to build an audience as this can lead to sales. Having some idea about the niche you are getting into will also help you create content that resonates with your audience. No experience may render it harder to reach them and bring that traffic to your store.

On the other hand, you can also outsource these blog writing tasks to ghostwriters or someone equivalent. But most entrepreneurs do this, especially when starting out to keep costs low. As mentioned previously, getting into selling a product you somewhat like and having some expertise in the niche can help motivate you, in the long run, to sustain your business, especially if the money isn't hitting the profit margins like you desire.

FB Search

Another tool you can use is FB search and this tool can help you determine the amount of engagement your posts actually get. You can also use this as a competitor analysis tool so you can see the posts of both your competitors, as well as customers, make. You can also look up at the brands that are within your nice. Search using specific keywords to search. Your search will turn up based on people, pages, photos, videos, links, and marketplace. When you look at these pages, you can see the number of followers. It will also help you understand the kind of frequency your Facebook posts need to be, which is somewhere between 1-2 posts per day to maintain a competitive advantage and scale quickly.

Browsing the pages that come up in your search also gives you an idea of the direction of your marketing strategy, looking through photos helps you understand the kind of material you need to create and the markets you can target.

Continue your research

Here are several other things to consider before you start building your store. You want to make sure that you have an audience for your niche even before you were spending hours on marketing your website and buying ads online. Here's a quick list of what to look for:

- What kind of social platforms do people market your niche?

- Are there dedicated Facebook groups for your niche?

- Are there targeting options you can use on Facebook for this niche?

- What kind of forums exist for people to discuss the niche?

- Do people host events for this niche?

- Do influencers post about this niche?

- Are there fans for your niche?

Pinterest, YouTube, Instagram and of course Facebook are all popular places to look if your niches are talked about on these platforms. It is always better to put your content where it is seen, heard and speaks because there is where your audience spends time on.

Another thing is, all these platforms have one element in common. They are all heavy on visuals which means, stunning images and video attract your audience faster.

Step 2: Create a Website or A Blog

Designing a website or a blog requires planning, and it needs a robust and good plan. Although setting a website or blog through Wordpress is free, you'd still want something that is lasting and memorable, even if this website or blog is for personal use.

On a piece of paper, just use at least 20 minutes to articulate your Mission Statement. You will want to have a few things determined for your site, so you have the focus to your site and you know the content you want on it.

Here are a few things to establish:

- What will you do with your site?
- What kind of content do you want on it?
- Who do you want to read this?
- How often do you plan on posting and adding content?

Depending on what your site is supposed to do, you will need to consider what kind of information you are willing to share and post. You would also want to include some contact information, so your visitors can contact you-unless you don't want them to do so.

Choosing the Right Domain Name

The domain name and the domain extension go hand in hand. Once you have decided on your domain extension, you need to figure out what you'd like to call your site which will be your domain. Your domain name is what your website's URL will consist of when someone types it into the browser's address bar.

Here are a few crucial points to consider when devising with your Domain Name:

- Matching Names: Essentially the name of your site as well as the URL must match.

- Short: So it's easier to remember and can be typed into the browser

- Consistent Branding: Your domain is a reflection of your brand. Keep it consistent and memorable.

- Memorable: Well, a website must be easy to remember and memorable, so you want it to stick the first time when your visitors come to your site.

- Catchy: It must be easy to pronounce and roll off the tongue easily. Your domain name must also describe what you do.

- Includes Keywords: You want it to be Search Engine Optimized (SEO).

Essentially, you want it to be easy to remember and easy to type. Your domain name must correspond with what your business does or what your personal online agenda is for your site.

Customizing and Personalizing

To make your site 100% your own, you can choose to personalize and customize the theme. Usually, customization is done on the fonts, the colors, and other simple design elements, without altering the layout of the site.

To customize the theme you have selected, you can go back to the Appearance section and choose the Customize link. Here, you have the option of doing a variety of things to your site to make it sync in with your branding needs. Usually, most themes allow you to change the logo, the colors and backgrounds, the fonts, the header image, the menus and the widgets.

In this chapter, we will investigate the various ways in which you can customize your site based on what can be changed. If you are not experienced in coding, it is best to leave the customization to the selected options. But if you do know coding and can take your site's customization to another level, then go ahead- there is no stopping you and the sky's the limit!

Step 3: Choosing and Signing up for an Affiliate Program

When you sign up for an affiliate program, you will need to ensure that it fits your needs, your site as well as your audience. There are affiliate programs for whatever route you go for and for whatever products you choose, whether you're a blogger for electronic products, a review site for vacation home rentals, or even coupon codes for makeup.

Stick with programs that suit your needs and your site

When you find an affiliate program, it does not mean you need to sign up for it immediately. When you become an affiliate marketer, your credibility becomes extremely crucial and it also depends on how involved you are in the program you choose. The involvement you have in the program can become even greater when you start pushing the boundaries based the content you engage your users with. Marketing products and services that stay true to their selling features will bring you trusted, loyal fans; and doing the opposite will make you less of a star.

When you choose an affiliate program, stick with ones that are a natural fit for you and for your site. You will find that it is much easier to keep growing your audience with this approach, and you will also yield a higher rate in sales.

Assess the Customer Service Experience

When choosing an affiliate program, do a little bit of research on its customer service, You want to know what it is like for customers to deal with product or service issues, which will give you a good idea on how much value the merchant site places on customer service and how much value they place on customers. Merchants that value their customers will offer good customer service, which is a good sign for you as an affiliate. Everyone wants to make money online but to ensure that the income you get is consistent and sustainable, do things ethically, even if it means it will take a longer time to achieve the target you want. You want to promote a product or service that is ethical as well, so if you will not recommend a product or service to your own family, then it is best not to sign up for a program that you will not recommend to your site visitors.

Place yourself in your users' shoes- you should also be hesitant to purchase from a merchant that has bad reviews and recommendations right? So keep thing in mind when sourcing for a program to sign up for. Signing up for a program that has questionable reviews and low quality products would ultimately affect your own bottom line. Why does this happen? Because unhappy customers will return products and they will never want to buy from the same site again. They will also post their review somewhere on the Internet. Your merchant's credibility also affects you, so choose wisely.

The Commission Rate

Commission rates matter: and while this facet should not be the only thing to consider when signing up, it is part and parcel of making your decision of choosing an affiliate program. Commission rates are generally small but the more sales you make, the more they add up. If you have found a program that offers a smaller pay percentage consistently on particular items compared to others, then you are just wasting your time. You need to research commission rates for various products on different affiliate programs before you sign up with them. Different programs offer different rates-look for one that has the best rate with the best payment term and the best terms and conditions.

Average Order Size

The average order size may be a piece of information that is hard to find, but it will be useful for you to determine, even if they do not offer this information. The average order size gives you an idea of how business works on their site and what kind of opportunities you will have to gain more money. These little extras will add up to your bottom line. For instance, sites that offer free shipping for purchases over a certain amount means that buyers will be encouraged to buy a little extra to get their money's worth on the shipping bonus. And if you promote these items on your site, you get a little extra incentive to gain more money because the chances of buying are higher.

Payment Threshold

You must also get to know the kind of payment threshold involved with your program especially when you have different affiliate programs and networks that you are interested in. It makes the decision-making easier. Affiliate programs are individual merchants, whereas networks denote groups of merchants under an umbrella.

The payment threshold for the program and the network could be identical, but you are more likely to meet the threshold in a network at a much faster rate as it will include your commissions from multiple merchants. The profits you earn add up much faster than acquiring sales from just one merchant. This means you get paid more often from different merchants.

However, it does not mean you should avoid individual programs. It also depends on the product you have chosen as well as your audience. Choosing to stick to a program may be beneficial for those who do not have that much of time promoting several different programs from various different merchants. Also, a program may suit an affiliate who wants to make an average side income of a few hundred a month.

Understanding the threshold for programs or networks is essential nonetheless as it will give you a better understanding of how much you can potentially make and how else can you maximize your earnings. Not reaching your threshold also means you may be penalized for it.

Cookie Length

When doing your research on affiliate programs, analyze the cookie length. For some affiliates, the cookie or tracking code lasts for a few hours while for some, it could be months. If a customer makes a sales sale while they cookie is still there, you will earn a commission even if it wasn't a direct sale from your site. A longer cookie length however does not mean it is a better affiliate program. It is just useful knowledge to know what your program entails and how you can utilize it to gain more profits. Your cookie length must relate with your product- some products take smaller decision making time to purchase whereas some take longer. Your cookie length needs to match the consumer's purchasing habit.

Terms and Conditions of the Affiliate Program

You will want the terms and conditions of your chosen program articulated in a clear fashion. You don't want unnecessary surprises and hurdles just to get paid. You must read and understand your choice of program before signing up so you know what you are agreeing to from payment terms, cookie length, and payment threshold, and so on. Weed out the bad programs by reading the fine print, so you can make the best decision with the best programs available.

Step 4: Creating Content and Using Social Media To Promote Your Website

There is no such way a business can survive without social media. Practically every type of business, big or small with the intention of moving forward, is adapting and seeking new opportunities and customers need to have at least one social media account.

From our previous chapter, we know that Facebook takes the cake when it comes to social media dominance so much, so that even an old business serving a small neighborhood community has at least a Facebook mention or a street address on Facebook.

Social media is a great tool in generating leads, and as a marketer, you should pay a good amount of attention in amplifying your social media presence so that it can play a significant role in generating leads in your marketing campaigns and strategies. Social media can drive niche web traffic from those that are actively seeking the kind of information you are projecting. Using social media monitoring, advertising, networking and content creation will bring you the kind of leads you need to maximize your online sales.

A) Using Social Media to Build Strong Networking Ties

Harnessing the power of social media takes time. To generate leads, you must invest in interaction, affection, communication and time. How do you create ties?

1- Follow prospects on Twitter and LinkedIn

Following prospects and industry leaders in this platform help builds authority, and it also produces interaction. Users visiting your Twitter or LinkedIn pages will see the kind of people you follow and create a perception that you are keen and passionate in the line of business you are in. You as the account holder would be able to communicate, share, engage, like and comment on these prospects pages. All these things will be viewed by current and potential customers.

2- Make friends on Facebook

You'd be surprised how people view friend requests on Facebook. It is sort of like giving a business card to people-you offer it to them with the hopes of either receiving a call or so that they will remember you when a business opportunity arises.

3- Utilize Google Hangout with Industry Leaders

Google Hangout is the professional version of Facebook. When you do share email contact with other business leads of a company whether an employee, the CEO, marketing executive, and directors - Hangout with them on Google. Share ideas, presentations, conduct virtual training classes, and invite them for company cocktail events and the like. It presents a more interpersonal approach from one employee to another.

4- Host a webinar

Hosting a webinar creates authority, increases trust and positive perception on your brand. Hosting webinars also lure the niche crowd you are targeting which increases the chances of this select crowd signing up for your service or purchasing your product.

5- Answer questions on your social accounts

Opening social media accounts and not interacting with your community and clients is social media suicide. Social media gives consumers a means of communicating with brands on a more personal level. Not answering any questions or comments posted on your account or not even participating in discussions on your page does not create a wholesome image for your brand.

B)   Influence connections for content sharing

Publishing and sharing content exemplifies one of the best ways to increase lead generation. Here are some great ideas to help you to create content:

6-   Writing ebooks and include forms

Ebooks, whether free or paid, provide an excellent way to share your content with your target audience. Usually, a short accompanying blog list post would help in increasing the download of the ebook, too. The blog post itself entices the reader, enables sharing, and fosters keywords optimization. Writing ebooks also increase your authority on the subject and credibility.

7-   Retweet

Found a tweet that promotes your product or service? Retweet it. Locate a negative comment on your product or service? Read no.5.

8-   Make visual content

In our previous chapter, we discovered that Pinterest was the biggest network featuring shared content. Optimize your content to make it easily shared on Pinterest. Visual content also makes the amount of time to make a decision to share or comment or tag someone lesser, thus increasing conversion rates.

9- Don't always talk about you, your product or your service

Nobody wants to constantly read about things that you sell or do. Sometimes, it helps to create content on helpful information. For example, if you sell cars, write content about how to maintain different car engines or where is the best place to get car parts. Link with other service providers into your post, and you'll work on no.2 on this list.

10- Optimize for mobile viewing

As a result of smartphones, information is now in the palm of our hands. Any content you create has to be optimized for mobile viewing first and desktop second. Your consumers are more likely to view your newsletters, product updates, emails, statutes, and tweets via mobile then they will be on their desktop. One of the things to consider when optimizing for mobile viewing is also when to publish your content, so the chances are higher for your clientele to pick up their phones and read it. 3 am is not the time, in case you are wondering.

11- Utilize Slideshare

Increase your credibility and authority on your subject matter and industry by creating relevant and shareable content on Slideshare. Again, this content must not be about your product or service because then it's just selling your stuff. Talk about information that would subtly help your business. For example, if you sell cars, then mention things like DIY servicing, how to care for second-hand vehicles, how to change black oil and so on. People will naturally flock to your site at the end of the presentation for more details.

C) Utilize social media monitoring

Listening to your audience on social media helps to uncover plenty of information on how receptive they are towards your brand and how your brand relates to them. Listening in this sense involves seeing the interaction between consumer and brand and reacting to this through offering information or expertise helps increase the sales, without the pressure of selling. Here's how to monitor for lead opportunities:

12- Monitor industry trends

It is essential to keep up with trends in your industry to stay at the top of your game. Trends can help make your product or service more visible. For example, if you sell shoes and the latest trends are fringe products, then highlight shoes in this category through your newsletters and blog posts or, link an article featuring fringed items and connect it with your product.

13- Monitor discussions about your product category

Reddit, Buzzfeed, CNET and Google Alerts are great places to monitor conversations of your product category. Google Alerts, for example, gives you alerts on any news items that are related to your keyword search. Staying updated on what's happening in your industry helps you not only to make more informed marketing decisions, but it also allows you to interact proactively with your customer base.

14- Monitor questions and conversations about your product category

Questions and conversations about your product category regularly help you tweak your product to better suit your target market's needs. Conversations often takes place at comment sections in social network such as Instagram, YouTube, Facebook and even commerce sites such as Amazon and EBay. Just keep an eye out on what your audience is saying.

D) Use social ads to generate leads

Of course paid advertising and sponsored Tweets as well as promoted content on Instagram, Facebook and Twitter can help generate leads. It will assist if you have a new product or service or an event that you would like to reach out to new audiences.

Here are ten examples of how to do it:

15- Use a Facebook ads & Promoted tweets to drive traffic to your website.

Facebook ads and promoted tweets are perfect for new

businesses entering this incredibly popular social network platform. If you have a new product or a new event you want to promote, use the ads. Facebook and Twitter ads are relatively cheap, and you can also create ads to target specific type of audiences based on their location, age and even, content that they search on the Internet.

16- Create an ad on LinkedIn

LinkedIn ads are perfect for promoting webinars, seminars, training as well as talks. Use ads on LinkedIn wisely for the right type of content because the people you are targeting are different from those on social media accounts like Snapchat and Facebook. If professionals or business people are what you are looking for, then LinkedIn is the place to advertise business content that you know will help them.

17- Make ads for Pinterest

Within the US, Pinterest's audience is made up of 52% Millennials, 68% of women aged 25 to 54 and 69% of moms and 36% of dads. Knowing this piece of information, tweak your ads to be visually appealing and made for this target audience. Clothes, shoes, baby products, vintage accessories, and art are the best kind of products to be advertised on Pinterest. No matter what you do, make sure your headline corresponds with your images.

18- Advertise on forums

Depending on what industry your product or service is in, advertise in them. There is a forum for practically everything on the internet from Crockpots to homemade baby foods, GoPro cameras, hand woven silk, drones, short story writing, second-hand furniture, garage sale, old books and novels and so much more. Understanding your clientele also means knowing where they 'hang-out' online and where they get their information. People often tend to rely on information found on forums because it's mostly from other users who have utilized them before.

E)   Search Engine Optimization (SEO)

Last but not least is SEO, which is a huge driver to your online sites. A combination of the right keywords, social media content, blog content and a good website can all boost your SEO. With better SEO, you are able to reach out to your target audience much easier as they can find you more easily.

Always remember to ensure that this is always on your checklist when it comes to Search Engine Optimization:

- Cross-linking your post to your Facebook or Twitter accounts (or both)
- Using appropriate keywords on your LinkedIn page
- Applying relevant keywords in your headlines
- Utilizing tagging and specific keywords for your images
- Sharing your ebooks with relevant keywords and phrases
- Integrating visual content by using infographics, YouTube videos, and Instagram-worthy images
- Connect and share through Google +

Bottom Line

Like it or hate it, social media is here to stay. As the year goes by, there will be newer platforms that will make their ways into consumers' smartphones, and mobile applications; in turn, businesses must keep evolving with this technology. Social media has presented a relatively cheap, fast and convenient way to share, post, update, and advertise to the masses and brands must take advantage of this. One of the major takeaways for social media is that it allows a deeper and more personalized connection between brands and consumers, which also mean brands must be ready to react, respond, and connect with their target audience at any given time.

By connecting with your audience, you enable them to see a more human side of your brand, and that also means you get to let your brand personality shine.

Millennial want this. Millennials want a genuine connection with the things they use, the brands they come into contact with and the products and services they use.

This is why cheesy stock photos do not relate anymore to the consumers of today.

If managing several social media accounts give you a headache, move on to the next chapter to discover what tools that you can utilize to maximize your productivity, marketing and also managing several accounts at one go.

Step 5- Optimizing your Content

Increase Traffic with Better Headlines

Online marketing and content go hand in hand. As you know by now, content is a key decision maker on whether a user will click on a call to action or a blog post, an article, a video or an image. What is it that makes certain content more clickable and shareable than another?

This chapter focuses on data mined by CoSchedule on over 1 million headlines of blogs and social media content. The research was conducted on headlines that have at least a total of 100 shares across major social networks. Below are the results of their findings. As a result, you can learn how to tweak or change the headlines in your own content.

Result 1: Majority of content does not get shared that much

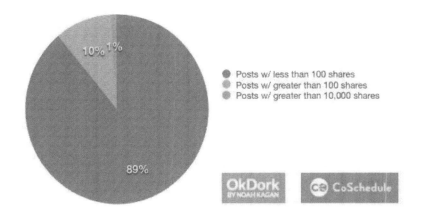

The results here are astounding. 89% of the content you create is never shared for more than 100 times. This is a major indication for content creators and online marketers working together that things need to be done differently.

But what about the 10% that was shared 100 times and the 1%

that was shared more than 10,000 times? What is it that made those headlines top performing? Knowing these essentials will help you to create your own content and position your website among the top high-performing sites on the Internet in your selected field.

Result 2: What common words/phrases are used in highly-shared headlines?

Most Popular Words/Phrases In Highly-Shared Headlines

Word/Phrase	# of uses	% of headlines
List Post	787	11.10%
You/Your	478	6.74%
Free/Giveaway	255	3.60%
How To	205	2.89%
DIY	197	2.78%
I/Me/My	153	2.16%
Easy	137	1.93%
Win	104	1.47%
New	97	1.37%
Ways	75	1.06%
Why	60	0.85%
Video	51	0.72%
The Most	17	0.24%

CoSchedule also compiled a list of common words and phrases used often in headlines to figure out what made them more attractive to share. As you can see, the results again are telling.

Takeaway #1 – List Posts are in Demand

It goes to show that people find list posts are shared much faster 1,000 times. This despite the fact that list posts only make up a total of 5% of the posts actually written by marketers. It reveals that content creators don't create enough of these types of posts in the first place.

Takeaway #2 – Identify with You and Your

Headlines that utilized the words 'you' were shared extremely well and very frequently. Posts that used 'I' or "Me' were shared three times less. It shows that content written in the second person point of view resonates with the reader as if the content is speaking directly to the reader. It makes it ideal to be shared compared to content that comes from a first person view, and that usually means it isn't about the reader but about someone else. It also denotes that readers like to envision themselves in what they are reading.

Takeaway #3 – Help Your Readers Imagine A Better Life

People will love content that helps them to create, do, or learn something wonderful. It's even better if the post comes in words like 'Do this in a few minutes' or 'How to' or 'Win something' or 'Share this for free gift' or '10 Hacks to.' All these posts contain promising words to attract readers by subtly or overtly telling them that if they read this post, they can learn, buy, win, or create something. In essence, this tactic increases their likelihood of sharing your content.

Do common headlines change depending on social network?

There is a trend regarding how posts are circulated among social media networks. For example, Facebook, YouTube and Google+ are very much home-oriented therefore you would find plenty of 'How-To's,' DIY videos, homemade posts and recipes. Twitter is more business and technology focused, whereas Instagram tends to veer towards lifestyle and fitness.

Common Words/Phrases In Highly-Shared Headlines, By Social Network

Facebook	Twitter	Google+	Pinterest	LinkedIn
things	google	chocolate	chicken	google
recipe	facebook	butter	chocolate	facebook
about	giveaway	recipe	recipe	should
video	about	peanut	butter	social
should	should	google	wedding	about
reasons	social	cream	peanut	chicken
homemade	media	cookies	cookies	things
healthy	reasons	chicken	homemade	apple
every	twitter	cheese	salad	ideas
people	android	cookie	cream	media

■ = Possible list-posts
□ = Shows a unique characteristics of this social network

OkDork   CoSchedule

Takeaway #4 – List-posts Do Best On Facebook, Twitter, and LinkedIn

We know that list posts are shared quickly and easily but which of these networks work excellently for posts like these?

Using the common terms guide above, it becomes obvious that certain words indicate that list-based posts work excellently on these networks. Words like 'Thing', 'Should' and 'Reasons' feature prominently on Twitter, LinkedIn and Facebook.

Using this information, you can easily think about headlines you've seen on these platforms:

- 10 clever ways to use binder clips

- 5 hacks for better SEO

- 15 places to visit in Colorado

List posts often use highly emotional terms, which is a strong reason why they are shared.

Takeaway #5 – Video Is Most Popular On Facebook

Facebook is by far the most popular platform to feature video content, apart from YouTubr. This is also due to the fact on how Facebook easily allows videos to be embedded into its newsfeed. Taking advantage of this, lately there has been plenty instructional video that is not more than 1 minute long, as seen on things like Tasty or Crafty.

Takeaway #6 – Customize Headlines For Each Social Network

As you know, each social network has its own demographic and its own audience therefore each of this platform should be catered to individually. We realize that Facebook and Pinterest are more home-oriented whereas LinkedIn and Twitter are much more business oriented whereas Snapchat and Instagram are more lifestyle based. Each of these platforms caters to different audiences and therefore they require different types of content.

To accommodate this, writing custom headlines for each social network is essential rather than sharing the same post with the same title for each network. For Twitter, whether you like it or not, you already need to tweak your headlines to fit its 140 character limit. So while this may sound tedious, tweak whenever necessary.

Which platform does the world's most popular headlines get shared?

To understand how shareable headlines work is also to understand how users will ultimately share your content. Here is how users on different social networks share content. As you can see, Pinterest is the leader in sharing and pinning content and why wouldn't it be as the platform was created for the sole purpose of bookmarking things on the internet in the most convenient way possible.

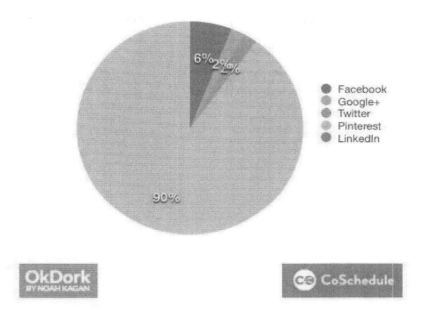

Takeaway #7 – Pinterest Offers HUGE Shares If You Can Reach The Audience

Pinterest is huge, but in order to get your post shared on Pinterest, you need the right type of content. Words alone will not cut it. Pinterest thrives on beautiful images as well, just like Instagram's carefully curated, expertly shot mobile pictures. However, creating the right content with the right headline and images will get your post picked up and pinned- plenty of times.

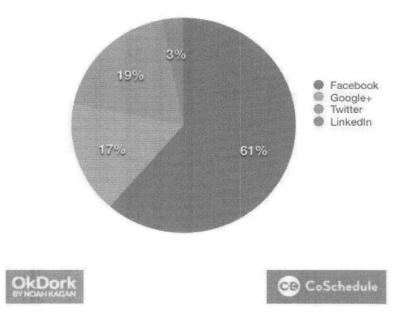

Takeaway #8 –Facebook is still the frontrunner

When you remove Pinterest from the equation, you get Facebook coming in second place as the most popular network for shared content. So when it comes to shared content, you want to gain a bigger portion of both Facebook and Pinterest.

Can a marketer predict the popularity of a headline?

Just like there's an app for everything, there is also a web tool for everything. As an online marketer, you need to take advantage of resourceful tools that make your life easier. The same goes to testing headlines to rate them if they are going to be an attention grabber and well-shared post. The Emotional Marketing Value Headline Analyzer was created for this purpose by the Advanced Marketing Institute. This web tool allows a marketer to identify how emotionally driven your headline is by using the number of emotional words used in the phrase as a measurement yardstick.

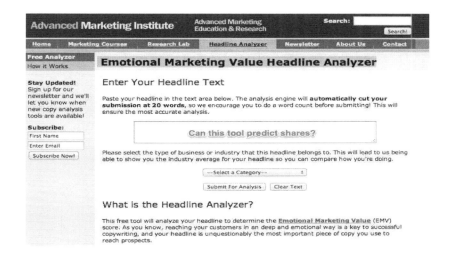

Above is a screenshot of the website. This tool is easy to use as all you need to do is copy and paste your headline into the box, and it'll give you a score of your headline based on the EMV scale.

The analyzer works by rating your headlines according to the emotional marketing value or EMV.

Here were the results:

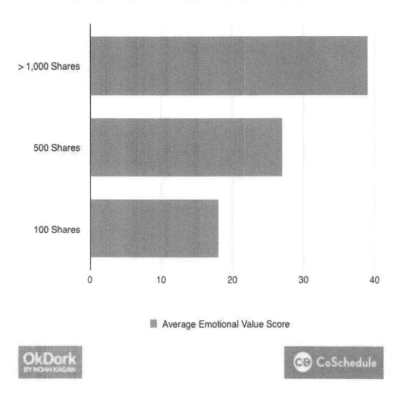

Average EMV Score For Headlines Based On Shares

Posts with a high number of shares usually have an EMV Score of 30 or 40, which are several points more than posts with fewer shares.

Takeaway #9 – Emotional Headlines are shared more!

As the numbers of shares increased, the EMV score on a post also increased. There is a direct connection between the quantity of emotional words used and the probability of being shared more than 1,000 times. This is something marketers can enforce for future posts.

Headlines with more emotional words connect to readers even more making them share posts like this faster. CoSchedule also conducted a quick research on the five more shared posts and the five least shared posts on some of the world's most popular blogs to find out with the EMV score would still continue to be a good indicator of sharing probability and here is what they found:

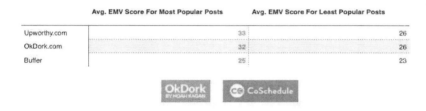

	Avg. EMV Score For Most Popular Posts	Avg. EMV Score For Least Popular Posts
Upworthy.com	33	26
OkDork.com	32	26
Buffer	25	23

The answer is yes. Even the least popular posts earned a pretty good EMV score.

Takeaway #10 – You Can easily measure The Emotional Value Of A Headline

Based on the results above, it looks like every post should be having an EMV headline of at least 30 or above to make it shareable. An EMV of 40 will definitely increase the chances of the post being shared. So if you don't know if your headline is good enough, then use the checker tool to assess. The headlines of a post are the first things a reader will look at, followed by the accompanying photo, so when you create your post or content, make sure the headline correlates with the image poster.

A good way to create good content is to always check the virility of your headline by analyzing the EMV score for your current posts, so that you can create future posts that have a higher value.

Chapter 5- Examples of Affiliate Marketing

In this chapter, we will look at real life examples of successful affiliate marketing endeavors to get you inspired and motivated to build your own site and work on affiliate marketing as a substantial side business.

- **Nerdwallet**

Considered a veteran in the affiliate marketing scene, Nerdwallet has a gold rank if you want to get inspiration. Plenty of marketers will tell you that they favor this affiliate website as the content is genuinely useful and it does exceedingly well in a competitive market. If you want information on financial products and where to get what you are looking for, NerdWallet is your source of information. This is a site you can go to if you need advice, reviews and information on everything financial from insurance to investing, mortgages to credit cards. Their content is stellar, their user-interface is exceptional and they also have a really good marketing team behind them. Nerdwallet is the gold-standard for affiliate marketing sites because they have a niche focus which is finance, they service a consumer niche which are people looking for information on financial products and services, and they also have a goal which is to help these people pick the best option for financial matters. This site currently has 10.6 million visitors a month.

Nerdwallet is a 100% affiliate site, there are no ads and they also do not sell their own financial products.

What can you learn from Nerdwallet?

- ❏ Nerdwallet's most engaging content comes into will form. They give a great user experience and their tools attract plenty of links. SEO plays an integral part of this site.

- ❏ Nerdwallet also updates their key pages constantly. Their most popular contents are updated annually, making it relevant and enabling their marketing team to market it again.

- **Money Saving Expert**

With a website URL that directly says MoneySavingExpert.com, you're bound to be getting plenty of visits just for your URL alone. This site gives out advice and information to help users make informed financial decisions. They operate the site as a financial education site that explores opportunities for people to get more bang for their buck. Kicked off in 2003, this site was created by Martin Lewis and is currently ranked as one of the most influential affiliate websites for consumers in UK. The site currently amasses 8 million unique visitors a month. MoneySavingExpert sets apart itself from the rest of the pack thanks to quality of content as well as the passion of helping consumers. The goal of this site is to help people make better financial decisions with ethical, accurate and updated financial information. The site is financed by monetizing affiliate links. The monetize their site by using several approaches. Firstly, their use of coupons. MoneySavingsExperts curates a list of deals and coupons for a variety of retailers, making a cut from each sale. Their site also has plenty of 'Best of' guides that feature products and services from banks and credit cards and it takes cut from each sign up from these affiliate links. They also take a cut from their 'Cheap XX' guides that help users choose the cheapest consumer products of a certain category. On the MoneySavingsExperts site, you'll also see a number of calculators from mortgage to loan calculators and each time there is a recommended financial product, MSE gets the cut. MSE also utilizes Amazon discount finders as well as Skimlinks in forum threads.

What can you learn from MoneySavingExpert?

❏ You will see that the MSE website if very well designed and organized. Their articles are also heavily formatted so as to make it as easy as possible to browse.

❏ They also stand out due to their strong editorial code of ethics which identifies correct affiliate links and minimizes any misinformation.

❏ They also maintain 'hero' pages which are highly visual pages that allow readers to get a quick glance of their best options. These hero pages are used-focused and always rank well on search engines.

❏ Each blog post, calculator, content and product has a call-to-action. There is no unnecessary fluff for users to address. Users can immediately go straightforward to the desired information.

- **The WireCutter**

A New York Times Company, the Wire Cutter is a review affiliate website that is a favorite for people looking for gadgets, electronics and related consumer goods. Started by Brian Lam, the former editor of Gizmodo, this site puts all reviewed products through innovative and strenuous tests. Known on the Internet as 'Mythbusters for Gadgets', the WireCutter has grown to become one of the top 6,000 online sites that feature the best products in each of their listed categories. Their product niche is to showcase consumer product reviews and their main goal is to enable people to find the best consumer products in their selected category. Their website currently sees a visitor rate of 3.6 million a month. The Wire Cutter explains clearly how their monetization model works under their 'How to Support Us' page. It is a really simply model that focuses on affiliate commissions through BestBuy and Amazon. Like the MoneySavingExpert and NerdWallet, The Wire Cutter also does not do any sponsored posts or any advertisements; it also does not sell its own products.

To monetize their site, they also have 'Best of' product pages full of product recommendations for each category and this gives Wire Cutter's bulk of profits. For each recommendation, there is an Amazon link and for every affiliate link that is clicked on, Wire Cutter takes a cut. One unique thing about Wire Cutter is that they answer readers' questions constantly, extending the customer service experience and they get a cut from the product sales made. Wire Cutter also uses other reputable retailers, other than Amazon, and they also utilize Skimlinks to make money online. Wire Cutter indicates that there are some forms of advertising, but these details are not readily available.

What can you learn from Wire Cutter?

❏ The Wire Cutter has focus. Instead of creating plenty of new posts on gadgets every month, they focus instead on in-depth reviews.

❏ Their clever use of design makes browsing reviews easy and fast for users.

❏ Their focus is quality and not quantity. Their tests are innovative and extensive tests on products increase their credibility and they live up to their name of testing all products to be the best in their class. Wire Cutter also produces an average of 6 to 12 posts a month.

- **Dating Advice**

The dating scene on the Internet is an extremely lucrative one, but it is also filled with plenty of scam and spam sites that send traffic to other affiliate offers. DatingAdvice.Com sets itself apart from the rest by focusing on a niche. Their site is fun, clean. Their main focus is on expert advice and they emphasize on answering real questions users usually will have. So in essence, their niche is to provide dating advice as well as dating website reviews with the goal to improve people's dating skills and find the best dating sites that fit their needs. Their website amasses a monthly visit of 413 thousand people.

atingAdvice.com makes the bulk of its profits from referring its users to dating websites such as eHarmony and Match.com. All of its recommended sites are mainstream and wholesome. Apart from that, DatingAdvice.com also has its own 'Best of' lists as well as best websites, best apps, products for dating and takes a cut for any sign-ups or sales that have been made. The reviews of popular dating sites also attract plenty of reads and they make money out of the affiliate commissions. As far as revenues go, these two types of content bring in the profits for DatingAdvice.Com. They also have sponsored posts that bring in some money for them.

What can you learn from them?

❑ The main thing that DatingAdvice.Com does spectacularly well is to keep their site clean. They keep a healthy, wholesome image without any scams, spams and sexual content. The designs, the colors and the use of faces in practically all posts goes a long way in telling users that this site is safe.

❑ Another way they keep it clean is by having no banner ads anywhere on the site. Banner ads have a long history of being spammy and it can also cheapen the design of a site: and for DatingAdvice that has a very cohesive design, it will definitely hurt, especially if you are monetizing your site with affiliates.

❏ They also have section for 'As Features in,' which has logos of mainstream, well-known publications. This helps the site establish credibility and sincerity and it also affirms the mainstream nature of the content. This social proof is excellent in maintaining a credible, trustworthy site.

❏ Lastly, DatingAdvice focuses on expert advice. Their advice is not from any random person but instead, features relationship experts as well as dating and marriage counselors. This also adds to the credibility of their site and gives authority.

- **PC Part Picker**

When you look at this website, you'll notice the design itself sets itself apart from traditional affiliate websites. It is not just another content targeting site that has 'the Best of'. Not that best-of listicles are bad- they are great and everyone loves them, but PC Part Picker is on a league of its own because they've managed to build something that provides extreme value that enables the site to market itself. The website's focus is basically as a tool for users who want to build their own computers, with the focus on gaming computers. The difficult part about building computers is getting the right information without browsing too many websites and getting information overload. New computer parts are constantly out in the market and finding the latest ones that fit your budget and needs take time to research. Plus, you will also want to know their compatibility.

What PC Part Picker does is just that- picks all the information apart for you. The site allows you to shop for the latest computer parts based on budget and performance and it also cross-references products to check compatibility. This site operates as a tool but it also has a nice blog that dispenses advice and other information on computers. PC Part Picker has a niche, which are computer parts. They have a goal to help people build computers and they have a website that enables these two elements to come together. The website receives about 3.3 millions visitors on a monthly basis.

PC Part Picker monetizes their site through affiliate links via user-created or expert-created PC builds. They also focus on individual reviews on computer components. In the expert-created PC builds, experts put together a PC for you on the site via a blog post. If users like what they read, they can click on the affiliate links to purchase the component.

Individual component reviews on the other hand use historical price data to help people make better purchasing decisions for their computer parts.

What can you learn from PC Part Picker?

❏ Their site is built as a tool. While they do have a blog and valuable content, their main game is the PC - building tool.

❑ Their main focus is on user experience. Everything from the tools to the parts is geared to help users achieve a specific goal, which is to build a PC that has no compatibility issues and within a certain budget.

❑ They make it easier for users to shop around for the right component. By being a member of various affiliate programs, PC Part Picker can help users to gain the best component at their desired price range and they even go beyond just recommending products on their site- they also help readers to achieve a good shopping experience.

- **50em.com**

This site has just 7 pages. It does not have a well-established team or a large budget. It also lacks existing audiences. 50em's main goal is to help readers choose between two of the most popular automation tools currently on the market which are InfusionSoft as well as Ontraport. These tools represent a huge spend for any marketer and they also run into hundreds of dollar every month. 50em, by crafting an ultra-focused, hyper-targeted content makes the selection process between these two easier and of course brings in the profit for them. This site is a master-class in creating high-impact, high-value product reviews.

There are plenty of things you can learn from this site. Primarily, they have a focus which is automation software reviews and their main goal is to help marketers choose between Ontraport and InfusionSoft.

Wondering how they make money? The monetization method for 50em is the same like the rest- through affiliate commissions. Both InfusionSoft and Ontraport are expensive, starting from $199 to $297 a month. A single sale is wildly lucrative. To make these commissions, 50em creates in-depth reviews for both Ontraport as well as InfusionSoft. These are texts as well as videos to explain each product well and it gives plenty of value to their readers.

Apart from this, 50em also gives high-quality head-to-head comparisons, if the reviews themselves are not convincing enough for you. You can compare both products against each other, by reading in-depth breakdown of each software's weaknesses as well as strengths.

Users will be able to read recommendations apart from the comparisons and reviews. On the site, there is a self-serve page for recommendations, enabling you to select a product that meets your needs. Last but not least is the 'Ask Me' tool which enables 50em to give their users an option to get direct answers to any queries they have on automation.

What can you learn from 50em?

❑ They selected the right niche. All they ever talk about are just two tools- InfusionSoft and Ontraport and nothing else clutters the site. It's straightforward and hyper-focused. While extremely narrow, this niche brings in high profits even if the sale volume is low.

❑ 50em provides users with first-hand experience through their reviews, comparisons and the Ask Me feature. While there may be plenty of text, you'd find that none of it has fluff but offers value overall.

❏ 50em also invests a lot of time in their copy. Their content is easy to read and fun and not at all boring.

❏ It helps users choose easily and wisely. The recommendations, reviews, and comparisons take a lot of time to write and create, but the outcome makes it easier for readers to choose the right software for their needs.

- **This is why I'm Broke**

  With an extremely quirky name, This is Why I'm Broke is an affiliate marketing space that was among the first affiliate websites to materialize on the internet and their focus is on novelty and gift aggregation angle. This site taps into pop-culture and finds strange and unique gifts that appeal to people's sense of fun, excitement and strange. You can find the unique to the bland on this site, but it generally delivers more exclusive stuff than anything else. It is difficult not to click on any of these affiliate links.

This is why I'm Broke is great because they focus on their product niche, which is novelty items and gifts: and their goal is to source the web to find the weird, the wacky and the unique for people.

As an affiliate site, they make most of their money through affiliate offers, especially through Amazon Associates Program. They also generate their money through selling stuff on Etsy, appearing as an affiliate there. They also do not add links on every page or article, so it does seem that they do not monetize all of their pages.

What can you learn from This is Why I'm Broke?

- ❏ They have the fun factor, which is a natural marketing. This is does not do active marketing but it does attract its fair share of people coming in from natural links and shares on their posts. This is mainly due to the fun factor in their articles.

- ❏ The fact that they do not monetize all their content is a source of credibility and authenticity, keeping in line with the fun factor of the site. Some posts are just for fun which provides a great user experience and goes a long way in terms of boosting the site's reputation and credibility.

- **Making Sense of Cents**

This is another financial matter site that was created and run by Michelle Gardner. This is not so much of a big finance site like the others on this chapter. Making Sense of Cents is written entirely by Michelle which makes the advice on the site more personal, rather than advice coming from a team of experts. Using her own writing in the content has paid off for her big-time. Michelle publishes her income reports on the blog and the last one showed an income revenue of $125,000. In terms of an individual blogger doing well with affiliate marketing, Michelle has proven that you can get all the way up there. Her niche is personal and family finance, and her goal is to help people budget and save money.

Of course she makes money through a variety of affiliate marketing as well as selling her own courses. She also earns money through advertising on her blog but the main revenue comes from Affiliate Marketing.

What can you Learn from Making Sense of Cents?

- ❏ Firstly, by taking a personal angle, this blog differentiated itself from other competitive content blogs. Finance is a hyper-competitive market and Michelle can compete by making her content and style personable.

- ❏ She has her readers' backs. Plenty of Michelle's top content enables her readers to earn a little bit of money through saving and budgeting effectively. It is not about reviewing products but more about helping people.

- **The Points Guy**

The travel and finance avenues make up some of the biggest affiliate sites to date. The Points Guy focuses on social traffic which rakes in plenty of organic traffic via social sites. Their niche is the use of credit cards for travel purposes and teaching people how they can benefit from the use of credit cards for getting better service, or free fares or travel luxuriously on a cheap budget. The Points Guy is extremely popular, thanks to its super-focus on helping people do extremely specific things- which is to get stuff for free!

This site is a master-class in combining solving a problem and recommending products to earn an affiliate commission. Their niche is credit cards and travel and their goal is travel and credit card hacking. The affiliate program of credit cards and travel is how The Points Guy makes money. Their focus is directly on people using credit cards to earn travel rewards.

What can we learn from The Points Guy?

❏ Solve a problem with your site. Just because you are an affiliate does not mean you can blindly write about products and services that you do not believe in. Take a focus and actually help people solve their problems and you'd enjoy free marketing and ever-growing popularity thanks to your genuine output, the desire to help as well as producing content that is valuable.

❏ Place your best products in the limelight just like the Points Guy has a 'Top Cards' Section that lists top travel credit cards. It does not bring as much traffic as some other content, but it definitely helps. It gives people an easy place to find the most valuable products for people specifically looking for this type of information.

- **Just A Girl And Her Blog**

This blog is your cut and paste affiliate website- this blog uses Amazon Associates program to sell things about crafts or organization or anything related to DIY. Immensely popular, this blog has enabled her to earn at least $40k a month through affiliate marketing. Her blog works because of the niche- organizing and DIY and her goal is to help people organize, simplify and beautify their lives. Abby makes her money through Amazon Affiliates and it is also hosted using BlueHost. Another way she makes her income is by selling courses related to her niche.

What can we learn from Just a Girl and Her Blog?

- ❏ Her blog is a like a guinea pig. She tries various things and details her experiences, so her readers do not have to go through the process of testing things on their own. She eliminates this problem. She also recommends products she believes in along the way.

- ❏ Social media is a big useful tool for blogs. If you are in a niche that works well in social media, then you need to utilize them.

Bottom Line

The sites listed here is just a handful of the best practices and examples on the internet where affiliate marketing is concerned. All of these blogs and sites have one thing in common- an invest of time in quality content and the need to address a specific problem. Your involvement in the affiliate marketing channel you choose is entirely up to you, but it also depends on the product or niche you have chosen on the kind of income you get. If you want positive outcomes, then invest in good content, time and a good site.

Chapter 6- How to Achieve $10,000 a month through Affiliate Marketing

We all have aspirations of making it big, or at least making our ventures successful. We all want things to work out for the best, and we all want to get profits with whatever endeavors we invest, so it is not a surprise if we think about hitting that golden $10k in revenue through affiliate marketing.

Affiliate marketing takes a good investment in time to make it sustainable and credible. Plenty of good and positive stories are around to make good money with affiliate marketing, but what can you do as a beginner? Can you actually hit $10k?

The immediate answer is a resounding YES. If you know how the basic function of affiliate marketing works, how to use the Internet and the basic requirement of a computer-you are already one step ahead of the pack to start making money with affiliate marketing.

In this chapter, we will investigate the things you can do to ensure you get profit. Keep in mind that this is not a one-size-fits-all template. Affiliate marketing also depends on your tenacity to market your site as effectively as possible.

You can achieve 10k a month by doing very simple things on your site.

But first, answers these questions:

1- Have you selected your niche?

2- Have you identified what problem you are solving with your niche?

3- Have you chosen a program or network to join?

4- Have you optimized your blog/site to fit your needs and your niche?

Once you have all your bases covered, let us look into deeper details to help you stay at the top of your game:

- Stay Ethical, Keep things legal

It is important to protect yourself. Depending on where your business is located, you are bound by terms and conditions and legal issues related to affiliate marketing. In the US for example, you need to disclose that your link is an affiliate link. The affiliate disclosure must be part of the link or as close as possible to the link itself and not at the bottom of your posts. Failure to disclose is an accident waiting to happen and whatever you have earned may end up going for legal fees if you do not do your business ethically and legally. It may seem tedious, but it will save you time and money in the long run.

- Cloak your links

Most affiliate links are very messy with all sorts of numbers and words. As an affiliate, you want to create links that are not confusing and also easily searchable on search engines.

Getting custom URLs for your products or cloaking them helps you gain visibility and credibility as well. Use Pretty Link Lite to cloak your affiliate links. It's free to use and once you've done so, it is easily to find your affiliate links and also, with cloaked links, your content is less spammy. People will trust your domain and are more likely to click through your links.

- Recommend things you will use yourself

You'd have more passion to continue what you are doing and promote what you love only if you believe in the product. Genuine love and enthusiasm is what will get you more and more people coming to your site. You cannot fake this for a long period of time- maybe for a short time but what happens when you run out of ideas of content? Promoting a product/service that you genuinely like will help you get more of the product- what are its benefits, its pain points, what the audience is saying and so on. You want to make more and more ethical decisions as your business grows and promoting something you know and use will help you make better decisions in your business to increase profits.

Knowing your products and giving your feedback and review will bring you more fans. When brands notice this, they will be more willing to give you a higher cut for every sale. You may have two products that you need to review and both has its fair share of advantages, but you have a better understanding of a product and its best features, so you may want to recommend that on a genuine point of view compared to another product.

- Expertly weave in your links

When you do affiliate marketing, you have a choice of your involvement because your involvement determines your profits. Do you want to go all out and provide excellent, quality content in return for high profits or do you want average or low involvement which also translates to low profits? This choice is yours, but when you do promote products and services, you want to masterfully recommend these products in a way that is non-spammy. When you provide content that is not spammy, your users are more likely to believe you and trust what you are saying.

When you deliver content that is helpful, they are more likely to share your content because they have found value in the content and they believe others will to. So when you use affiliate links, make sure to weave them in as naturally as possible. It's all about context. Put yourself in your user's shoes and look at your content- is it something you would read yourself?

If you want to make money with affiliate marketing, content and context is key. The affiliate links you use must make sense in your post. Randomly dropping them in your content is not very helpful

- Add affiliate links to your popular posts

As we discovered from 50em or even WireCutter in the previous chapter, updating content and marketing them is one way of staying fresh. You can freshen up your posts but updating them with affiliate links and adding new content in them.

Keep in mind NOT to over-link your post though. You can also try linking your top-converting blog posts with affiliate links. Tutorial posts, best of's and cheapest kind of posts really work in this avenue. You do not need to make complex articles just to add links- updating what you have sometimes goes a long way.

- Resource Pages

Your resource page gives you a wealth of links. You want to create a resource page that lists all the products you recommend. Say for example if you are a makeup blogger, then there can be a page full of makeup products you love. You can even make a list of makeup products that are vegan and cruelty-free or best makeup for skin color or best makeup for traveling. Get the idea? There are plenty of ways you can add your link and the resource page denotes one of them.

- Target audience

One of the best ways to make sure you get profits and reach your 10k target is to make sure your target audience and your niche are aligned. What are you promoting? To Whom are you promoting it to? What problems are you solving for them? One reason why you may not get the kind of money you want through affiliate marketing is the misaligned audience and niche. You are probably recommending a product your target audience does not need. Say for instance you are a vegan blogger. What would your main source of income come from? It wouldn't be on kitchen gadgets would it? It would probably be on recommendation on vegan food guides, vegan travel tips, vegan restaurants, and vegan products.

This is because your target audience is just like you- people who are foodies but want vegan alternatives. To be successful in affiliate marketing is to keep your audience needs in mind. Always think- how am i solving my audience's problems today?

- Experiment with different styles

Affiliate links come in many different formats and styles. You do not want to stick to just one even if they yield the most traffic for you. You want to diversify so you can reach a wider audience. Use product images, simple links, coupon and discount codes as well as cleverly placed banner ads. You also want to play around with your content format and recommend products in different ways from lists to photos, stories and video. You may want to choose both formats (write up and video) if your product needs it.

- Newsletters

Some people prefer reading long-format articles right from their inbox or they prefer getting notifications of your new post from their inbox. This is where you can include your affiliate links into your email campaigns. Add in your affiliate links where appropriate into your newsletter. You can also send out newsletters on affiliate products that you love but make sure to include them in a good way such as in an email challenge or a social media giveaway. We all know how hard it is to build an email list and get active subscribers so do not let this go to waste. Use your email marketing as best as you can.

- Lead Magnet

Another way to ensure you get your 10k mark in terms of profit is to add your affiliate links to freebies or lead magnets. Lead magnets have been proven to be extremely effective for all age groups. You can definitely bet that your audience, or at least a majority of them would be consuming your lead magnet and when it is relevant, weave in your best affiliate links in them.

These tips are all great ways to ensure that you content and context is sustainable. You need to do these things in order to make your site visible and credible, so you will have a continuous stream of audience coming in from all corners of the Internet. Always make sure to try and test different formats, links and such so you will know what works and what does not.

Making your $10,000 Sustainable

- Scaling Your Business

In order to reach your goal of $ 10,000 revenue in your affiliate marketing business, one needs to know when the time is right to scale your business. Only by doing so can you be able to generate a larger revenue that meets your business goals at the end of the day. The best way to grow your drop shipping business is to relook back into the ads that are performing well.

Redirect a portion of your profits into those ads to capitalize on the ads performance to your intended customer pool. Reinvesting the profits back into your business will ensure that you keep your money rolling within it in order to make it more successful in the long run. In the start, it is usually the norm that business owners do not take a salary (maybe in the first year or two). They keep channeling their profits into the business to grow it further until it becomes more sustainable and competitive.

- Outsourcing

For any new business that is starting from the ground up, it becomes vital to be economical as possible. This is to ensure that funds and profits are first and foremost invested back into the business to generate growth, be competitive and increase revenue.

Once you've scaled your business and the revenue stream is sustainable and growing, you will need to start looking into the possibilities of hiring extra hands to manage the business. This is because time is limited and there aren't enough hours in day to accomplish all tasks relevant to your business. Hence, outsourcing or adding on manpower into your business is one way to ensure the business operations run smoothly and you will be able to focus your energy into growing the business and generating revenue.

- Growing Your Business Using Data

In any business, be it the traditional or online method, data is vital in growing the business in order to stay relevant and to stay ahead of the competition. Using Google Analytics and Facebook conversion pixel data, you will be able to track every single data to grow your business. You will be able to know specific details of your customer, for example their locality and the path they took to your website which generated the sale in the end. This will in turn allow you to determine what works and what doesn't work on your website to enable a farther reach to a larger pool of customers.

Chapter 7- Tips to Becoming a Successful Affiliate Marketer

What does it take to become a successful affiliate?

It's always hard for me to come up with an answer.

However, I always try to devise some sort of plan for an answer.

So here are the steps to become successful in affiliate marketing!

Selecting The Right Merchants

As an affiliate marketer, it is not a priority at the start to select a merchant that pays the highest commission but it is more important to select one that has a reputable product and a good and stable reputation. Another factor that should be considered is to differentiate the merchants between their sell-through rate.

Importance Of Integrity

When you start to promote a product or service, its always important to note that, never ever sell something that you wouldn't buy for yourself. It doesn't matter which type of channel you use to sell your brand, be it via a website, social media platform, email or a blog, you don't want to promote and sell something that you wouldn't buy for yourself or recommend to your friends or family members. You should be selective on this as carrying a lousy product will only do more harm to your name and business.

Being Niche

The best way to generate income through affiliate marketing is to get more people to visit your website or online store. The more people, the likelihood of more sales is much higher. It is okay to have some competition with other brands or affiliate marketers but you don't want to take on a product or service that already has a saturated market. The key here is to identify a brand that is niche and only serves a particular market segment. But be careful of this as, some brands may not have any competition and that can be an alarm bell as having no competition means that this particular product or service isn't highly sought after by the community.

Being Brand Relevant

To ensure success in affiliate marketing, it is important to ensure that the content on your site and the brand you are promoting are relevant to each other. You cannot promote healthy based foods but have affiliate links and banners on your site promoting fast foods and pizza. These two key areas should be relevant and tie into each other in order to attract and convert potential customers.

Do Not Overcrowd

It's vital that the content on your page is not overshadowed by over excessive banners. Having rows and rows of banners will tend to push potential customers away from your site, and it makes your page look less attractive.

Personal Recommendation

To achieve better sales results, it's best to make a personal recommendation on brands, products and services that you have tried yourself and completely endorse.

Monitor Results

Being a successful affiliate marketer means having a good relationship with your merchant. In order to achieve that you need to have a merchant that has a good track record and is performing. If you affiliate with a merchant that cannot deliver, you are bound to receive many complaints from your customers and drive your business downwards. As such, it is critical to partner with a merchant that has a good track record to ensure your business keeps growing.

Work With Multiple Merchants

In any investment, the main advice you hear is never to put all your eggs in one basket. The same holds true for affiliate marketing. You should not just work with one merchant, but focus on diversifying and having multiple agents have the same item or different items.

Original Content Creation

Having original content is important to an affiliate marketer as Google constantly looks for websites with duplicate content. While you can source the Internet for free content, if your blog or website is identical to others, Google will indefinitely penalize you. As such, always try to be creative and original with your content.

Changing Content

For a new site or blog, you will have immediate traffic once it's up but it will start to dwindle down over time. This is because Google will visit your site; and if there are no new changes, it will start to rank your site lower every time. Therefore, changing and updating your content is important for search engines to rank your platform higher.

Choose Good Products

When starting out as an affiliate marketer, never try to register with many affiliate programs. Since you will be new in this, it can get very overwhelming very fast if you try to promote more than you can. So, you need to carefully select your products and try to understand the market needs and also pick brands that you understand and identify with thoroughly.

Use Many Traffic Sources to Promote Products

Apart from using just ads on your blog or website, you may also opt to use other traffic sources to assist you in promoting your products. With more traffic to your page, you can expect more generation of revenue in the long run. One such tool that can be of use is Google Adwords. It can be used to direct traffic to your webpage. All you need to do is to make an ad using your Adwords account and link it using your affiliate link to the target URL page of the ad.

Learn About the Product And Service You Are Promoting

Always research and learn about the product and service that you will be promoting and selling on your blog or website. Acquire its benefits and disadvantages and what makes it stand out against other brands.

Understand its features, and how it can benefit the user. It is also key to understand the market and the customer demographics that you intend to sell it to. Never carry or promote a product that you lack knowledge of or have never personally used.

Create A Strong Brand Name For Your Niche

As an affiliate marketer, don't just stop after building a one-page campaign. You will also need to work on building assets, funnels and any things that add value to your business. Focus on one particular niche and master it. If you keep doing this, you not only ear your visitor's trust but also open the doors to work with exclusive advertisers to stay ahead of your competitors.

Have A Plan

When starting any business, it is always important to have a plan. Before promoting any product, put yourself in the shoes of the owner. Look from their viewpoint. If you owned that offer, what would you do differently and why? This is particularly important in choosing the right merchant, the right product the right ad campaign and soon on. One tool you can use is to emphasis the usage of the 5Ws, which are the What, Who, Where, When and Why.

The Learning Process Will Take Time

Never expect to make a quick buck out of affiliate marketing in your first few months. As with every learning process in life, things take time. Likewise, you will need to take baby steps in your journey as an affiliate marketer. You need to understand your product and services, the market space, your customers, managing websites and ad campaigns. All these take time and can be from a few weeks to months or years before you are successful.

Failure Is Your Friend

Failures are a part of business and you will encounter moments of ups and downs in affiliate marketing. However, failures always teach us a lesson and we should always rise up from each situation instead of quitting. Try to figure out what went wrong and correct your mistakes. Never ever give up and always try something new and be consistent with it and a solution will surely present itself for every problem that arises.

Developing a Positive Attitude in Business

Today, positive thinking is applied in many different fields from business to sales, marketing to advertising, health, sports, education, motivation, inspiration, national allegiance, psychology as well as self-image. Many of the twenty-first-century authors apply positive thinking in various areas. Some of these famous ones are:

Anthony Robbins' seminar and speeches using the knowledge of psychology and positive thinking. Robbins' is a motivational speaker and advisor to many world leaders and have helped ordinary people to achieve success or lead more positive, and fulfilling lives.

Steven Covey is the author of *The 7 Habits of Highly Effective People*, and his points are regularly quotes in businesses and personal development. These seven habits can be used above and beyond the business realm, applying it to almost anything in life.

Louise Hay is the author of *You Can Heal Your Life* and several other motivational and self-improvement books. She promotes the use of self-healing to use the power of our thoughts to enhance our lives.

Wayne W. Dyer employs the teaching of Tao Te Ching of Change your thoughts, change your life which directly influences use to lead and live a more balanced and fulfilling lifestyle. Dryer is the author of *The Power of Intention.*

Why Positive Thinking is important for one to truly live and abundant and productive life

How many times have you failed at something and someone- a friend, teacher, classmate, parent, or partner tells you not to give up and focus on the positive?

Sometimes you think that advice is easier said than done. The truth is, focusing our mind on being and thinking positively is fairly straightforward- it is all about controlling your thoughts because of the understanding that a positive attitude leads to a fruitful, and happy life is already a high motivation to change. Having a positive outlook on life will enable you to cope much easily to the affairs of the everyday life from the moment you wake up until the time you go to sleep. A positive outlook gives you an optimistic approach and makes you worry less and think less negative thoughts. It will further enable you to experience the silver lining in the darkest of situations.

A positive mind is a state of mind that is worth developing because everyone can benefit from it and who knows where it will take you?

A positive attitude is noticeable in the following ways:

- Optimistic thinking.
- Constructive thinking.
- Creative thinking.
- Optimism.
- Drive and energy to do things, accomplish goals.
- An attitude of happiness.

A positive mindset can help you in many ways:

- Expecting success as failure is not an option
- The feeling of inspiration in everything you do
- Gives you strength to keep going and not give up
- Helps you overcome obstacles you face
- Gives you the ability to look at failures, mistakes and problems as a blessing in disguise.
- Keeps you believing in yourself, your abilities, and your talents
- Radiate self-esteem and confidence
- You look for solutions instead of dwelling on problems; you seek opportunities when it comes

Positive thinking is a game changer- you can transform your whole life if you always look on the bright side of life instead of wallowing in self-pity and allowing yourself to think negatively. Positive thinking is infectious! It not only affects you but each individual around you- people want to be with you and make friends with you and hang out with you because you've got the drive and energy and positivity, making it so easy to be your friend. You will end up changing the life of those around you, uplifting them and encouraging them to become the best version of themselves. Positivity is a strong emotion, so if you are positive, then you radiate positivity!

Even more benefits of a Positive Attitude:

- You achieve more of your goals easily
- You achieve success much rapidly
- You bring in more happiness in your life and those around you
- You have more energy to deal with everything life throws at you
- You have more faith in your abilities and have higher hopes for a brighter future
- You can inspire and motivate everyone around you
- You feel you encounter fewer obstacles and difficulties compared to other people
- You are much more respected and loved by all those around you
- Life smiles at you

The bottom line is, if you exhibit a negative attitude, then you will only bring in more failure and more difficulties. However, if you radiate positivity, you are bound to be attracting good energy and success so the time is NOW to change the way you think and the way you react.

Negative thoughts, behaviors and reactions do nobody any good. If you have tried to become positive in the past but you have failed, then you have likely not tried enough.

Chapter 8- Top Affiliate Marketing Trends of 2019

Content

In the coming years, content will play an even more important role in affiliate marketing. It won't just come down to what you put up but how it engages your target market. As such, the content has to be not only creative but also eye-catching as well. It will also have to incorporate both audio and visual tools that appeals to the target market but will also need to be relevant the search engines as well. As such, you will have to employ various tools such as video demos, pictures and even slideshows to be a step ahead of the competition. However, traditional approaches to content should not be pushed aside and forgotten, as these tools are still needed to provide the necessary information and descriptions.

Affiliate Marketing Discounts

In 2016, the U.S Department of Industrial Policy and Promotion (DIPP) introduced a ban to online platforms in offering discounts. As such, these platforms could not offer the utilization of cash to give huge discounts or subsidize certain products. Since this ban was introduced, online marketplaces started to look at affiliate marketing as an option to provide indirect discounting. Top affiliate marketing websites generate their revenue by increasing traffic into their online stores. A commission is then charged and directed back towards the website. It is through this commission that customers can enjoy benefits like in the form of discounts and cashbacks. This has shown to be a huge appeal to customers looking for good deals on products and services online.

Use of Artificial Intelligence

The usage of artificial intelligence is quickly becoming a useful and important tool in affiliate marketing. The technology is often used by affiliate marketing to ensure smooth communication and also to help in monitoring performance. One example of this is IBM Watson and WebGains, an affiliate marketing platform came together to create its first chatbot. It is evident that within the next few years and with the improvements in technology, we will be seeing this tool becoming more effective for affiliate marketers.

The Use of Voice Search

The use of voice searches has increased exponentially ever since tools such as Google Home and Siri have entered the market. As such, Internet searches are moving more towards voice searches and affiliate marketers will need to invest more time and money into optimizing voice searches. Converting from normal search engine optimization (SEO) methods is easier said than done. As such, developers will need to look at all possible avenues such as natural languages and long keywords that are more likely be used in voice searches. Big names such as Apple, Amazon, Google and even Facebook have already jumped on the voice search bandwagon, and other players will soon follow suit.

The Use of Influencers

With the huge rise of social media platforms like Facebook, Instagram and Youtube, it has also given birth to a new trend of social media influencers. These influencers use their popularity to market products and service to generate income. An influencer is an individual who has a huge popularity or followers that listen or emulate them. They collaborate with marketers to promote products, services and even events to their followers. Apart from that, links can be placed in these influencers bio or comments sections to channel traffic to the specific website that they are promoting. As such, it has become the latest trend for the younger generation. This has pushed many ad agencies to increase their budget on social media influencer marketing to catch this trend.

Mobile Phones Market Is Growing

In a recent 2018 survey, research revealed that the mobile phones made up of 61% of all online views as compared to 52% in 2015. In developing countries especially in Asia, growth is more profound due to the influx of new mobile brands such as Oppo and Huawei that are challenging for the market space. As such, affiliate marketers will need to ensure that they construct their webpages as mobile-friendly to users and also prevent any clickloss when traffic is directed to their webpages.

Use of Keyword-Rich Reviews

Another important trend involves product reviews that are keyword-rich. This is particularly important when customers are reading through testimonials, which indicates that they are one step away from getting a purchase. To help make this push from search to purchase, high-quality and honest reviews are needed from the affiliate marketers. And as an affiliate marketer, it is vital that you provide good content and also ensure that all the reviews are real and honest. It is also imperative that you work with individuals who are interested in posting reviews of your products and services.

Native Advertising

Some of the challenges advertisers face is customers not being attracted to banners on websites. Moreover, publishers have moved towards creating valuable content using native advertising. Using native advertising, affiliate marketers can focus on sharing information in a way that is more attractive to the visitors to the website. Native advertising can also be utilized for directing traffic to your website and also for content promotion.

GDPR Aftermath, Privacy, and Data

The General Data Protection Regulation or GDPR is a regulation on an individual's personal data that came into the picture in mid-2018 and has had an impact on affiliate marketing. When this regulation came into play, many types of campaigns and tactics became redundant overnight and caused affiliate marketers to rethink their strategies. With the growing awareness of privacy data, you as an affiliate marketer will need to ensure that your website won't increase your visitor's privacy fears. For this reason, a Secure Sockets Layer or SSL needs to be used to create an environment where potential customers feel safe when making purchases and sharing their personal data.

Anti-Fraud Tools

In 2018, it was estimated that about $19 billion was wasted online due to ad fraud and Pixalate is estimating that it will make up about 17% of online traffic in 2019. As an affiliate marketer, this can be negated by analyzing bot behavior and monitoring patterns from data. Also, to battle ad fraud, make sure any traffic source or tracker that you choose is well-equipped to battle ad fraud.

Emails For Affiliate Marketing

Many affiliate marketers have their own lead list used to market and communicate with their customers that will be interested in their products and services. There are many types of lead lists that these affiliate marketers integrate. The first one that is commonly used is the list containing regular visitors of the affiliate marketer's website. These visitors enjoy the content that the affiliate marketers deliver and they are more likely to make a purchase when they receive email notifications on a product update or review. The next type is when business owners or companies share their lead list with affiliate marketers for their promoted products and services.

As an affiliate marketer, when receiving these leads, it's best to classify them into segments to make sure you are getting high quality leads from the business owners to make this work. Always bear in mind that the end game is create ad campaigns that attract potential customers and convert them into making purchases. The better and higher quality leads will lead to higher chances of making a sale. Many business owners predict that the trend of using email for affiliate marketing will continue to grow and evolve into better ad campaigns to target specific customer markets.

Live Streaming And Interactive Ads

The use of live streaming and interactive ads can also help to direct traffic and potential customers to your website. By employing various incentives, affiliate marketers can makeshift offers when conducting live streaming demonstrations. A couple of segments that are useful for this are the fitness and personal care industry. Potential customers can purchase these products by going to the weblinks that appear during these live streaming demonstrations.

Smaller Networks Will Get More Attention

It is predicted that in 2019, many smaller affiliate marketing websites may start giving larger platforms a run for their money. While these smaller networks lack the marketing and presence as opposed to the well-established affiliate marketing websites, their strength will come from the fact that they serve a specific group of customers with very niche products and services.

The Rise of SaaS Products

Software as a Service or called SaaS for short is the process of marketing software and applications to companies and individuals that require them. This application still hasn't really caught up with affiliate marketers, as it's quite hard to market. But many affiliate marketers are beginning to use this app in 2019, so it's becoming more popular.

Affiliate Diversification

Previously, many business owners targeted their focus on at least one or two affiliate companies that already had a wide array of products and services. In keeping with changing times, these methods are proving far less fruitful and currently there is a change by these business owners to diversify their pool of affiliate marketers. Business owners are now targeting smaller, niche affiliate marketers in order to market their products and services.

Working With Agencies

Another rising trend in 2019 for affiliate marketers reflects the use of influencer marketing agencies. These agencies are the ones that are responsible for connecting influencers and bloggers with the products and services. These agencies will source for products and services that influencers are interested in and also identify influencers for their customers.

Experts (Individuals) of Affiliate Marketing

Brian Marcus, VP Global Marketing at TUNE, says that with an advertiser's need to increase growth and engage more customers, one will start to venture into more mobile-savvy performance-based partnerships. For affiliate marketing, there is also a large untapped market in e-commerce, travel and finance industry. He also states that new innovations in marketing will rise from mobile-online partnerships as customers can experience new and cross-channel offers with just a click of the button.

Kevin Edwards, Global Client Strategy Director of Awin, further contends that affiliate marketers must create a safe online environment for their customers, so that they will be comfortable making purchases and sharing personal data online. This is in wake of the numerous data and privacy breaches that have happened prior to this.

Todd Crawford, VP Strategic Initiatives from Impact, also suggests that partner marketing will take a step forward in 2019 and onwards. He infers that partner marketing has begun to mature and has expanded; he asserts how more brands are moving towards this trend to grow their business.

Julie Van Ullen, GM of Growth for Rakuten Marketing, goes on to say that ad tech companies will need to focus their energies to create an enjoyable customer experience, which will also enable them to serve their publishers and advertisers in 2019. Some other trends that she also sees are: -

- Transparency – websites that place priority on transparency in performance and data will create a winning working relationship between publishers and brands.

- Data Driven – a meaningful customer experience can only be created when data is used correctly to target customers and build attractive ad campaigns.

- Artificial Intelligence – the use of this tool is so important to manage the affiliate business

Choots Humphries, Co-President & Owner at LinkConnector, expects that compliance will play an important role for affiliate marketing in 2019. As the industry starts to mature and compete with other areas of marketing, compliance will play an integral role between business owners and affiliate marketers.

Scott Kalbach, Founder & CEO from AvantLink, notices that there will be a significant increase in sales authentic publishers. It used to be coupons, deals, and loyalty sites that dominated the market space for the last several years, but a strong presence of content publishers are slowly making their mark in the arena.

David Naffziger, the CEO from BrandVerity, expects to see the following trends in 2019:

- Increasing awareness of compliance in affiliate marketers – affiliate marketers are taking more responsibility to ensure their partners comply with the policies of their advertisers.

- Increased privacy regulations – With the implementation of the GDPR in EU countries, affiliate marketers in the U.S are also striving to ensure they keep up with the regulation to create a safe environment for their global customers.

Swim Song, Director of Traffic Operation for Mobvista says that focus for affiliate marketers should be turned towards the consumer. As such, he stresses that attention should be made towards mobile content such as games and e-commerce products that suits the individual's daily needs and lifestyle. He also thinks that advertisers will prefer platforms such as Cost Per Sale (CPS) and Cost Per Lead (CPL) as it is a simpler pricing model.

Beatriz Gonzalez, Business Development for Toro Advertising, suggests that e-commerce will play an important role in affiliate marketing as it already represents 10% of total retail sales in the US and it expected to grow up to 15% every year.

Emanuel Cinca, CEO of WHAT THE AFF, also identifies his money of e-commerce as an important trend for affiliate marketing in 2019. He says that both brand owners and affiliate marketers will start investing more into e-commerce to increase the success potential of their respective businesses. He also suggests that in building an e-commerce store, working together with influencers will also be critical due to the huge following they have.

Ada Pizzaro, Digital Marketer for Mobsuite, sees a more direct relationship between the advertiser and the source in 2019. These relationships will allow them to create more exclusive deals and also build trust within one another. She also predicts that 2019 will bring a new light into online shops, native advertising and increased social media presence.

Michael Xu, Founder and CEO of WebEye – envisions a more in depth focus into the use of artificial intelligence to create better ads for both publishers and advertisers. He also estimates it being used in fighting against ad fraud, estimating customers' interests and analyzing data collected. He also sees an overspill of the GDPR compliance effect altering the affiliate marketing landscape. Data and privacy matters will take an importance as affiliate marketers try to dispel the doubts customers have regarding the security of their transactions and data over the Internet.

Adam Esman, Business Development at Evertrack.io, feels that regulations in privacy will continue to increase and gain momentum in 2019. Thus, it will affect the way data is mined and used for advertisers and affiliate marketers alike. He also states that he is starting to see affiliate marketers becoming more open to the use of technology to track and optimize the performance of their business.

Chapter 9 - Tools to Help you in Affiliate Marketing

Tools help you make the best of your time and effort when it comes to marketing. In this chapter, we will look at the tools to help you make full use of your time, efficiently market your site and promote, your affiliations online. Most tools listed here give you a free version (with limited capabilities) or a trial version before requiring you to purchase the full license to use.

If you feel like this tool has met your needs, then sign up for a full package.

- Flippa

This essential tool can help you get into the process of building a sustainable and successful affiliate site from scratch. This site is created as a bidding marketplace for people to buy and sell websites. For affiliate marketers especially, you get to buy sites that already come with strong backlinks and an optimized SEO growth. Keep in mind that you need to conduct a full backlink audit before you purchase a domain from Flippa to ensure that the domain isn't inflated by unethical SEO practices.

- CJ Affiliate

Affiliate marketing begins with a strong partnerships with sites that are in need of sales. CJ Affiliates is a number one resource for affiliate partnerships as it connects affiliates with merchants wanting to drive up sales for their products. Affiliates get paid for each phone call, or lead, or website when visitors peruse a merchant's site from the affiliate links discovered. CJ Affiliate is a great starting point if you want to seek partnerships.

- SEMRush

If you are looking for keyword research, competition analysis and even fixing SEO errors then SEMRush is a tool needed in your affiliate marketing arsenal. This tool is a favorite among marketers who want to understand what kind or type of content drives the highest ROI for their competitors as well as analyze on-page SEO issues. SEMRush is great for finding top performing content from competitors that you should be writing about too, monitoring keyword rankings weekly, and running SEO audits to watch for issues on your website that could potentially hurt your SEO rankings. What's more, you can use SEMRush to monitor press mentions.

- Ahrefs

Ahrefs is another keyword research tool that you can use just like SEMRush. It also provides on-page audits and competitive content analysis. What's different with Ahrefs is that it places a deeper emphasis on backlinks than on-page

SEO. Ahrefs gives marketers insights about lost as well as new backlinks as well as sites that are linked to broken pages on your site. Marketers will find it useful to use Ahrefs for reviewing new and lost backlinks, assessing competitor link profiles, and also obtaining new link building opportunities.

You can also use Ahrefs to find sites that are linked to broken pages and of course finding top-performing competitor content. You can try out both SEMRush as well as Ahref's to build on your SEO optimization. If you can invest in both-great but if you cannot then think about what you really want to track first. If you are an industry leader in your niche, SEMRush would prove to be worthwhile. Since both SEMRush and Ahref have trial periods for their software, you can use both and see which works best for you.

- Yoast SEO

Yoast SEO gives you advanced SEO functionality in each and every page which includes the title tag and meta description which you can customize, canonical link customization, sitemap customization as well as meta robots customization. Yoast is a free tool; but if you want 24/7 support, then you can go for the paid version. They also have a redirect manager in the paid version that allows you to redirect broken pages or pages that you want to be removed from search results.

- Grammarly

This example exemplifies another useful tool to have if you are publishing content on a regular basis. It is good to have a tool that can check your spelling, grammar as well as plagiarism all in one go. Grammarly is a master-class tool in spell-check and grammar. It sports incorrect word use as well as comma usage. All in all, it makes your written content even better.

- Duplichecker

If you are part of the content team for your website, then running your article through Duplichecker will help you spot any kind of plagiarism. Of course Grammarly also does this task, but if your intention is only to check plagiarism, then Duplichecker is a good investment tool. Accidental cases of plagiarism can prove to be a painful legal issue, so it's best to get your content checked.

- Hemingway

Another amazing content review tool, Hemingway, helps you to simplify your writing. It is based off the writing style of Ernest Hemingway, hence the name of the software. Whatever content you write, especially the ones that go on the Internet, needs to be simple, straightforward and easy to understand. Your readers what the point to come across fast and their want insights, which means you do not want fluff tossed into your content just to make your sound intelligent. With the Hemingway software, you can simplify complex sentence, and it also points out complex words and adverbs that you can replace with simple ones.

- Sumo

One of the main things you want your site to do is attract visitors and with Suno, you turn your visitors into customers. Most website visitors are not ready to open their wallets and make a purchase with their credit cards when they reach your site, especially if it is their first time visiting. How can you possible get money from them? You sell them things that they are ready to buy. The best way most successful affiliate marketers do is to scale to build their email list. This enables marketers to drive repeat visitors back to their site and also to purchase products over a period of time. With Sumo, you can have easy to install email capture forms on your site.

- Google Adsense

Earning money for each referral you get is wonderful isn't it? Want to elevate this experience? Use Google Adsense! With Google AdSense, you get a second revenue stream as you continue to scale your business. AdSense basically allows you to create ad blocks that you can use throughout your site that other sites can pay to utilize. You can also select payments based on per ad in a variety of manners such as through CPM (cost per thousand impressions). Applying this method, you get paid a flat fee per thousand website pageviews for a specific ad. The rates can range between $1 to $3 and this rate can go higher based on niche categories. Another way which you can do this is through CPC which is cost-per-click. This way, you get paid each time an ad is clicked on your site. The rates for this vary between one industry to the other.

- AdThrive

Getting money from Adsense is slightly tough, but if you have a good website, Adsense can give you a second revenue stream no doubt. What if you're only making a few dollars in ads and only have about 1,000 website visitors? You can also use AdThrive to optimize your ads so you get better performance. AdThrive delves deep into your analytics to understand the advertisers who have the best performance on your site. From this, you can see higher CTRs on your ads and this will enable you to generate more revenue.

- InfusionSoft

InfusionSoft is a paid software and a little on the pricey end, but it is a powerful tool to use for any marketer and manager. Its finest feature is the automation that makes extremely efficient marketing campaigns for you. InfusionSoft is a robust yet costly email marketing tool that would benefit any small business looking towards reaching out to a bigger audience. The startup fee for this software is at $2,000. After this, maintenance would cost anywhere between $199 to $599 a month depending on the package you choose.

In brief, InfusionSoft saves you plenty of time. For first time users, it takes a little while to learn how to use the system and set it up according to your needs. But once setup is completed, you are pretty much set up for a smooth ride. InfusionSoft is renowned for its high deliverability rates and its ability to scale no matter what the size of the campaign.

- Keyhole

Keyhole offers a detailed analysis of the hashtags that you use for your marketing campaign. Instead of randomly using hashtags with your campaigns, Keyhole enables you to track and analyze hashtags in real time, shows you how influential it is, as well as its engagement, reach and popularity. The trial is free, but paid versions start at$132 to $799 a month. Let's face it- marketing campaigns nowadays thrive on hashtags. Not only can you track hashtags, but you can also get analytics by account, keywords, mentions and URL. This is a useful tool to have if you are always working on marketing campaigns targeting heavy social media users.

- Buzzsumo

Buzzsumo enables marketers to source the most shared content on specific topics and websites. Marketers can also refine lists according to the type of content such as blog posts, news items, or just infographics. The advanced feature includes 'monitoring' and 'influencers' that marketers can use to get ahead of the competition. The free version of Buzzsumo gives you limited results. However, the pro version starter plan is ideal for small businesses and bloggers, as it costs $99/month. But if you want something deeper and significant, then the Advanced feature at $299/month comes with API access and many more incredible features.

Content marketers would love this because it helps in searching for trending topics and subjects on the internet easier and plus, it allows content creators to analyze headlines for their effectiveness. Buzzsumo helps content marketers understand how to create the next viral topic.

- CoSchedule

CoSchedule is a software that helps you plan, organize and manage your marketing campaigns, your content and your strategies. Any marketing campaign needs to be planned and executed according to schedule, and with CoSchedule, you can streamline this process easily. CoShedule works great with Chrome, Google Docs, Wordpress and Evernote too! Coschedule ranges from $15 per month for personal use to $600 per month for larger agency users. Coshedule allows you to stay organized and it saves time. It is excellent for large companies or small agencies to manage deadlines, share notes, stay up on to their day to day tasks and get updates on campaign progress. Timelines are easier to manage, any alerts are prompted by CoSchedule.

- Pingdom Website Speed Test

Website speed is a crucial element in retaining a user's visit to your site. Website speed is one of the fastest ways to improve your SEO rankings and increase conversion rates. With Pingdom's, marketers can test their website speed, and it also gives a free report that gives you an in-depth analysis of your site as well as tips to improve it. The test itself is free however for a full on website monitoring service; it will cost you anywhere from $13.95 to $454 per month.

Full-time monitoring is essential and useful for large websites that receive plenty of traffic. A few more minutes of downtime or crash can cost you revenue as well as traffic. You can save a lot of money by investing in a monthly plan with Pingdom to continuously check your websites' status, give you alerts and monitor and report on site speed.

- Canva

With easy to use designing software available to us, most of our company's basic design materials can be made ourselves because let's face it: not everyone can afford a graphic designer on a retainer basis. If Adobe Photoshop and Illustrator is too complicated to us, then Canva is an easier alternative that makes design easy and fast. Canva has templates that are created especially for social media sharing and posting, and these templates are stunning. A few clicks here and there and you have eye-popping visual.

If you use its cloud-based software, it costs nothing. But there are premium features that come, and it is a 'pay-as-you-go 'method. If you feel your business needs constant designing but hiring a graphic designer is too much, then opt for Canva For Work. It has advanced features and a variety of other tools that you can utilize for a mere monthly subscription of $12.95.

Great visual design can create a huge impact on your target market so if you are embarking on a big marketing campaign, do not skimp on hiring a graphic designer. But if you need visual content quickly and it's something that you can easily put together quickly, then Canva will help you make your content look stunning.

Conclusion

So how do you feel now that you've covered the most relevant details of affiliate marketing? Ready to start? Well, I'm hoping that you do! Affiliate marketing takes time to build, and it depends entirely on your level of commitment- how involved you are with your marketing and promotions and how much money you want to make. If you want to make more money, then you need to invest time and effort to get things off the ground.

Starting up is a little hard simply because you need time to understand things, the mechanics of how it runs and so on. But once you have covered the bases, you are good to go! Also reading as much as you can (which includes this book) helps you build a solid foundation of affiliate marketing. Building your credibility is the most important thing in affiliate marketing, next to creating good content. With the arsenal of excellent content as well as credibility, working your way towards a consistent and increasing profit base is achievable.

Passive Income Ideas

35 Best, Proven Business Ideas for Building Financial Freedom in the New Economy

Chapter 1 - What is Passive Income?

Earn money while you sleep? That strategy sounds like a dream, doesn't it?

The idea of passive income has been a goal for many, and it has long been the ideal way of generating income for entrepreneurs looking to generate a healthy income, without working the traditional 40-hour weeks and dealing with the pressures of daily duties and accompanying responsibilities

When an income revenue is passive, it means that you do the work upfront once, and it requires very little or no maintenance to keep the money flowing. This doesn't mean that maintenance can be forgotten or completely ignored. Most passive income models still require some sort of maintenance, and it is critical as an entrepreneur to track every bit of passive income you have, no matter how automated it is.

Passive income is real, and it certainly is achievable. In my early 20s, I was able to build a business that currently generates over six figures a year passively. But for those who never built a business before, the fear of uncertainty and failure can cause them to not take action.

Once achieved, passive income is great, but to getting there certainly isn't easy. You definitely need to invest some amount of time to get things started: and the truth is, time is far more valuable than money because time can only be spent once, then it is gone forever, unlike money which can be earned over every time.

Before we transition and cover the many aspects of passive income ideas that you can create to automate your revenue, we must first understand the concept of passive income and what it is and is not. You'll find plenty of posts on the web talking about ideas of passive income, how to go about it, and what it takes to get there but they never really go in depth. In this book, we're covering each one in extensive details.

- Passive Income and Interest

When money is lent in an S-corporation or into a partnership acting as a pass-through entity by the owner of that entity, the interest gained on that loan into the portfolio income qualifies as passive income. According to the IRS, self-charged interest can be treated as passive income or passive activity deductions, only if the loan proceeds are utilized in a passive activity.

- Passive Income and Property

Very often, rental properties are considered passive income. There are a few exceptions to this rule, though. If you're a real estate professional dealing solely in properties, then the income you make on the rental is actually your active income. Also, rental income is not considered passive income if you're self-renting. It does not constitute passive income unless the lease has been signed before 1988.

- Passive Income and the No Material Inclusion

If an investor invests $100,000 in a bicycle store with the agreement that the investor gets a percentage of the earnings by the owners, this venture would be passive income for the investor, as long as the investor doesn't contribute or participate actively in the business operation, other than placing an investment.

The true benefit of passive income lies in the records of profits or loss. When a taxpayer records a loss as a passive activity, only the passive activity profits can be deducted instead of the entire income as a whole. It's wise for a person to ensure that all his or her passive activities are classified as passive activities, so that one can make the most out of tax deductions.

- Passive Income and Grouping Activities

Grouping activities happen when a person groups two or more of one's passive activities into a larger one. This forms the 'appropriate economic unit.' According to the IRS, when a taxpayer does this, they would only have to provide material participation for the activity as a whole and not in multiple activities.

Chapter 2 - How to Create Passive Income Streams

It's not hard to understand what passive income means. While it's easy to understand the concept, it does require work to produce the results. Passive income requires some form of investment of time, energy, and of course, money to make it worth the long run of minimal maintenance ahead.

Based on the Internet's capabilities, building a passive income stream has made this process easier. There are plenty of online passive income ideas you can embark in, and I personally believe the internet is the best place to start. So how do you create successful passive income revenues? In this chapter, we'll explore how to go about creating a plan to produce this form of income, especially now that we have a better idea of what passive income is.

It may not be easy, but it's worth the effort. Here are some step-by-step ways to ensure you're on the right path to acquire and work on your own passive income stream:

Step 1 - It starts with an idea

Of course, the first thing you should do is select the idea which you can work on the best. Later in the book we'll discuss 35 business models that you can generate passive income with. I recommend you pick one from there. Which one you decide on is entirely an individual decision as it involves the unique situation including your passion, interest, skill sets, etc. If you have the means to purchase real estate or business investing or even in dividend stocks, then great. If not, you can look at other choices you have. For most people now, passive income is built from an online business. One of the biggest reasons being that there are plenty of ways that you can create passive income online that doesn't require such a huge investment upfront. So, go through the business models listed in this book, then start by writing down which one works best with your situation now, and identify what resources you have to make this idea happen.

Step 2: Setting your goals

When you've selected on the passive income business you want to build, your next step is to set measurable goals and to start taking action. You need to invest a good deal of time to bring your idea to fruition, so you'll want to do proper research to make sure you understand as much as you can about the business.

I recommend everyone to purchase a proven course/program on the chosen business model and start following it. There are courses on almost everything right now. All you need is the willingness to research and to start implementing what you learn.

It's also vital to clearly write down your goals because setting goals on pen and paper are much more powerful than setting them in your mind. Setting goals arbitrarily in your mind will often lead to failure. Keep in mind though, failing is ok and a normal part of the process. It serves as a learning experience for you to get better and push you towards success. So set your goals, take action, and keep failing forward towards your goal.

Step 3- Planning your Steps to get there

Once you've decided on your passive income business as well as set some hard goals, it's now time to plan effective steps on reaching these goals. How will you achieve goal one? How will you get from point A to point B? What can you do to get there? What are the actions you need to take?

Again, you've articulated all these steps onto paper, so it'll help you bring the gap between dream and reality a little closer. Keep in mind that nothing materializes quickly - if it does, then it'll burn out just as quickly. Don't chase get rich quick schemes, as the business also disappears quickly. Make sure you're selecting a business that is proven to last for the long-term, like the ones I list in this book. The step by step plan you put into place must be consistent and persistent and as long as you know what's going to take you to get there, you're setting yourself up for success!

Step 4 - Have Income Backup Plans

Creating and beginning your journey towards financial freedom can be daunting, and it can be easy to give up after not seeing the results you want initially and instead focus on work that gives you consistent pay (like a job). It might take a while to build, but once you've successfully established your passive income stream, the rewards are great. You'll achieve not only more money, but more time and location freedom as well. On the journey to get there, however, you need backup plans. Getting into your passive income stream without any monetary backup plan is a fool's game.

In the entrepreneurship space currently, especially online, you'll commonly hear many so called "guru's" preaching to people that you need to go ALL IN. That you need to quit your job, invest all your life savings, wake up at 5am, go to bed at 2am, and work on your business 16 hours a day.

Many people who've never built a business before overestimate how much it takes to actually do so, thus, believing in BS advice like this. Yes, you have to put in a lot of time, effort, and sometimes money (depending on the business you've chose), but doing it like this going "all in" will only lead to a burn out. What's more important than a short burst of massive work is CONSISTENCY. It's much better to put in a consistent, focused few hours a day while maintaining your normal life, rather than dropping everything for your business. This is actually most successful people built their businesses, so don't get tricked by the lies the few "guru's" that are vocal that you see online.

Ok enough of my rant, let's get back into the topic. Like I said, you need to keep your active income and just work on your passive income on the side, slowly and steadily building it up till it reaches a point that enables you to quit your active income if you want to, and rely on your passive one. However, completely retiring at that point is still not a wise decision. It's smart to continue reinvesting your profits and creating other passive incomes sources, so that you don't rely on just one source of income.

Be sure to always have a fallback plan, even if your passive income pays your bills and feeds you more than what your active income can bring to the table. You always want to be ready for the change in the market, and seeking new opportunities. If you do keep your active income work but work on passive income on the side, you can slowly and steadily build it up. For example, if you're starting a new blog, don't quit your day job. You can make a ton of money from blogging, but not many people do, and it takes time to get there. In sum, be sure you have a fallback plan until that passive income source is paying your bills.

Step 5 - Exemplify Successful Online Marketers

Online marketers are good examples of people who build passive income streams. In fact, many successful online marketers usually have multiple different passive income revenues. If you're trying to succeed in business, you'll want to be like an investigator. Seek out those who are successful and learn exactly what they are doing. Then all you need to do is to do the same thing, to get the same results. You don't have to reinvent the wheel here. Ask yourself, what and how are the most successful online marketers doing to generate passive income? How have they managed to build their sales funnels and sell products on autopilot? Do plenty of research prior to starting your own online passive income stream. Some people teach you to just get started and figure it out later. I don't believe in this approach. I always like to take the time to research and really get a good idea of the business before I dive in and get started. The time you invest to gain the knowledge, understanding, and wisdom will be worth it.

Step 6 - Join mastermind Groups

Apart from learning from the master online marketers, another step I encourage is to join online (or offline) communities with other entrepreneurs and form a mastermind. You can search on places such as on LinkedIn, Reddit, Facebook, as well as networking groups offline, which you can find by using google, meetup.com or attending business seminars.

When I was making around $1000 a month from my online business, I decided to invite 3 other people I knew who were in the same business making around the same income and formed a little mastermind facebook chat group. We talked everyday and shared everything from new strategies we tried, what worked, what didn't, etc. All four of us were making around $1000 a month when we started, but in about a year, we were all making over $10,000 a month. I believe being in a mastermind was one of the single biggest factor of succeeding in my business. I formed mine with others who were making around the same income, but if you can collaborate with a mastermind with those who are more successful than you, that is better.

As the famous quote by Jim Rohn asserts, "You are the average of the 5 people you spend the most time with." This premise recommends the more time you spend with those who have already built passive income streams, the faster it'll accelerate your results as well.

Ask as many questions as you can (without being annoying) and more often than not, someone in the group would be happy to share knowledge and expertise. People often perceive successful people as "greedy," but in reality you'll find that they're normal people just like you and me and are happy to help you whenever they can. You'll also notice that you don't have to be a genius to become successful, and will help you feel confident that you can also build a successful business as well. You might even end up buying an online business or even partnering up in a business with someone in your mastermind - Remember, your network is your net worth. Gather tips, tactics, strategies, and advice to help you along your journey.

Step 7 - Find a mentor

On your path to success, you may hit stumbling blocks and get frustrated. It happens. Being in groups and learning second-hand from successful people who've built passive income streams is one thing but having a mentor guide you every step of the way is by far the fastest way to creating the same results yourself. Being in your groups and forums helps as you can find a suitable mentor along the way. But keep in mind that many people, especially online marketers, portray success, when in reality only a few actually achieve it. What's worse is that these same people will sell mentorship/coaching packages for a ton of money. You don't want to pay these people for mentorship obviously, as they haven't even achieved success themselves.

When you do find someone whom you can connect with and has a few successful businesses under his or her belt, ask if you can take mentorship with this figure. This person may take you up on your offer. Do not get discouraged if you don't find one - good things come to those who wait. It's better to take your time in forming a good partnership with a reliable mentor than to hastily connect with one who's not a good mentor at all.

Step 8 - Scale like the wind

The last but certainly not least, of things to do in creating your passive income stream is to scale. When you find a business that works and you start making money, you need to start scaling like the wind. Part of ensuring that your revenue stream is sustainable is making it scalable. The good thing about passive income is that it can be scaled whether it's a blog, online courses, or audiobooks. All you need to do is reinvest back into what's working and scale. It won't happen right away but through persistence, you'll reach the goals you want.

Chapter 3- Passive Income Ideas

Idea #1 - Affiliate Marketing

What Is Affiliate Marketing?

Affiliate marketing is the process of earning a sum of commission by promoting someone else's products or company. If you find a product you like, you promote it to your channels, and in the process, earn a piece of profit for every sale that you make. You make a commission each time you share, recommend, or promote another person's product, service, or company. Each time that company gets a sale, you get a cut! The great part about affiliate marketing is that you do not need to create your own product or company or invest the time and effort into something to sell it.

Who is it for?

Affiliate marketing is perfect for those who need to work from home. It's an ideal home business simply because it doesn't require much costs to get started and you do not need to stock or ship or produce any kind of product, inventory, or even do any delivery or service. You get paid for referring new clients and customers. While affiliate marketing isn't hard, it still requires some knowledge, a bit of planning, and consistent effort to make it worthwhile and yield significant income.

How much money can you potentially earn?

An affiliate marketer's payment depends largely on the commissions they receive from the company that they acquaint themselves with. Buttons, links, and banners of the product that they sell contain unique user ID embedded into the HTML code of your blog to enable ads to that business appear. Essentially, an affiliate marketer can earn anywhere from $300 a day to even up to $3,000 a day or more; this profit depends entirely on how much effort they put in and what their profit goals are.

How does affiliate marketing works?

- **Find Your Niche** - Your niche should be a product or service that you have knowledge on or something that you**'re** passionate about because then you'd already have an idea on whom to target, how it works, what methods to use, and so on. This niche does not need a mass audience as long as there's some kind of audience looking for the product or service, you're good to go.

- **Research & Identify Affiliate Opportunities-** Once you've selected your niche, it's now time to look for affiliate partners. These are the companies that will pay you to promote their businesses on your site. Most affiliate programs are free to join and you can find them in many ways such as through affiliate marketplaces like Rakuten and ShareASale. You can also join affiliate programs such as Amazon Associates and Overstock and sponsored post programs like Blogvertise.

- **Build Your Website -** A website is an integral part of affiliate marketing especially if you want most of your work and marketing to be done online. Your website is a key component that acts as your marketing channel as well as the home base for your business. There are plenty of website services available currently that allow you to create a website easily such as WIX or SquareSpace.

- **Create Affiliate Content -** Once you have your website, it's time to assess the content you will feature. Start crafting authentic content that speaks about your niche and promotes your affiliate products. You can work on various types of content ranging from product reviews to How-To Guides, recipes, and even do give-away discounts.

- **Add Marketing Channels to Extend Your Reach -** Your website shouldn't be your online means of marketing online. Affiliate marketing needs to be split across different marketing channels as this is an ideal way to target, reach, and build your audience. Once you start your website, connect it to your social media channels and blog. Once you've gained a substantial amount of following, start a newsletter, too. People prefer reading about certain information on specific platforms.

Myths about Affiliate Marketing

- **It's Easy -** So what are the myths about affiliate marketing? You've probably heard about them during your research. Firstly, by the way it's described, it sounds like affiliate marketing is easy. The truth is, it becomes easier once you learn the process. But managing affiliate marketing is probably the easiest aspect. Other than that, affiliate marketing is competitive and time-consuming. There are no shortcuts to this and you need to put a good amount of hard work to get the ball rolling.

- **Plenty of traffic means plenty of profit** - Many newbies think that their main marketing goal is to continuously drive traffic to their website. While this is important, it isn't the only thing you can and should world on. It is also about how appealing your target market feels about your product which would then increase your sales ratio. Advertising at the right channels where your target audience is one way to get their buy-in.

- **Popularity on Social media ensures success** - You may be popular on social media to attract a new audience and reach a wider depth. But customers want to buy your product and will continue buying your product simply because they deem it as good quality and also meets their desired specification.

Idea #2 - Blogging

What is blogging?

The term "blogging" has evolved since its inception. In fact, it's more than just a personal online diary and its uses have evolved dramatically from an avenue where you just write your stuff down on a daily basis to a medium of income, news, and information. Even the appearance of blogs has changed from merely an online diary to now a site that has exciting marketing and social features. ProBlogger describes a blog as a type of website that displays content in chronological order. While the very essence of blogging still remains to this day, you need a variety of skills in 2019 to run a successful and sustainable blog, from not only knowing to write engagingly but also the aptitude to use visuals and PNG files and buttons and links as well as the ability to market your blog professionally.

Who is it for?

Blogs are for anyone and everyone who wants to talk about a certain topic or document something, curate information, and generally craft and share their views, opinions, daily life, and just about any topic under the sun. Anyone can open a blog, but it also takes a great deal to keep it sustainable with new and fresh content. Blogs are great for startup companies, tech companies, bakery stores, hobbyists, photographers, crafters, event planners, marketers, doctors, ballerinas -

anyone. As long as you have content to write and talk about, then blogs are a perfect platform to do that.

How much money can you potentially earn?

When blogging was relatively new, carving out your name on internet retail space was relatively easy. Now, it takes a little bit more work because the market is saturated with blogs of various kinds. Many of today's blog income earners have been building their blogs back when it was still new. It's a different story altogether, but the cash flow is lucrative still, albeit a little harder to get. It's not something that you can get rich quickly, even if you do work on your blog full-time. If you want to make a living out of blogging, you need to do some really good research and work on content that appeals and sells. According to a survey done by Blogger.com in 2012 found that 17% of bloggers could sustain their lifestyle and family through their blogs, whereas, 81% never even made $100. The balance of 2% spent less than 2 hours blogging but made $150k. ProBlogger also conducted a survey among bloggers and found that 9% made $1000 to $10,000 a month but the vast majority made less than $3.50 per day. How much you make depends on several factors, such as how often you blog, how competitive the topic is, and your effectiveness of building an audience and also generate the right traffic. Success will not come quickly.

How does blogging work?

Step 1 - Open an account in any blogging site you like:

1. WordPress.org
2. Wix
3. WordPress.com
4. Blogger
5. Tumblr
6. Medium
7. Squarespace
8. Ghost

Step 2 - Choose the kind of layout you want.

Step 3 - Customize your blog according to your needs, content you plan on posting, and interest

Step 4 - Click on New Post and start writing your content. It's that easy!

Myths about Blogging

- Blogging is just a quick fad - By now you already know that it's not a fad. The landscape of blogging has changed quite a bit and even Fortune 500 companies use blogs. Blogs can drive actual and profitable business so long as you're willing to work on them.

- Your posts should never be over 500 words - It's false. Your blog post can be over 500 words as long as it's engaging and something your readers want to know. Having in-depth articles on your blog actually improves your SEO rankings so don't worry about your word count but instead worry about the quality of the content.

- If you can't write well, you can't blog - You may have an English degree but that does not mean you are a great writer. There are different kinds of audience looking for various things only and different ways of indulging in content. Depending on who your target audience is, as well as the kind of content you want to write about, you don't necessarily need high-end college-worthy writing skills.

- You can't write a blog post in an hour - Every piece on your blog does not have to be a masterpiece and it doesn't need to be a certain amount of words. You write because you have things to say on your blog and as long as they serve the value your audience is looking for: you can take any amount of time to write engaging, purposeful content.

Idea #3 - Dropshipping

What is Dropshipping?

Dropshipping is an element of retail fulfillment practice in the standard retail model that allows a store selling products and merchandise to not hold its own inventory; in other words, do away with keeping their products in stock, or shipping their products to their customers on their own or owning a warehouse to store its products. In this case, whenever there's an order for the product, the seller purchases its item from a third-party vendor and this third-party vendor ships it directly to the customer. This retailer partner with a dropship supplier does the manufacturing, warehousing, packaging, and shipping of these products on the retailer's behalf. The merchant doesn't see or handle the said product.

Who is Dropshipping For?

If you're a first timer entering the online business, then drop shipping is a great business model to begin with initially. It's low-risk and low-investment which is great for novices starting their business. It doesn't involve much monetary gamble. It's ideal for someone who is the current owner of a retail store and already has an inventory, but looking to reach newer, wider markets. This business model, however, doesn't give you amazing results from the get-go. Dropshipping margins are relatively lower so this might not bode well for a startup brand because these businesses do not have ultimate control where customer satisfaction related to brand experience and branding is concerned.

How much money can you potentially earn?

Depending on how much work you put into and the effort of time and some money, you can earn anywhere from $1,000 to $1,000,000 in a year or more. For example, if you get a product at $15 and you sell it on your site for $30. Minus the shipping and advertising costs, your profit is $10. To make $100,000 in a year, you need to sell at least 1000 products each month. This means $10 x 1000 orders = $10,000 per month. You can potentially earn $120,000 if your idea, product, and strategies work well.

How does Dropshipping work?

- **Finding your Niche in Dropshipping -** It may sound overwhelming to find your niche in business because there are plenty of things that you can get involved in at first. An evergreen niche is a niche that most retailers would like - it stands the test of time. Things like gaming, beauty, fashion, and weight loss are very evergreen niches. However, on the other hand, trending niches have instant profits and surge, but it also falls in popularity pretty fast.

- **Looking and Finding the Right suppliers -** In the world of dropshipping, it's critical to work with the right supplier, especially since suppliers are a crucial element of this entire drop shipping process. But like everything in life, drop shipping suppliers also come in different sizes, needs, and interests. To identify good suppliers is to place small orders to get a sense of their processes, sales reps, and professionalism. This way, you can pinpoint:

- o How efficient their ordering process is
- o How fast items are shipped out
- o How efficient they are in following up with an invoice for tracking information
- o How good the quality of their packing is

- **Setting up your Business** - One of the biggest pull factors is that you don't need stock or even to handle the things that you are selling and you can also start with limited funds. In its very basic idea, dropshipping requires a website optimized for e-commerce and ad from the merchant you purchase items from a third party supplier who then fulfills an order made by a customer on your e-commerce website. This cuts operational costs and also frees up your time to focus on other aspects of the business such as customer acquisition - marketing and promoting your website. A site optimized for e-commerce is extremely crucial in the drop shipping business model. One of the simplest platforms that you can use is Shopify, as it comes with built-in, customizable apps to help you create a website, increase sales, and even market your website. It's a very easy plug-and-play option.

Myths about Dropshipping

- **Dropshipping only works for low priced, general products** - The truth is, dropshipping now offers entrepreneurs looking to sell something the ability to offer specialized, high-quality items. If you find a niche for your products, you've definitely found a market that values quality products.

- **You need to have an in-depth understanding of coding and all things IT-**Any knowledge can be beneficial for your business but you don't need to be a tech-expert to run a dropshipping site. The basic idea of crafting a well working site as well as knowledge in marketing can help you kick off your business. Over time, as you gain knowledge and expertise as well as money, you can hire experts to help you fine-tune your business.

- **All you need is to list products on your site and the sales will roll in** - If that were true, then anyone can make a living with dropshipping. Unless you've hit the golden ticket with your product, chances of getting a profit immediately are quite dim. Dropshipping is not a get-rich scheme. It takes time to build and reach markets as well as target audiences. However, once you've got your footing, it'll be much easier.

Idea #4 - Amazon FBA

What is Amazon FBA?

On Amazon's FBA site, you'll see the tagline - you sell it, we ship it. The Fulfillment by Amazon, or for short, FBA, is a process where you store your products in Amazon's fulfillment centers, and they'll pick your products, pack it for you, and ship it for you as well as provide customer service for these products. When you list your products on FBA, customers are eligible for free shipping and qualified listings are shown using the Prime logo. Customers browsing your site know that Amazon will do the packing, delivery, and everything for the product.

Who is Amazon FBA for?

If you love shopping and also love taking advantage of amazing shopping deals, then you might want to look into starting a business that can bring your extra income. Amazon FBA gives the opportunity to earn money all through shopping for items and then reselling them. If you like certain products on Amazon and you'd like to sell them, you can do it via Amazon FBA but you don't need to worry about storage or customer support, sales, or shipping because Amazon does this step for you.

How much money can you potentially earn?

It depends on the amount of inventory you begin with because your profits will vary. With a good strategy, you can earn a good few thousand dollars in your first month of selling on FBA and up to $10,000 or more a few months later as you scale your business.

How does Amazon FBA work?

Step 1- Set up FBA

You can start by setting up your 'Selling on Amazon' account and then add FBA account to this. You can set up your account at this link.

https://sellercentral.amazon.com/

Step 2- Set up your product listings

Here, you can add the products you want to sell to the Amazon catalog either one at a time or in bulk. You can also integrate your inventory-management software using Amazon's API.

Step 3- Preparing your products

All your listed products need to be 'e-commerce' ready, so that Amazon can safely and securely transport them to the customer's location. You can also get Amazon's preferred prep and shipping supplies if you ever need it delivered right to your location.

Step 4- Shipping your products to Amazon

Here, you need to create your shipping plans and also look into discounted partner carriers. You can use your partners to ship and track your shipments to Amazon fulfillment centers where Amazon's online seller tools can help you through the process.

Step 5- Ordering, picking, packing, and shipping

When customers order your products, Amazon picks it up, packs it, and ships it for you. Prime Amazon customers get fast and free shipping on your products. However, all customers can qualify for free shipping on orders that are eligible. Orders are quickly and efficiently filled using web-to-warehouse, high-speed picking and sorting system from Amazon. Customers will receive tracking information directly from Amazon.

Step 6- Customer support all throughout the way

The great aspect about using Amazon FBA is that they offer amazing customer-service that provides inquiries, refunds, and returns on their orders on Amazon marketplace. This service is provided 24 hours a day, seven days every week.

Idea #5 - Self Publishing

What is self-publishing?

Self-publishing is publishing your own book using platforms such as Amazon Kindle. As a self-publishing author, you need to produce your final draft, supply the funds to design your book, market the book on your own, as well as distribute the book. You also get to decide how many copies should be printed and how much each would cost.

E-book publishing has opened up a new avenue for authors as online readership keeps growing the more and more people are moving away from regular books to online reading. Self-publishing eliminates the costs involved with printing and distributing physical copies, and it is also accessible worldwide.

Who is it for?

Self-publishing is useful for authors who cannot get a publisher or agent. This option is also ideal for people who have marketing prowess, which means there are times that you need to give your book away for free or publish your book in series or even look into effective marketing strategies that traditional publishers may not be aware of.

The money you earn from self-publishing could also be much better. Most authors price their books slightly cheaper or even the first of the series is free and charge the others at a certain price. It's also great for people who love writing and would like their books published on an online avenue and have a niche audience read their books.

How much money can you potentially earn?

Like all the other passive income methods listed here, self-publishing is also not an easy path to make a huge amount of money overnight. The Self-published author has the potential to make over $100,000 a year if the business is built correctly; and that's also because many self-published authors have plenty of books already published and collectively they make the amount.

Some authors also end up making less than $500 a year. With a publisher, you could end up with 10% or less but when you self-publish, you can keep 50 to 90% of the profits and this also depends on the distribution channel you use. If you use Amazon Kindle Direct Publishing (KDP), it gives you 30 to 70% to authors.

How Self-Publishing Works

Self-publishing is like building a house entirely on your own, with little to no help. It is actually quite satisfying to write your own book and publish it and create an audience that loves your work. In today's market, there are several ways to publish your book.

Essentially, here are the basics of self-publishing your book:

Step 1- Write your book - Of course, you need to start with writing your book. Pick your genre, write your draft, and work on your book.

Step 2- Edit your Manuscript - Self-edit your manuscript as much as you can. Enlist the help of reliable friends and colleagues who have the gift of word and grammar to help you analyze your words, sentences, and even your story.

Step 3- Designing the cover and formatting of the interior- The cover of your self-published book helps sell it and authors of both kinds of publishing - the traditional versus the online ones all heavily depend on a well-designed book. You can hire the services of a designer of UpWork or Fiverr for a small fee or you can even use online design services such as Canva or Pressbooks.

Step 4- Self Publish your Book in Print or as an Ebook- Before the internet, if you want to self-publish a book, you'd have to get a print run done which would involve paying up front for thousands of copies of books to be printed. You run into a risk of having copies of books you struggle to sell. Thankfully, with the internet, you can simply publish your book on Amazon's Kindle Direct Publishing. You can also Print-On-Demand through either KDP or IngramSpark or offer your book as an eBook.

Step 5- Master the Kindle Store - Mastering the Kindle store is akin to understanding and mastering other online platforms that you use to advertise, talk, and market yourself or your blog. Just like every other online platform nowadays, Kindle also has its own set of algorithms and knowing this will help you understand what works and what doesn't when you publish your book.

You must also know what a good price range for your book would be, so it will sell, as well as how to compose a good book description. The latter is key as it's the first contact for a potential reader of your book.

Step 6- Marketing your Book efficiently and effectively - For people to know your book and to reach the audience that wants to read your content, you need to craft a creative and effective marketing strategy. Employ different routes of marketing from social media to digital media, email marketing to on-ground meet and greet. All of this will enable you to get to know your audience and learn from whatever tips and mistakes you might make.

Myths about Self-Publishing

- **You can tell if a book is self-published -** Unless the book has plenty of errors, a badly designed cover and margins that do not exist, it is hard to tell if the book is self-published or not. Just because you're a self-publisher doesn't mean you have to do everything on your own. Your expertise lies in writing, but you can always get help from family and friends to help you in fields where you expertise, such as designing and editing. You can also easily hire an editor or book designer, should your budget permit, to look through the final draft of your book before you click on Publish.

- **Publishers do not like Self-Published authors -** This is a huge myth, one that needs to be squashed. A self-published author who has hit success will make publishing houses notice you, and it will also tell them that there's a market for the genre of your book. It also tells everyone in publishing thatyou've got what it takes to not only write a book but market it as well. You might just end up with a full-fledged publishing deal.

- **Self-Publishing is just an author being vain –** Oh, how the mind runs. There's more to self-publishing than just satisfying one's sense of importance. Self-publishing gives life to books nobody thought had a readership. While publishers do have their area of expertise, they will, more often than not, stick to certain types of genres that guarantee a mass following. Publishers also have specific capacities regarding the number of books they can assume in a year, which means books with merit are excluded.

- **Self-Publishing is merely the process of making a book -** The real work really begins once you have a self-published book. For any author, the biggest challenge would be to sell, distribute, and market your book, and most of the time, book stores and distributors prefer to work with publishing companies and not authors. This also means that self-published authors need to look at other means to get their books to their intended target audience and it takes a great deal of hard work to get there. So, when you're writing your book, you should also look into how to sell and market your book.

Idea #6 – Shopify

What is Shopify?

Shopify is a platform that offers potential retailers a comprehensive e-commerce site where they can create, design, promote, and sell products to customers in any part of the globe. This platform comes with plenty of ready-to-go templates that will suit your business needs and the products or services you plan to sell. Due to its use and integration of today's popular applications and practices, Shopify is a fast growing crowd favorite. For example, it utilizes 70 payment gateways with checkouts in over 50 languages, making product sales quick and hassle-free for customers anywhere in the world.

Who is it for?

Shopify is a form of drop shipping and it is great for novices starting their own business. It doesn't involve much monetary gamble. It's ideal for someone who is the current owner of a retail store and already has an inventory, but looking to reach newer, wider markets. Shopify is a plug-and-play e-commerce store. They have all the necessary tools, plug-ins, and templates that enable anyone to open and operate an e-commerce store.

How much money can you potentially earn?

To put it briefly, if you're only selling one digital product, then Shopify may not be the platform for you. You would be better off using a PayPal button or even a WooCommerce plug-in on your blog. However, if you're planning to run a full-fledged online store that requires a multi-product e-commerce support with inventory, customer records, marketing tools, and so on, then Shopify is the go-to platform for you, which will definitely be worth your investment.

Depending on how much effort you put in, your Shopify store can bring you anywhere from around $500 to $100,000. There are plenty of successful Shopify stores which you can use as examples, however, keep in mind that you'll only reap what you sow, so your success rate depends on how much time and effort you're willing to put into your shop.

How does Shopify Work?

Step 1- Setting Up your Shopify Store

To start with Shopify, you must first sign up for an account. Visit Shopify.com. You'll see a signup form. Use the form to create an account. Enter all the details required and ensure that they're accurate. Afterward, click the **'Create your store now'** button. At this step, you must select a Unique Store Name, as well as your preferred store template, and include all necessary details.

Step 2- Add Your Products to the Store

It's time to add your products to the store! To do this step, navigate to the bar on the left of the store and select **'Products'**. You'll then see '**Add a product'** in the top right corner of the page. You can use this screen to add in the details of your product. Put in relevant details for your product and focus on words and texts that can help with SEO such as description, name as well as URL. Include as much information as possible so your customers are informed of your products, but you don't need to write a long story. Succinct and useful information is the best.

Step 3- Selecting your preferred payment gateway

With a payment gateway set in place, your customers can make their payments via your website. Different gateways have different prices and commission rates, so it's important to know what features each gateway offers before taking on their service. Not all payment gateways are equal as they all serve different needs and interests.

Step 4- Get Your Online Shop "LIVE"

A few more details are required before your site can go live. These details are about your company and how you plan to make your product deliveries as well as pay your taxes. Once you're done entering all these details, test your site from purchasing an item to shipping an item and using your payment gateways. When you're satisfied with the results, click enable to make your site go LIVE!

Myths about Shopify

- **Shopify is a rigid platform** - If you're are worried that Shopify doesn't give you room to explore and expand your e-commerce site, just take a quick look at all the successful online retailers and what they did with their own sites. Shopify does seem rigid to the advance CMS builder but for novices and people who want a built-in an e-commerce site with minimal coding and HTML headaches, Shopify can do this and so much more.

- **You cannot integrate Shopify with advance back-end systems -** As your shop grows, you'll want it to look more polished and offer more user-friendly features to make shopping, searching, and purchasing easier. Shopify knows this which is why you CAN integrate Shopify's platform with more sophisticated CRMs such as Salesforce or ERPs such as NetSuite.

Idea #7 - Freelance Virtual Assistant

What Is It?

As the name indicates, a freelance virtual assistant is an individual who is hired by a business to assist with either the daily tasks of the business or a specific role from a remote location. Many small businesses, as well as online platforms, typically seek virtual assistants to help with these roles so that they may do away with the need to hire additional staff into their workforce. A function of a virtual assistant is vast and dependant on the nature of the business interested in hiring a virtual assistant. It can range from replying emails, clerical work, or managing personal schedules. At times, the job role for a virtual assistant is quite specific and can encompass the following responsibilities, depending on the hiring business:

1.   Managing Social Media Accounts

2.   Market Research

3.   Finance Management

4.   Content Creator

5.   Web Design

6.   Writer

7.   Personal Assistant

Who Is It For?

Those who take up the option of becoming a virtual assistant are usually those individuals who fall into one of the following categories:

- You have the freedom to work from anywhere and are not confined to any office space as long as you have a laptop and an Internet connection.

- You can work for yourself and decide when you want to work. This enables you to spend more quality time with family and friends.

- Prevent brain drain that comes with mundane and monotonous daily office tasks.

How much money can you potentially earn?

The earning capacity for anyone becoming a virtual assistant is unlimited and isn't hindered by the number of hours that you work with your client. This is because once your freelancing business grows, you can hire someone else to do the work for you and you keep a cut of the profit. In most cases, the top-earning virtual assistants usually have more clients and tasks than they can handle.

As a beginner into this industry, you'll need to start from scratch and slowly build up your credentials and portfolio with your respective clients. Once you acquire a good amount of reference and experience, you can start charging anywhere from $20 to $40 per hour based on your skill set and experience. Some experienced virtual assistants have even charged clients in excess of $50 to $100 per hour. However, it's important that you also ensure that the rates you'll be charging are not too exorbitant than the local pay rates when you are starting out at first.

How it works - Step-by-Step

Many virtual assistants begin their paths by promoting themselves through sites such as Linkedin and Upwork. There are also sites that focus largely on virtual assistants like VAClassroom and agencies like Zirtual. However, before you embark on your journey into the virtual assistant world, you may want to consider the following steps:

- Never quit your 9-5 job right away when you initially begin. Always ensure that you have enough income saved for at least six or nine months for living expenses depending on your situation.

- Determine what tasks suit your prior experience or what you enjoy most doing. You may want to test your suitability and strengths for low-risk assignments first to determine what you would be good at.

- Open an account in a professional website. Highlight your skills and experience. Once you start getting jobs, add in testimonials and samples of your previous work to attract new clients.

Myths about Virtual Training

Here are some common myths uncovered about working as a virtual assistant:

- **Virtual assistants are expensive -** The cost of hiring a virtual assistant can differ, depending on the kind of work that a client is seeking. If the client is looking for a niche or specific skill set, then he or she should be prepared to pay more. But if one is looking for someone to do just general clerical work, the costs will be much cheaper. On that note, it does save organizations money as you only need to pay these virtual assistants the cost for completing the work and excludes other benefits that they pay their normal staff such as year-end bonuses, medical claims, and so on.

- **Virtual assistants are always work-at-home moms -** Being a virtual assistant allows one to have the flexibility to work from anywhere; for parents, it enables them to work from home and spend more time with their children. However, not all who pursue this path are parents, since some are professionals who still work at their day jobs but use this opportunity to generate more income and others choose this career to travel and work from any location.

- **Virtual assistants are just online personal assistants -** It's be short -sighted to think of virtual assistants as just merely secretaries or personal assistants as they can perform a wide range of tasks that help a business. Here are some of the key roles that a virtual assistant performs:

a.   Creating social media content

b.   Sales support

c.   Email management

d.   Proofreading, writing, editing

e.   Web design

f.   Graphic design

Idea #8 - Creating Online Courses

What is it?

An online course is a platform in which an individual can provide information or tutorials on a vast array of subjects that he or she either has a passion for or experience. This can range for a variety of topics from culinary arts, music, software, fitness, gardening, and soon on. Contrary to popular belief, you don't have to be an expert in your field to come up with an online course. You just need to have more knowledge on the subject than most people. While some individuals have shared their knowledge through books, blogs, and online videos, creating an online course is a great method of generating passive income. Many people have made tons of money through their online courses over the years. According to global industry analysts, online learning will be a $240 billion dollar industry by the year 2021.

Who is it for?

Creating an online course isn't limited just to the professional or experts in a given field. In our day-to-day life, we're already sharing our knowledge and information to those around us through daily conversations, our Instagram posts or Facebook feeds without even knowing about it. We reiterated that we all have knowledge in a certain area that someone else does not have and wants to learn. Are you already sharing your fitness regimes or travel recommendations on your social media accounts? Then it's probably high time you invest your time to combine all these details into an online course. A popular online learning platform called Udemy already has over 35,000 instructors offering 80,000 courses. As such, if you have a passion or knowledge in any areas of your life, you might want to consider applying into a course as you're probably already teaching others and not even aware of it.

How much money can you potentially earn?

The average worker in the U.S makes an average of $25 per hour. With an online course, your income potential is unlimited. This happens, because after completing most of the initial work up front, you can continue to generate revenue every time you sell a course over the period of the next few months or even years. And the more courses you create and sell, your revenue keeps increasing.

How does it work?

If you're thinking of diving into the world of selling online courses, you can follow the steps below to prepare yourself:

- Topic – First, you need to figure what you know or what you're passionate about. Try to think of subjects that you constantly help your friends and families on or even a hobby or sport that you've been doing for some time. Make a list of these things.

- Do Market Research - The next important step is to conduct market research on the topics that you have listed out in the earlier step. Here you'll need to determine if people would be willing to spend money on the topics that you will be teaching.

- Structuring The Outline Of Your Course - Prepare modules and lessons that will cover all important aspects of your course. These modules should dwell deeply into the subject matter and help the reader better understand the course.

- Teaching Method - Identify the best format that you will use for your online course. Will it be by text, audio, video or worksheets? Certain topics will require only one format, while others will require two or three more formats to better convey the information.

- Drafting Your Lessons - When creating your online lessons, consider creating a visually appealing content that will attract the reader. Also, always proofread all texts and watch all videos to correct errors.

- How To Sell Your Lessons - For starters, you may want to opt for an easy alternative by using online platforms such as Skillshare or Udemy. You just upload the content of your lesson on these sites and then they'll take care of marketing these courses interested individuals.

- Keeping Course Information Up To Date - Every now and then, do a quick check to ensure that the content in your course is relevant with the current times. Continue to update and make changes to ensure that you don't receive any negative reviews that can derail the sale of your course.

Myths about Creating Online Courses

It's imperative to note that while it may seem easy and cheap to start an online course, you must be aware that there are many other individuals who are also providing a similar course online. As such, you'll have to market your content aggressively, which will require time and money on your part.

Idea #9 - Building an Application

What is it?

In this day and age, almost every individual owns a smartphone. And with the usage of smartphones comes the usage of apps that are created by third-party developers on both the Android and iPhone platforms. Since apps have made their debut, it's estimated currently as a billion-dollar industry, and it doesn't seem to be slowing down anytime soon. Creating an app starts with an idea, and it'll also need to encompass some basic knowledge in coding.

Who is it for?

Individuals who are already familiar with the basic coding language or have developed basic apps have a head start in this area. But for a non-coder that has an idea that would work, it's best to learn the required coding skills that will be important in creating an app of your choice. Kevin Systrom, the founder of Instagram, learned coding at night to build Burbn, which in time turned to Instagram and was sold to Facebook for an estimated value of $1 billion.

How much money can you potentially earn?

It is estimated that in 2016, the revenue generated from apps is somewhere in the region of $46 billion. A large chunk of this revenue comes from mobile app games. For the iOS platform, it is estimated that 25% of the developers earn anywhere between $5,000 per month and about 18% of developers on the Android platform earn the same number. There are multiple ways to earn revenue through the apps on both these platforms. They are:

a.   Provide a free version of your app but charge a certain amount for the premium version.

b.   Allow ads to be displayed in your ads to generate income.

c.   Collect and sell data to organizations that require info   for   their   businesses.

How It Works - Step-by-Step

Once you have devised an idea for an app and some basic coding knowledge, you can follow these steps to create your first app.

1.   Set A Goal For Your App - Using a pen and paper, ask the following questions:

a.   What exactly do you want your app to do?

b.   How are you going to make it appeal to users?

c.   What problem is it going to solve?

d.   How will you market your app?

2.   Turn Your Ideas Into Sketches

    a. With the answers from Step 1, create visual representations of your thoughts into what your app will look like.

b. Make decisions if you're going to include ads to generate revenue or will your app be a paid download.

c. Sketch as many ideas as possible.

3. Market Research

a. Research your competition to make your app better

b. Read the competition's reviews.

c. Make changes to your ideas and sketches to make necessary changes based on the info collected.

d. Determine your target market and how will you market your idea.

e. Look for new and refreshing designs for your app.

4. Creating A Wireframe

a. Now, you'll take all the ideas and sketches and provide them with more contexts.

b. Using a wireframing website, you can start to put some functionality to your ideas in your app.

5. Designing Your App's Back End

a. Once the wireframe has been constructed, you'll need to delineate your servers, APIs, and data diagrams.

b. For the novice, you can source the web for app builders that will provide you the necessary tools for   this.

6.   Get Feedback

a.   Give a demonstration of your app to your family and friends. Get their feedback on areas to improve.

b.   Their feedback will be crucial in finalizing the overall structure of your app and functionality.

7.   Putting The Pieces Together

a.   Once you have gone through the above process, you can start finalizing your app using your app builder.

b.   Now is the time to create an account with Google Play and Apple, so that you can create your app on the market

c.   At this stage, you may want to engage designers to create your user interface for your app.

8.   App Testing

a.   At this stage, it is important to test both the functionality and user interface of your app.

b.   You can use platforms like Proto and Pixate to test your app.

c.   Make any changes and adjustments to your app based on the test results before moving on to the beta testing phase.

d.   During the beta testing phase, you may use both Android and iOS platforms to test the app in a live environment.

9.   Releasing Your App

  a. You can now start adding your app into both the Android and iOS stores.

  b. For the Google Play store, you will be immediately selling your app.

  c. For the iOS store, it will be reviewed first before it goes live.

Myths about Building an Application

- Mobile Apps Are Cheap - Development of simple apps are by no means cheap as there is extensive effort and time that goes in the development of these applications.

- Apps Are Usually Aimed At Smartphones - While the largest users of mobile applications are individuals with smartphones, mobile apps can also be used for tablets, handheld consoles, and smartwatches.

Idea #10 - Online Auctions

What it is?

Another popular method of generating passive income is through the use of online auctions. Using this platform to generate revenue is fast becoming a favorite, as it's relatively simple compared to the work that you would put in. To do this, you would just need to create an online profile and begin to sell your merchandise to interested individuals. Plus, in recent times, users are quick to use the drop shipping options that are offered by many companies. You become the middleman by displaying the goods from the supplier on the online platform and once it's purchased by the interested party, the goods are directly shipped from the manufacturer to them. Hence, you make the money without the need of keeping inventory.

Who is it for?

The best thing about using this method to generate revenue is that it can be done by anyone with a laptop and an internet connection. Anyone that has either goods or craft items to sell can utilize this method. Plus, you can also purchase highly sought items from manufacturers and resell them on these websites or through an auction.

How it works - Step-by-Step

The first key step in generating revenue from an online auction is to research, research, and research. You don't want to sell stuff where there isn't any demand; hence, it is vital that you look for goods that are highly sought after and can be sold at a premium.

The next step in generating revenue and increasing your profit margin is to find out the starting bid price for your item. The trick here is to determine how popular the item that you will be placing for the bid is. If a certain product is high in demand, you can start the bid at a low price. But if there aren't going to be many bidders for a particular item, then you should go with a price close enough to the actual price of the item.

Next, to attract the attention of potential bidders, you will need to come up with a catchy phrase for your listing. And it'll also help to give a little description of the product so that potential bidders will be more open to placing a bid for it. Also, to ensure success to your online auction, you'll need to ensure that each product is listed in the right category to verify that you only attract the right bidders who will be more prone to purchasing your items.

When you start, your auctions will also have an effect on its success and failures. It's recommended that you begin your auction on Thursdays and have them run for ten days straight. This will allow your auction to be open for two weekends straight. This will ensure more traffic time to your auction site.

Myths about Online Auctions

Here are some points to dispel the typical myths associated with online auctions:

- Items will not fetch their fair market value - Those who usually buy items online are pretty seasoned buyers and will have probably done their homework in terms of the price of that specific item. As such, they will normally purchase these items at their fair prices.

- Selling with an online auction platform is expensive - Contrary to popular belief, there are many online platforms that are willing to negotiate on the commission rates that are reasonable depending on the item that you are selling.

- Auctions only attract buyers looking for a bargain - Not all online buyers are bargain hunters. Many of them are always on the lookout for items that are considered collectibles and hard to find. As such, if you have these kinds of items, you'll surely attract serious buyers.

Idea #11 - Online Survey

What it is?

An online survey is a set of questionnaires for an individual to complete on the web. These surveys are a set of questions that are created using a web form that is eventually connected to a database that will store all responses which, in turn, will be used as a statistic for further analysis. Many organizations employ these online surveys to gain a better understanding of their target customers. The feedback provided by respondents in these surveys will help organizations improve their products and services. Surveys serve two distinct functions; one is to collect more data on the demographics of the customer base. The other is to gather feedback on a certain type of product or service provided by the organization. Online surveys are widely used these days as opposed to traditional surveys as there is a much broader outreach to respondents at both local and international stage. Most organizations usually will provide cash incentives to individuals to participate in their surveys.

Who is it for?

In online surveys, the organization is looking for individuals that fit into the character of their sample. As such, when you register to an online survey platform, you'll first need to undergo a pre-qualification test. From here, these platforms will start sending your surveys based on the demographic that you qualify into. So, if you have plenty of spare time on your hands, you should first sign up to as many online surveys websites as possible to expedite.

How much money can you potentially earn?

- Vindale – One of the best survey companies in relation to pay and time spent. Between $150 - $200 a month.

- Earning Station – Between $120 - $180 per month

- PineCone – minimum $3 for per survey

- Paribus – Between $70 - $100 per month

- My Survey – Between $150 - $200 per month

The major benefit is that you can take these surveys during your free time while watching a movie, having a meal at home, yet still earning a substantial amount.

How it works - Step-by-Step

To help you in generating income from online surveys, we recommend the following steps:

1. Register as many free online survey companies as you can. The more you join, the more surveys will be sent to your email and more revenue you will be able to generate.

2. Do not lie when you register on these online survey sites.

3.   Always keep your profile updated to eventually allow more surveys to be sent to you.

4.   Read and answer all questions carefully. Every survey has qualifying and quality questions to ensure that the respondent is giving this or her honest answers.

5.   Each survey has a designated time frame to complete it. As such, do not rush, but instead, take your time and answer each question after reading it thoroughly and carefully.

6.   Do not take multiple surveys all at once. Complete one at a time. Since some surveys have a limited timeframe, completing multiple surveys at one go may prevent you from completing a survey within the allotted time frame.

7.   Always ensure that you complete the survey at one go. Most surveys are only available for a certain period of time only. Once a predetermined number of surveys are collected, the survey is no longer available. Hence, it's vital to complete a survey from start to finish at once.

<u>Myths</u>

Online surveys are an excellent way for many people to make some extra money on the side. In turn, an influx of people have signed up to participate in online surveys, which has perpetuated a number of myths. Here are some typical examples:

- Online survey sites are nothing more than a scam – Contrary to popular belief, there are more legitimate sites than scams when it comes to online surveys. Legitimate sites are free to join and they will not ask you to pay anything upfront and most legitimate sites use PayPal as a means for payment transactions.

- Online survey sites only hire experienced individuals – Not true. Anyone can qualify for a survey and experience is not a means for qualification.

- It only takes a few minutes to answer a survey – Most surveys will take some time for you to complete them properly. Remember, answer honestly as you risk losing your account if you just barge your way through the survey.

- Online surveys are a get rich quick scheme – No, don't go and quit your day job over online surveys. Online surveys help to provide a supplementary income stream and it is by no means can get you rich overnight. To generate more revenue, it's best to register with as many online survey companies and participate in as many surveys as possible.

Idea #12 - Online Consultancy

What it is?

Online consultancy is a highly broad terminology, and it covers a huge number of topics and roles. The need for online consultancy usually stems from market demand. Some of the fields that usually require online consultancy are:

- Accounting
- Advertising
- Auditing
- Business
- Business writing
- Career counseling
- Communications
- Computer consulting
- Editorial services
- Headhunting

Organizations often seek online consultants due to these primary reasons:

- Consultant's experience and expertise
- A different outlook and solutions to the issues being faced by the organization
- The temporary overhead for a short period of time

Who is it for?

Honestly, everyone with a decent knowledge on a particular topic can become a consultant on it. In short, you really don't have to be an expert with many years of experience. But you shouldn't resort to unethical practices when providing your knowledge and insight on a particular field or topic.

How much money can you potentially earn?

These top online consulting sites below demonstrate the range of typical online consultancy charges for their services:

- Clarity – a minimum hourly rate of $60. A site for upcoming entrepreneurs and consultants are usually seasoned experts.

- Maven Research, Inc – a minimum hourly rate of $25. Consultants for a variety of subjects.

In 2013, the market size for online consulting was estimated at around 39.3 billion, and it shows no sign of slowing down presently. In 2013, 42% of organizations planned to hire more online consultants and another 5% planned to increase their budget to spend on online consultants.

How it works - Step-by-Step

In becoming an online consultant, you're required to provide feedback and advice to individuals or companies that may range from a broad range of topics or a particular niche subject. If you desire to become an online consultant, you may follow the steps below to launch:

1. Identify your niche – You'll not only want to define in what areas that you have the knowledge and experience that can be beneficial as a consultant but also an area of particular interest.

2. If required, get the proper certification and licenses – do some research and find out if any formal licenses or certification is required for your field of interest before going online as a consultant (i.e. accounting). You'll also need to check local licenses and regulations that are required before embarking on this path.

3. Have patience – Every business takes time to grow. If you lack the patience in growing the business, you'll be doomed to fail. Thus, it's essential for you to establish your long term and short-term goals.

4. Identify your target market – Please ensure the area of your intended consultancy has ample demand and is profitable. Otherwise, your business is set up for failure.

5. Research – As in all businesses, you will need to do massive amounts of research. From identifying your target market, scoping out your competition, how you will market your services and how will you help your potential customers.

<u>Myths</u>

Here are some common myths usually associated with online consulting:

- It's expensive – Getting started with online consulting is relatively inexpensive. All you need is a laptop an internet connection and you're good to go.

- No personal touch – A large part of online consulting requires one to be good at selling yourself as well as the services you provide. And not to mention, you'll need to be in touch with your customers regularly to meet their requirements.

- You need to be an expert – This myth is relatively untrue; however, you'll need to pair the knowledge and experience you have together with something that you're passionate about to truly stand out as an online consultant.

Idea #13 – Cryptocurrency

What is it?

Cryptocurrency is a digital currency that, as the name suggests, that uses cryptography for security purposes. In sum, a cryptocurrency is very difficult to duplicate. The basis of cryptocurrencies is based on what is known as a blockchain, which is a distributed ledger connected by a large network of computers. Cryptocurrency has one unique feature. It's uncontrolled by any central banking authority of any country. At present, there are many cryptocurrencies in circulation and one of the most popular ones is Bitcoin.

Cryptocurrencies enable payments that are made online to be secure and are usually referred to as "tokens.. Various encryption algorithms are used when cryptocurrencies are used for secure payments online.

Who is it for?

or starters, starting with cryptocurrencies can be a little tricky as there is a lot of jargon that you'll need to understand in order to make a profit from this. In a nutshell, if you have some substantial amount of cash that you would like to invest in cryptocurrencies without the fear of making losses, then, by all means, this is for you. But, if you prefer to have your money placed in more conventional investment methods, then stay clear of cryptocurrencies.

How much money can you potentially earn?

Cryptocurrency has been the craze over the last few years, and its value is ever increasing. In 2017, Bitcoin went from $750 to $10,000 by the end of the year. If you would have invested about $10,000 of your savings into Bitcoin in January 2017, you would have received returns up to $133,333 by December 2017. The total market value for all cryptocurrencies was valued at $500 billion at the end of 2017.

How it works - Step-by-Step

Before diving into cryptocurrencies, it's important to consider several factors below:

1. Which cryptocurrency will be suitable for you? Specifically, consider how long it has been in the market, its market share, and also its purpose.

2. What type of investment will you be into? You need to determine the duration of your investment. Is it going to be short-term or long-term?

3. Research – Study the market and patterns of cryptocurrencies to determine if you'll be in it for the short or long term

4. Determine the amount of money you will invest – Always ensure you only invest what you are willing to lose. Don't go dive head in and put all your eggs in one basket in hopes of making a quick fortune.

Myths about Cryptocurrency

Here are some myths regularly associated with cryptocurrencies:

- Cryptocurrencies are mostly used by criminals – The security features in cryptocurrencies negate this myth, thus making it totally secure.

- Cryptocurrencies can be shut down by the government – Not true. Unless the entire Internet decides to come crashing down, no government entity can shut down cryptocurrencies.

- Cryptocurrencies are illegal – While some countries like Russia have banned the usage of cryptocurrencies like Bitcoin, many others have encouraged the usage of cryptocurrencies as a means of a payment transaction.

Idea #14 - Make YouTube Videos

What is Youtube?

How many videos have you watched today? Chances are an average of 5? Or maybe 3? If by now you don't know what YouTube is, you're probably not one of those people who are always on online. YouTube, simply put, is a video sharing platform. Sustain all contractions No matter the number, you know that video content makes the arsenal of content marketing. It was the success of many campaigns in 2018 and it will likely continue in 2019. YouTube is an essential tool for plenty of industries. Even before YouTube, brands and companies have been creating videos to showcase their products and services: and now with YouTube, it makes it much easier for both brands and individuals to create and upload videos.

Who is YouTube for?

To answer this question, you need to ask yourself a series of questions. Firstly- do you have visual content? Is your brand, company, or product something your target audience can see, touch, hold, or hear? What industry are you in and what is your target audience? Are they 65-year olds and above? Are they toddlers? Are they fathers who have daughters? The kinds of videos there are on YouTube are of different types from how-tos to DIY to tutorials to promo materials to information, edutainment, interviews, and so on. Answering the questions above can ultimately help you decide whether or not you should be on YouTube.

How much money can you potentially earn from YouTube?

n Youtube, consistency is crucial if your main aim is to grow your channel. Much like blogging, the more consistent you are at posting content on your channel, the higher the probability of reaching a wider audience. A strict publishing schedule is what most YouTubers stick with - they post at least one video each week on a specific day. The truth is, anyone can upload a video but not everyone can make a fortune out of it. To give you an idea, SuperWoman Lilly Singh raked in $10.5 million in 2017. Daniel Middleton earned $16.5 million through YouTube videos and Logan Paul made $12.5 million.

How does YouTube Work?

The steps for using YouTube are quite simple:

Step 1- Start by watching YouTube videos either anonymously or by logging into your Google or Facebook account. Get a feel of the types of videos on YouTube.

Step 2- Get an Account to Broadcast Yourself or your brand

Step 3- Use YouTube for basic activities such as liking and commenting

Step 4- Browse and watch YouTube videos

Step 5- Craft and create your own videos

Step 6- Upload your videos

However, there's more to it than that if you want to use YouTube to make money. You need to optimize your video content in order to establish your YouTube channel. Before you get started on creating videos, take the time to do your research on keywords as well as video content so you can create a video that fits these keywords for the audience you want to target.

- Make Compelling Titles - Your video can be so awesome but without a title to hook a viewer, nobody is going to click on it. Having a killer title is so important because this is the first time a viewer will see.

- Create Perfect YouTube Thumbnails- The second most important thing viewers look at is your thumbnail. The right kind of thumbnail will attract a reader to click on it, making your video trend as well as make your channel recognizable. Just like the title, your thumbnail should be relevant to the content as well as correspond with your video title. Attractive thumbnails result in higher clicks. Also, include short descriptions in your thumbnail, so viewers can understand what your video features.

- Limit Videos to no more than 10 Minutes - The total watch time of your videos is also crucial. Long videos that have content repeating itself will not help. So if your videos are longer than 10 minutes, you need to ensure that it gives a good enough reason for your viewers to want to continue being interested in your videos. However, it is a great idea to make the video just over 10 minutes long, because once it goes over 10 minutes, you can place more ads in the video and significantly increase your ad revenue.

- Brand Your YouTube Channel - Let's face it, YouTube viewers and channels are so sophisticated now that there is no way you can get away with not having a consistent image for your channel. If YouTube is going to make a big part of your marketing arsenal, then you'd better brand it, so it's consistent with your other platforms and digital spaces. You need to make it visually attractive to not only encourage your visitors to take your brand seriously but also want to brand it so that it's cohesive and delivers the same consistent marketing message across all platforms - both online and offline. Branding also increases brand recall and awareness.

- Include Calls-to-Action (CTAs) - Adding calls-to-action to your videos will help you create more engagement on YouTube. They can also be irritating, so try to use them in the right way. No matter what goals you have, to get more likes or more subscribers, be clear and concise about key actions people need to take.

- Share Videos via Social Media -To grow your channel, sharing is important, whether you share on your social channels or people share your videos. You need to publish your latest videos on your other platforms as well as engage and stay active on your social communities and groups. Each social platform has its own distinctive culture. As a savvy marketer, it's your job to find out what this distinction is and use it to your advantage.

Myths about Youtube

- ou get paid based on the subscribers you have.

  Not true. Subscriber counts have no bearings where Google Adsense is concerned. The mechanics here is that YouTubers get paid for the amount of pre-roll ads that are viewed each time their video is seen, which if you look at it, the more views a person gets on their video means the more people will click on ads. From that perspective, subscriber numbers are imperative, but it doesn't mean that YouTubers get paid per subscriber.

- No violent or provocative videos are allowed.

  Pornography, abusive hate speech, nudity as well as dead bodies are all rightly banned, but there is still a multitude of other inappropriate content on YouTube from gun violence to car accidents and the like. While YouTube's community guidelines talk about the kinds of content that should be posted, the enforcement is not hard enough.

- Short videos get more views

  The type of video you post needs to be adequately long so that viewers know what you want them to see and that they get the information they want in good timing. Attention spans get shorter as time goes by and content can be attained at a rapid pace, however, short videos only work for the certain time of content such as those that are fun, fast, and entertaining. Videos such as how-tos, recipes, and even Ted Talks and debates can take longer than 5 minutes. What you don't want in your videos is FLUFF. Too much of unnecessary commenting and talking or too much of fancy video design can dull the mind.

Idea #15 - Online Fitness Instructor

What is an Online Fitness Instructor?

An online personal trainer is an occupation that allows you to take your fitness training offline to online. Via this way, you get to reach more clients who want to be inspired and have fitness content right on their mobile phones. Becoming an online fitness instructor also means that you can dramatically increase your income because you can train your regular clients face-to-face and also acquire an online following of clients who are anywhere in the world. Becoming an online fitness instructor allows you to make a living out of doing what you love, and it also enables clients to search for a trainer who best fits clients' fitness goals.

Who is it for?

Are you a fitness professional who loves training clients? Are you active on social and digital media? If you love training clients, motivating them to become better versions of themselves, and sharing your fitness routines and exercises, then this route to earn more and experience financial freedom is for you!

It helps if you have a certificate as this would give credibility to your skill set because if you are calling yourself an instructor, then a certificate would definitely give you an edge.

How much money can you potentially earn?

In most cases, the area you live in decides the factor of how easily you can earn as a fitness instructor. With online coaching though, borders are not an issue because you can reach a wider and more niche audience with your style and brand of fitness. Fitness instructors typically charge about $50 to $100 per hour for training sessions. To become an online fitness instructor, you need to create your own program and keep posting videos, content and other material to keep your clients informed of the plan, the level of commitment, as well as meal plans that come with it.

You can do this via asking them to subscribe to your mailing list where you can send them instructional videos and meals plans on a daily or weekly basis based on the plan that they have subscribed and paid for. You can earn an average of $200 a week to $500 a month. The stronger the following you have on the online space, the better your chances of improving your bank balance.

How to become an online fitness instructor?

There is no one-size-fits-all step-by-step guide in becoming an online fitness instructor because it depends on your brand of fitness. Some instructors focus on muscle gain for competition, some focus on lean bodies with good mobility, some instructors focus on HIIT workouts only, some instructors include martial arts into training, some focus on making you a better runner or ballerina or swimmer, while some focus on yoga or Pilates. As a result, there are guidelines you can use as a compass to help you get started:.

Step 1 Find Your Niche

As there are many types of fitness exercises out there, identifying your fitness niche is crucial so you can target the kind of audience who are looking for your brand of fitness be it HIIT, cardio kickboxing, yoga, bodyweight exercises, running, and so on.

Step 2 Determine your USP

Your unique selling proposition tells people why you and your fitness brand are unique. You may offer an exceptional type of fitness that is ideal for people who have little time on their hands to exercise or your brand of fitness may be perfect for postpartum mothers. Whatever it is, identify your USP because it'll help you get the right audience.

Step 3 Choose your Promotional Channels

In today's visually-charged world, certain platforms work exceptionally well as promotional channels for fitness. Tumblr was one of the channels used back before Instagram exploded on the scene and made video sharing workouts easily accessible. YouTube is also another way to get your programs available to your clients.

Step 4 Work on your clients

One of the ways Kayla Itsines's fitness programs is immensely popular is because her fitness program thrives on a community of positivity and geared towards health instead of achieving the perfect body. She also encourages her clients who do her workouts through her Sweat App to take before and after images showing the progress of their bodies. When it comes to your online fitness program, think about how to invest in your clients because they are the best form of marketing and publicity for you.

Myths about Online Fitness Instructors

- Fitness Instructors earn plenty because they have celebrity clients

  The moniker "Celebrity" Trainer is used when the trainer has clients who work in the public eye. While it's great to have a celebrity as a client, not all clients of a fitness instructor are celebrities and not all fitness instructors have celebrity clients. Some have none. Though having a celebrity client helps, the instructor doesn't rely solely on the celebrity client, so one's means of earning has to be varied, so that income is continuous. Most personal trainers make most of their living on average non-public eye clients.

- Fitness trainers love being in their workout clothes

  When we see an online fitness trainer, we always view them through the videos or photos they post on their blog or on social media and they are always in workout clothes simply because you observe them when they are working out. But like anyone else, fitness instructors also look forward to dressing up and wearing other kinds of clothing.

- Fitness trainers can also give you specific eating and meal plans as well as the right supplements

Most fitness trainers provide advice on what to eat it and how much as a recommendation, but they don't offer specific eating plans because this is outside their practice. This also relates to medication and supplements. The trainer always aims to education, but if a client wants to take a supplement, specific advice should come from a doctor.

Idea #16 - Renting out space via AirBnB

What is AirBnB?

If you have a spare room that you're not using, you are sitting on potential income. Did you know that? Your home is your asset and if you can monetize from it, it can defray some of your living costs. It could also potentially fix the problem of having a house too big for the upkeep.

AirBnB is an online avenue which allows people to rent out their spaces, spare rooms, or properties to guests. When space is rented, AirBnB takes 3 percent of the commission from every book from a host and 6 to 12 percent from guests. You can have different kinds of one-of-a-kind property on AirBnB from shared rooms to boutique treehouses, an entire house with different kinds of amenities.

Who is it for?

AirBnB is for anyone looking to make extra money from their living spaces and property. It's perfect for people who have a large house but would like extra money for the upkeep or those who like managing properties for homestays and unique accommodations but without the huge costs that come with purchasing and managing conventional properties such as hotels.

How much money can you potentially earn through AirBnB?

AirBnB, since its inception, has enabled more than 160 million guests to find the right accommodations through more than 3 million listings all around the world. According to Priceonomicthis, AirBnB hosts earn more than anyone else in the gig economy, with the average earnings at $924 a month. However, take note that earnings range depending on the property as well as the location. Some hosts even make more than $10,000 a month, while some make less than $500 a month.

How does AirBnB work?

Step 1 - Firstly, you need to own a space to rent whether a room, an apartment, or a house.

Step 2 - Next, you must register your listing on AirBnB and give them the specifications of your property such as the size, its area, number of rooms, and other details requested by AirBnB. You'll also need to open a host profile with a picture of yourself and go through scanning and verification processes.

Step 3 - You'll also need to check out the legality of listing out your space in your neighborhood or city because some areas have various laws on renting out spaces in a home for a certain period of time. So make sure to check your local laws concerning renting your home.

Step 4 - Once you have your profile ready and your information verified, you can continue with listing your spaces at the 'List Your Space' section. Here, you can describe the kind of lodging you plan on listing and information such as location, how many guests you can accommodate as well as the availability of your property. You can also set your price per night, per week, or by month.

Step 5 - List your property as best as you can and this also means posting high-quality photos of your listing, so customers will have a good idea of how the property looks like, how big it is, and if it suits their needs.

Once your listing is all set up, you'll be given AirBnB's variety of services such as Host Guarantee, insurance programs as well first aid kids and refunds. AirBnB also handles the payments. Payment options depend greatly on a country and can be paid through PayPal, wire transfer, or direct deposit.

Myths about AirBnB

- **Increased Wear and Tear -**The biggest myth going around is that your home, your room, or whatever property you rent out will be severely damaged. Yes, you've probably read news about how some property has been damaged but fret not, AirBnB offers insurance coverage for all property rented through AirBnB.

  However, the likelihood of a guest damaging your property is low because most people don't damage the place where they stay due to respect.

  With every business, there is a risk but the last thing you want to worry about is your property damage. Yes, there would be wear and tear but that is part of maintaining your space.

- **Tourism changing the locality -** It seems like a bad idea if an influx of travelers coming to your community, but tourism also brings diversity and opens the opportunity for new ideas as well as new income not just for hosts but also for the people in the community. AirBnB offers travelers and hosts alike a unique experience. Instead of huge hotels taking over both space and economy of the local community, hosting travelers with existing property enables the existing businesses to thrive.

- **You will end up with party-goers -** One of the main concerns of AirBnB hosts is the few bad apples that we read in the news. Yes, AirBnB homes are perfect for party and gatherings and out of 80,000 bookings per day, only on rare occasions would you read issues of a host's homes being irresponsibly used as party venues and guests not taking the responsibility to clean up or make good of the property.

Idea #17 - Becoming a Silent Partner

What it a Silent Partner?

A silent business partner is a person who contributes to a business financially but does not contribute any other ways such as in the day-to-day running of the business. The primary reason or motivation of being a silent partner is the return on investment. Silent partners want profits from owning a business, but they don't want to be involved in the actual management of the company.

While it's easy to assume that a silent partner's responsibility is only to provide the financial capacity of business, silent partners can also contribute to other tasks such as:

- Giving additional capital when a business is low in funds
- Offering the collateral needed to qualify for a loan
- Making connections to ensure business growth

Who is it for?

As a silent partner, you have the ability to earn a return of money when the business makes a profit. This is an ideal form of passive income for people who want to make money and own a business but don't want to be involved in the day-to-day running of the business. The amount of income you make will depend entirely on how well the business is doing and the arrangements you've made with the other partners. For instance, some silent partners take home a smaller share of profits than the active partner, and it also depends on the amount invested in it.

It's also perfect for people who have money but do not want to be involved in too many businesses and lessen the hassle and stress of running multiple projects.

How much money can you potentially earn?

For the initial investment made, silent partners will often receive stock in the company as well as a set percentage of the profits. The amount of passive income earned also depends on how well the company performs and the agreements made as part of the silent partner contract. More often than not, the silent partner earns a much smaller share of the revenue compared to active partners.

When it comes to losses and debts, all partners, silent or active, are responsible for the finances of the business; however, thanks to limited liability, silent business partners are generally liable for the amount or percentage that they invested in the business when it was formed. For example, a partner who has invested 15% in the business is only responsible for 15% of the losses and debts. The percentage, details, and agreement of the partnership must be decided at the initiation of the business to avoid any misunderstandings and legal disputes. Both the partners and the owners of the business must acknowledge each investment for tax purposes.

How to become a silent partner?

If you like the idea of becoming a silent partner, here is how you can do it:

Step 1 - To become a silent partner, you can do so by entering into a limited partnership agreement with a start-up or business owner. The other person is an active partner and this partner will be responsible for the daily business. Your participation in this is limited or essentially silent and the only thing you need to worry about it having money to be pumped into the business as and when needed.

Step 2 - When you enter into a limited partnership, you need a written partnership agreement drawn and all partners involved must agree to the terms of the contract.

Step 3 - You need to formally register your limited partnership with your local clerk where the business is located as well as with the Secretary of State. Silent and active partners are both obligated to be held liable for the business debts unless a form of limited liability partnership or LLP is formed. With the LLP, general partners will be responsible for business debts.

Step 4 - Once your partnership has been registered, you must next apply for an EIN or Employer Identification Number. This number allows you to pay your business taxes and also enables you open a business bank account for the funds for your partnership.

Idea #18- Cashback Rewards with Credit Cards

What is cashback rewards with credit cards?

Cashback rewards deliver an easy way of getting a little money with every purchase you make with your credit card, which is why it makes them appealing to customers. The main benefit of Cashback cards is the simplicity of how it works. When it comes to redemption, Cashback credit cards are pretty straightforward, and users do not need to think too much about how much they are earning. Most people usually just deduct their Cashback from their statement balance or just redeem their points via gift cards. Cashback cards come in a variety of options from bonus category, flat percentage Cashback cards as well as bonus category. Whatever the mechanism, all of them pay you back.

Who is it for?

It's ideal for people who want to make some money especially if they use their credit card plenty of times and for very big purchases such as airline tickets, cab fare, and groceries.

How much money can you potentially earn?

When you live on a fixed income, an option to make extra money helps. For example, you can use your Bank of America Cash Reward Card to bump up your bottom line. If you receive a $150 initial cash bonus after getting your card, you can earn at least 1 percent on all purchases you make via the card. Depending on the purchases as well, you get 2 percent if you get groceries or 3 percent on gas. What you get from your card enables you to purchase other things. If you're mindful of what you spend on, you can make Cashback worth up to $300 a year.

How do cashback rewards work?

Cashback is essentially a rebate of the purchases you make using your card. Card issues can afford a Cashback program because their merchants pay an interchange fee for every transaction made. For example, if you pay a merchant $100 using your credit card, then the merchant will only receive $97. A TV that you pay for $700 would give you a $14 net and a 2 percent Cashback card. And the merchant would need to pay a transaction fee of $21 since you used your card.

If it's a flat-rate Cashback program, every purchase you make earns the same percentage Cashback.

If it is the bonus cards and tiered cards program, then you earn different percentages depending on the category which means you earn a little bit more Cashback.

Merchants will know what type of spending qualifies for a percentage as there are merchant category codes that are four-digit numbers that specify the business type. These codes are used by credit card networks to categorize and track purchases.

Myths about Credit Card Cashback Programs

- **Applying for credit cards will hurt a person's credit score**

The only thing that will hurt your credit score is if you don't make your payments in time. Applying for a single credit card and making your payments in due time will make your credit score on the positive side. A credit card is worth applying for so long as you know your spending limits and spend wisely.

- **Canceling credit cards will definitely help my score**

Canceling credit cards will actually hurt your credit score because it'll reduce the total amount of credit you have been extended and it will also increase your debt-to-credit ratio. Canceling cards because you are afraid you'll go over the spending limit will also reduce your average length of credit card history. As long as you're not paying unreasonable annual fees, then it's wise to keep your existing cards on a good credit report.

- **Earning points and miles is not worth it**

One of the biggest reasons to use a credit card is to accumulate miles points. While it's true that airlines have limited availability of their awards seats at the lowest mileage levels and hotels try their hardest to hide blackout dates, it is still value for people who are willing to look hard enough for rewards. You can still sit on business class seats if you are flexible on dates and book your flights well in advance. Last minute flights can also give you great value when you compare it to walk-up and full-fare prices.

If you do your research properly, you'll find plenty of awards that you can use and book over the phone. Also, there are plenty of programs out there that offer awards with no blackout dates or even capacity controls, such as hotels from Starwood group as well as Southwest Airlines.

Idea #19 - Renting Out Your Parking Spot

What is it?

Got an empty parking space that's going to waste because you're not using it? Well, guess what? It's about to become yet another source of your passive income. If you live in an apartment that comes with two parking spaces and you've only got one car, this passive income option could definitely work for you. Or just about anyone with an extra parking spot to spare, really. Even better if this parking space happens to be near an event venue because you'll never be short of customers looking for the nearest parking available. You'd be surprised at how much some people would be willing to pay for convenience.

If you've ever wondered whether a parking spot could make a good investment in terms of generating passive income, the good news is *yes, they can.* In fact, just like real estate, a parking space is an investment that could potentially appreciate in its value over time while generating a steady cash flow stream for you every month (depending on where your parking spot is located of course).

How much you could potentially earn?

Passive income rates and how much you could potentially earn with this option would depend on several factors. The closer or more conveniently located your parking spot is, the higher you'll be able to charge. If your parking spot is highly desirable, for example, if it's near public transportation, in a high-security location, or covered car park, for example, you'd certainly be able to charge much more than if your car park was just located in an open air area.

Parking rates would also depend on the city that you're located in. Prime cities like San Francisco and New York, for example, have the potential to charge much more if the parking spot is located in a premium location. Parking spaces in this city can sometimes sell anywhere from $80,000 and more, especially if it's a standard parking spot located within a garage. Diving a little deeper into the San Francisco area, prime locations like Nob Hill or Russian Hill, for example, have parking spots which go for anywhere from $300 to $400 a month to rent. Depending on the needs of the customer you're dealing with, if one is looking to rent your parking spot long-term, there's the potential for long-term rental too, which means a consistent stream of income coming in each month. Even if you were to charge $5 per day for parking, you're still making an extra $150 a month.

How does it work?

Among the benefits of venturing into the parking lot rental business as a passive income option include that this is one of lower-risk "business" models that you could think about getting involved in. You don't need a lot of capital to get started if you do want to purchase a parking lot to start renting, and if you've already got a spare spot to spare, you don't even have to fork out any capital of your own at all! Another benefit is that this option doesn't require a lot of your time. You don't need to be there constantly having to manage or keep an eye on your parking spot. This is one of the few passive income options that just "sits there" and makes money for you without you having to do much at all. It's easy to get started renting out your parking spot. Here's how you get begin:

- Step 1: Start by advertising your parking spot online or on apps like <u>BestParking</u>, <u>Spacer</u>, <u>Streetline</u>, <u>SpotHero</u>, and more. Get the word out there that you've got a spot available for rent.

- Step 2: Check if your space can be used legally without a permit. If you need a permit, look into getting one before you attempt to rent your spot.

- Step 3: If you're renting an apartment with an extra parking spot, have a chat with your landlord to make sure they are comfortable with the arrangement.

- Step 4: Prepare a legal contract which clearly outlines the terms of agreements between you and the person who is renting out your parking spot.

- Step 5: Do a quick check to make sure if you're liable for taxes.

Myths about Renting Your Parking Spot

While there are no concrete myths about renting out your parking spaces, there are misconceptions that people will not be willing to pay to rent a spot to park. That's not entirely true; and in fact, if your rental charges are much cheaper than the rates that the city or town council would charge them, they'd be more than happy to come to you at the end of the day. Price it right and you'll have no problems finding renters and get your passive income going with this option.

Idea #20 - Network Marketing

What is it?

Would you like to be paid continuously for work that you would only need to do once? Who wouldn't, right? However, very few businesses these days actually afford us that kind of opportunity. If you're lucky enough to be blessed with the gift of being able to sing or write, singers and authors are great examples of individuals who get paid repeatedly for a job they've done once. This is known as *royalty pay,* and each time that their song gets played or their book gets published, they get paid a royalty or a commission for it.

Now, for those of us who haven't been blessed with these talented gifts, there's another option you can consider as an alternative to generating some passive income for yourself. *Network marketing,* and before you're quick to dismiss this idea as nothing more than a scam, stop for a minute and consider the possibilities.

Network marketing works on the principle that you will continue to earn an income based on the effort that you had to invest in the initial stages. Since network marketing usually involves products and services, your income is going to be based on the sale of these said products and services. In fact, network marketing has quickly become a very popular option among those who are seeking flexibility while making a little bit of part-time income in addition to their full-time jobs.

Commonly referred to as multi-level marketing, this passive income approach uses the method of selling products via teamwork through a tiered structure comprising of sales associates. Making money depends on two things, which are your ability to sell and your ability to bring in new employees. While this tiered approach works well and can generate a fair bit of profit for the early participants and the original promoter, those who jump into the game may find it more challenging to see a turn of profit as quickly.

The reason why many are so quick to dismiss network marketing as a scam is because they're selling the *wrong* kind of products. What you want to aim for is *consumable products,* which are the most effective approach to take with network marketing for one very simple reason. These products are a necessity, they are consumed quickly and customers constantly need to replace these products repeatedly each time they run out of their own supply. When you pick the right products, the sales start to happen, and you won't find it as difficult to generate a passive income for yourself based on this option.

How much can you potentially earn?

How much money you stand to make entirely depends on one thing - *you*. The more you sell, the more you make. It would also depend on the company that you're working with and the types of products you're selling. Established companies like Mary Kay and Avon for example, who already employ this distributed marketing approach, will most likely result in higher earning potential because the products have already established a reputation, compared to let's say a smaller, unknown brand or company perhaps. It could take a while before you start seeing a profit from the initial investment amount that you put in though, so you're going to need to be patient.

Anyone who is keen on making a little part-time money on the side can be involved in network marketing. What makes this option great is the combination of both the flexibility to choose your own hours, and you get a little bit of practice trying to run your own "business" in a way.

Getting started with network marketing is easy, too:

- **Step 1 - Researching Your Company Options**: You need to decide which network marketing company you would like to join and how to sign up. It is important that you spend some time researching the right company to work with, just like how you would invest the same amount of time deciding on which.

- **Step 2 - What's Your Why:** Network marketing is a business. Yes, it's working to generate passive income for you, but it's still a business nonetheless. Every entrepreneur who ventures into business must know their *why*, their reason for doing so, and so do you.

- **Step 3: Don't Skip the Trainings -** Once you've joined a network marketing company, take part in all the trainings and courses which are provided by the company, your mentor or your immediate supervisor. These opportunities offer great insight to help you get the most from your network marketing efforts.

- **Step 4: Advertise Yourself -** Once you've done all the above, the next step is to forget about being shy and just go for it. You must be confident enough in yourself and your products to be able to sell them. Introduce yourself, network, mingle, make connections, whatever opportunity comes your way, now is not the time to sit back and feel shy about it. Remember your *why* and your reason for doing this.

To answer the question, is network marketing a legitimate business? Yes, it is. It is *not a pyramid scheme,* which is a common myth associated with it because network marketing involves selling actual products. Unlike pyramid schemes that lure people in with the false promise of getting rich quickly with no basis for its claims, network marketing doesn't promise that you'll get rich through this approach, but it's good enough to bring in a little extra cash in your bank account.

Idea #21 - Storage Rentals

What is it?

Storage rentals are an excellent passive income option because of the "low maintenance and high returns" aspect. If you're looking for a piece of real estate to generate a steady source of passive income regularly, without forking out several hundred dollars or risking another mortgage payment buying a piece of property to rent, then storage rentals are easily your most affordable piece of real estate.

Who is it for?

Two perks associated with passive income generation reflect the freedom and flexibility benefits that come along with it. With storage rentals, you have the best of both worlds, *and* you don't have to invest a lot of time and money upkeeping the facility the way you would with an apartment or a house. With the growing population, the demand for storage facilities is on the rise, especially in city locations where, sometimes, you simply don't have enough space to store all your belongings. Storage facilities, therefore, offer the perfect solution. You rent out your facility to tenants who come to store their stuff until such time where they no longer need this facility. If you've got a little bit of capital to spare to purchase a storage unit, and you're looking for a low-risk type of property investment that is easy to manage, the storage facility rentals are the answer that you seek.

Quite simply, storage rentals are where you have a storage facility located outside your home. What you do is that you then rent out this space to anyone who is looking for a facility to store their belongings. The level of security provided in these facilities would depend on the provider, but generally, they are safe. Units can be locked, and they're easily accessible 24-hours a day.

How much could you potentially earn?

Storage facilities are one of the easiest ways for anyone to start creating a source of passive income. Financial experts like Robert Kiyosaki have even mentioned what a desirable investment option it is. How much money you stand to make would depend on several factors. Typically, storage facilities contain several hundred units in a single location, and these units can be rented out starting from $50 and upwards. The bigger your unit, the more you'll be able to charge.

To get started renting out your storage unit, here's what you need to do:

- **Step 1 - Purchase a Unit.** This is the most obvious way to get started. To rent out a unit, you must first *have* a unit.

- **Step 2 - Picking a Desirable Unit.** Your storage unit has to be appealing, or nobody is going to want to rent from you. When selecting a storage unit, some factors that you need to take into consideration include whether it's a climate-controlled unit, how accessible it is, the video monitoring facilities available, number of locks provided, whether in-person surveillance is available, size of the unit, overall safety and security, and lighting facilities. It's also a good idea to read online reviews about the facility before you make a commitment to it.

- **Step 3 - Advertise.** Start advertising your unit to get the word out that you've got a space to rent.

- **Step 4: Prepare a Contract.** A binding contract is needed to protect both your interests and that of the person who is renting your unit from you. A storage unit may not be an apartment or a house, but you are still essentially renting out a piece of property, and a rental agreement is still necessary.

- **Step 5: Checking If Permits Are Needed.** While most states generally do not require permits for any property that is less than 200 square feet, you should just do the same thing and check anyway if you'll need a permit for your storage facility.

- **Step 6: Get Insurance -** It's a good idea to get your storage unit covered by insurance just in case of any emergencies. It gives your renter peace of mind too, knowing that the facility you're providing is covered, if need be.

While providing storage rentals can be a great source of passive income, the myth that this type of passive income generator is a "cash cow" is exactly that - *a myth*. This choice is not an option you should go for if you're thinking about getting rich quick. This passive income source will generate some extra cash into your bank accounts.

It's also a myth that this is the "cheapest" business you can get into. While it's relatively low cost compared to a lot of other business models, depending on the location of your facility, it may not necessarily be as "cheap" as you think, especially when today's storage facilities are being constructed with higher quality material and provide a greater level of security. All these improvements are going to hike up the cost of your initial investment. So the term "cheap" really depends on the context. It's much more affordable if you're comparing it to purchasing a piece of property, but thinking that it's the "cheapest business to get into" is a myth that needs to be debunked.

Idea #22 - Develop Design Elements

What is it?

If you have a talent for design and you've got technology proficiency, developing design elements could be a great potential source of passive income for you. As a designer, you have the flexibility of options to increase your business without having to feel like you're piling up on your workload.

What's great about generating some passive income as a designer is that it reduces your dependency on clients to get paid. When you work as a freelance designer especially, it can be stressful constantly trying to search for clients, pitching your ideas, hoping they like your proposal and then going back and forth negotiating on the terms of payment.

Developing design elements that you can put up for sale on various platforms and online marketplaces, on the other hand, cuts out the bulk of your workload. You just need to design the content, put it up for sale, and anyone who's interested can purchase it immediately.

Who is it for?

This passive income stream is ideal for anyone who's got a computer to work with, is creative with tons of ideas, design software, and some spare time to work on designing. it's the perfect option for anyone who's already working as a developer, or a designer and is looking to make a little extra income as a side hustle.

How much money can you potentially earn?

How much money you potentially stand to earn from this would depend on the type of content you're selling and how often your content gets purchased. Another factor impacting your earning potential is the rates that you charge. More experienced, reputable designers have the luxury of charging slightly higher prices than those who have recently joined the scene. Design content can start anywhere from as low as $5 to $10 per content, and even be as much as a few hundred, depending on the quality and the intricacy of the work involved.

In the case of making passive income from developing design elements, the money you'll be earning is going to come repeatedly from the sale of one job. Recurring income is what makes it *passive* since you do no longer have to invest even more time working on developing and designing new content.

How to do this?

To start making passive income by developing design elements, here's what you can do:

- **Creating themes to sell on WordPress** - Designing themes and templates for platforms like WordPress is one way to go about producing a continuous income stream. The toughest part will be in the beginning, when you've got to come up with the ideas and put in the hours for the templates; but once you're done, each time someone purchases one of your templates, that's money in the bank for you.

- **Graphics To Be Used on Websites -** Another great option to consider, since there are new websites emerging all the time as new businesses and companies get formed. As long as websites exist, there will always be a need for graphics, and you could step in a fill that demand by developing these types of contents and creating a nice income stream for yourself while you're at it.

- **Selling Fonts -** Yes, there is even a demand for fonts. Develop and design fonts which are custom made, hand-drawn, in vector forms, airbrushed, fonts with extra characters, fonts which have embellishments, get creative and get designing.

- **Developing 3D Models -** 3D models are presently needed for all sorts of projects, so why not make a passive income option out of it? From animated models to architecture landscapes, if you've got a gift for designing and developing these elements, there could be a passive income opportunity in it for you.

- **Selling Stock Photography -** Design elements doesn't have to be focused on graphics or

Photoshopping alone. Selling stock photography is another way of producing a "design" element to sell online. The only equipment you'll need is a good camera, a creative eye for what makes a good photo composition, take a fantastic picture and put it up for sale. That's recurring passive income for you whenever your images get purchased and used.

Passive income through developing design elements can be a great passive income stream, but as with any other passive income stream, this is something that is going to take time to build momentum. If anyone has told you that you could get rich quickly doing lots of design work, then that's a myth. The kind of income you generate will depend heavily on how often your content gets purchase. Sometimes, you may get a high volume of sales, and then there may be times when you might not make any sales at all for several weeks. If you're looking for a consistent passive income stream each month, you might have to consider diversifying your options instead of just focusing on developing design elements alone.

Idea #23 - Website Domain Flipping

What is it?

Considering domain flipping as a potential passive income avenue? Why not, when there's definitely potential in it? If you've never heard of website domain flipping before, the concept is simple. You basically purchase a domain name with the sole purpose of trying to sell it quickly at a much higher cost. It's similar to what some people do with real estate: they purchase home, fix it up and then sell it at a higher cost with the intention to make a little bit of profit. The key to being successful with domain flipping though is to be at the right place at the right time *and* to have a valuable domain in your possession if you're going to charge premium prices for it.

Who is it for?

There are several reasons why anyone would want to buy domain names. Some purchase domains for the SEO value that they hold, others purchase them for events, current trends, and starting up new company websites. Some even purchase certain domain names because it happens to suit their business name much better. All of these little details are what you need to keep in mind when you start of making a go of this passive income idea. They'll help you tremendously when deciding which websites would make good purchases for future flipping.

How does it work?

To start website domain flipping as a passive income, you'll need to first learn the ropes. If you were working in real estate, for example, you wouldn't just wake up one morning and start selling houses right away. You'll need to learn how the business works. In the website domain flipping world, you're going to be just like a real estate investor, except for websites instead of property. What you'll require for this passive income business is a keen eye for detail and what could potentially be profitable domain names and profitable websites.

The next step of the process is to set a budget. Setting a budget will help you narrow down the list of options available to you, so you can then choose one that best fits your needs. If you have the skills and the technical know-how, you can even build a website on your own, reducing the capital that you would need to initially invest. If you're on a really tight budget, this one is a great substitute for purchasing a domain or website which has already been established.

Once you've done that, you can then move onto the next part of the process, which is to decide what type of domain or website you intend to buy. Do you want to purchase something that is new? Or wait until you come across some expired domains you can quickly latch onto the resell? Expired domains can be found at ExpiredDomains.net. If you're building a website from scratch, you're going to need a reliable web host as a place to store your website files.

Deciding what type of website or domain you want to purchase is another tricky bit of the process. Ideally, you want to look for domains or websites which have the potential to be more lucrative, such as forums, Adsense monetized sites, review sites, niche, book, e-commerce, and membership sites. Once you've found a website to purchase, you then need to get it registered before you can start looking for a buyer.

How much could you potentially earn?

How much you could potentially earn with your domain website or domain flipping falls into two different categories. For domain names, the value in them is determined based on the SEO value, the age and how well your domain is going to meet the needs of the person who is buying it. Websites, on the other hand, have their value based on the current and potential revenue, traffic, SEO, content, and more.

If you're wondering where you could flip your domain or website, there are several marketplace options that you could choose from. Flippa, WarriorForum, and DigitalPoint are examples of where you could seek out a potential buyer. If your website is high performing enough, you should be able to flip it fairly quickly. Other than that, your avenues of selling include spreading the word through channels like social media, emailing your contacts, and advertising on marketplaces online.

Myths about website domain flipping

The most common myths associated with this option are that people think you can be passive about flipping your website or domain. Unfortunately no, you can't. You still have to actively promote your website. You can't just sit back and hope the website is going to sell itself. Another common myth is that domain flipping is something that can be learned just like that (snaps fingers). Again, this isn't entirely true, because you're going to have to spend quite a bit of time learning the basics to master how this process works. It's time-consuming, but if you love it, it can be an enjoyable process, and the extra cash flow doesn't hurt either.

Idea #24 - Selling T-Shirts Online

What is it?

If there's one item that is universally accepted by men, women, and children everywhere, it's t-shirts. These items are a staple that *everyone* (no exaggeration here) owns at least one piece of, if not several. Take a look in your own cupboard and count how many t-shirts you own. Whether they're worn in the summer, underneath your jackets in the colder months, or for lounging about the house, t-shirts are a constant in everyone's wardrobe; in turn, selling t-shirts online is a great passive income idea. You're selling something that everyone needs, how could you go wrong?

How much could you potentially earn from this?

Now, how much profit you stand to make per t-shirt is going to depend on what your initial cost is and which platform you're selling your t-shirts on. For example, if the cost of your t-shirt was about $12 on average, and you wanted to sell your t-shirts on Amazon. If you log into Amazon, you'll see that the suggested selling price for a t-shirt is $19.99. This means that you could potentially earn around $8 in profit from just one t-shirt alone. Depending on the volume of t-shirts you sell, the more you sell, the more you earn.

Is selling t-shirts online a good passive income idea? Yes, *but* this opportunity is not necessarily suitable for just anyone. The ones who are going to benefit most from selling t-shirts online as a passive income option are people who love being involved in sales, artists, illustrators, and designers because they've got the creative advantage of being able to design their own unique t-shirts without having to outsource that part of the business and anyone who is willing to commit the time and the effort to selling t-shirts online as an extra income stream.

How does it work?

The beauty of selling t-shirts online though is the wide audience base that you have at your disposal. Men, women, teenagers, children, even babies, there are so many categories you could get involved in, potentially tripling your sale options. If you're looking to enter this business, here are the steps that you'll need to go through:

- **Step 1:** Find your niche market and who you intend to cater for? Are you only targeting a specific group? Or more than one? Where is your customer base located? What's the demographic that you're targeting?

- **Step 2:** Once you have identified your target audience, do your research to find a need that you can fulfill. What is it that is lacking right now? What does your audience want to see from you? What can you offer them that your competitor cannot?

- **Step 3:** Set-up your online store. With this, there are two ways that you can go about it. The first is to set up your own websites and the second is to sell on platforms like Amazon, eBay, Shopify, AliExpress, and more. It doesn't take long to set up and account either and if building a website from scratch is not your cup of tea, you could consider this option instead.

- **Step 4:** Be detailed in your product description and use as many keywords as possible. The more SEO-rich your content is, the better your chances of appearing in the first few pages of the search results that Google pings back to a customer who is searching for a product just like yours.

Among the challenges you might face with selling t-shirts online include having to constantly come up with fresh ideas that keep your target audience interested. Because t-shirts are purchased so often, and fashions come and go before you've even had a chance to blink sometimes, keeping your products fresh, on-trend, and in line with the current interest of your target market is how you keep them coming back for more. Another challenge is going to be, of course, the high competition. Google "online t-shirts for sale" or "buy online t-shirts" and you'll end up with more than a hundred thousand results listed in front of you. Competition is tough, and you're going to have to do a lot of hard work to get yourself in front of your customers, especially in the beginning when you're just starting to get traction and momentum.

Myths concerning t-shirt selling

Like with many passive income stream ideas, the biggest myth with selling t-shirts online is that it is a way for you to "get rich and get rich quick". It is not. It is going to take a while for you to build momentum, especially when you're not going to be the only person selling t-shirts online. There are literally *hundreds,* if not thousands, of other online shops and people who are selling t-shirts online, too. Bust out of that myth that it's going to be an easy side hustle business too, because it is not. Competition levels are high and if you want to make money, you're going to have to get active in promoting your merchandise for sale.

Idea #25 - Placing Ads on Your Car

What is it?

<u>Population Reference Bureau</u> revealed that on average, Americans tend to spend approximately 26 minutes daily commuting to work. If this is you and your means of transport involves a car, then you'll be happy to know that your car could potentially turn into a money-making vehicle. How? By letting companies *pay* you to advertise their ads on your car.

Who is it for?

This business is perfect for anyone who owns a car, drives a lot, and doesn't mind being seen in a car with random advertisements which sometimes cover your entire vehicle. You've seen those cars driving around town before, and if you don't mind being one of them, placing ads on your car could prove to be a good little side income for you.

Carvertise is an example of a car company who pays drivers just like you for the privilege of being able to place their ads on your cars. The company works on developing ads with many local businesses and helps these businesses connect with drivers who are in the targeted area. You would first need to become approved as a Carvertise driver, and once that's done, the company will then began applying color wraps and decals on your car for an agreed time period. When you sign up with companies like Carvertise, you will be prompted to fill out information which reveals your location, the type of car you have, and what kind of daily mileage you cover. Carvertise has a minimum 25-mile per day minimum requirement, which must be met before you can sign up with them. Other companies may have slightly different requirements which must be fulfilled before you can begin earning money.

How much could you potentially earn?

Now, here's how the money portion of this passive income option works - *the more you drive, the more you get paid.* That's because more driving increases your chances of exposure, which means businesses would be willing to pay more to those who cover more miles. Depending on the length of your commute, you could potentially earn anywhere from $100 to even $400 per month.

Another requirement from many of these companies warrants that your car still retains its factory paint job condition and that you have a clean driving record (you will be "representing" the business in a way, after all). Once you fulfill all the minimum requirements that the company is looking for, you can submit an application and the company will assess if you are a good fit for any of their upcoming campaigns. However, this process can sometimes take several weeks before you start getting anything going. Once you do get signed up with a campaign, however, the campaign can be anywhere from one month to six months.

When you sign up with these car companies to have ads placed on your car, often you don't actually get to choose the ad that you end up with. The company will decide this for you.

However, if you feel like the ad is inappropriate for your car or it is not something you feel comfortable advertising, you can always choose to opt out. Once you and the company have come to an agreement about the ad which will be placed on your car, a scheduled time to meet with a specialist to wrap your car is the next step of the process. Don't worry about the decals or wraps damaging your car, because they are often made with adhesives specially designed not to damage or scratch your car's original paintwork. Once you're done with the campaign, simply make another appointment to have the wrap removed.

With this passive income option, you'll want to be careful of scammers, especially the ones who promise big cash returns in exchange for placing ads on your cars. If it sounds too good to be true, then it probably is. The warning signs to look out for these scammers are if they ask you to deposit your own money first or if the links provided have no contact information. Look for legitimate companies like Carvertise and avoid any company that requires any sort of "upfront payment" for you to get started.

Idea #26- Using Instagram for Passive Income

What is Instagram?

Instagram, like many of today's social media platforms, offers businesses big and small the incredible opportunities to reach both massive audiences as well as the targeted audience to connect with them, engage them, and ultimately, convert them into customers. Instagram is a simplified version of Facebook albeit much more visual. It's all about posting photos and videos only.

However, the more and more brands join Instagram, the bigger the competition and the harder it is to stand out in a person's feed.

Instagram opened up its new ad feature in 2015, utilizing Facebook advertising's system. Accordingly, marketers and passive income entrepreneurs now have the ability to reach a niche segment of the population, which is currently at 800 million users and growing. Instagram ads have become an avenue for brands looking to increase their engagement and by extension, their profits, to the 500 million active users who use Instagram EVERY DAY.

Who is it for?

Are you passionate about a specific topic? Does your account acquire followers every single day and do you have plenty of traction on the content that you post from likes, shares, and follows? Are people commenting regularly on your post? Do you already own an online business? Or has a website or blog?

If you answered YES to one or more of the questions above, then you might want to think about using your Instagram platform as a source of income. In other words, you can become an Instagram influencer. You can use Instagram as a platform for affiliate marketing or use it to sell content such as hotel reviews, or sell your digital artwork or even quotes. The idea here is not to have thousands of followers but to sustain the most engaged followers. The more engaged they are, the better for your Instagram Marketing.

How much money can you potentially earn?

While the figures you earn depends on the extent of the marketing you do on your Instagram profile, a survey conducted among 5,000 Instagram influencers showed that 42 percent of them were charged $200 to $400 per post. Brands want to engage or do business with people who have a following that is engaged, so they can know if your audience is engaged with you or the concentration of engagement you have by looking at your analytics.

How does Instagram Marketing work?

- Define Your Target Audience: Who are you aiming to target through this platform? If you've already got a good idea of the kind of demographic you're going after, a good strategy to employ would be to start customer profiling. This will give you a better sense of what kind of content your target is after, the sort of hashtags they use and even what communities they are involved in on Instagram. Think of this stage as your due diligence. The more information and details you can gather to create your customer persona, the more definitive your advertising strategy will be.

- Define Your Objectives: The first question you should ask is what does your business hope to achieve by advertising on Instagram? What can you do on Instagram that you cannot with other social media platforms? How does this platform integrate with your other social media platforms and marketing strategy? Ideally, your objectives should try to increase brand awareness among your target audience, showcase your brand and company culture, shine the spotlight on your products and services (and why they're different), increase audience engagement and inspire brand loyalty. Your objectives should also seek to build a community that is more engaged, connect your brand with both audiences and influencers, increase sales by driving traffic to your site, and more. Your objectives will be the ones to help you navigate and decide on the next course of action.

- Use Your Hashtags Strategically. Before every post is sent out, ask yourself how many hashtags do you think would be best? Plus, which of these hashtags is going to benefit your ad the most? Having a quick think about these questions will save you a lot of time and prevent you from blindly hashtagging every word which you may think is going to help your post. Go with popular hashtags, but not the ones which are too popular where you run the risk of being lost in the tsunami of other content. 65,000 Instagram posts were analyzed by TrackMaven. This study discovered that if you want your post to receive the highest possible engagement rate, then 9 hashtags was the way to go.

- Building Brand Awareness (Goal): To achieve this goal, the accompanying advertising increases your reach and engagement by boosting your posts. For example, you could create a business ad that is aimed at the people closest to your business vicinity and try to reach as many people as possible. Creating ads which help your audience understand the value of your brand is a good way to start increasing brand awareness, especially among new customers.

Myths about Instagram Marketing

1 - Do not use hashtags

Instagram uses hashtags to curate content specific to its audience. Users also use hashtags to find content. It works both ways. Many people say that hashtags make content messy but in this day and age, people aren't worried about hashtags simply because they've become an everyday part of life. Also, hashtags help people find, so unless you are Kim Kardashian, use the appropriate and targeted hashtags for your content.

2 - Follow everyone, so they will follow you back.

This is not entirely true. It helps that you follow people on Instagram, but this has to be the kind of people that you find their content interesting, people that you can learn from, the people who also surf the same wave you are on so you can see what they are doing. You can also follow people outside your area of interest. Whatever it is, follow them with a purpose and not randomly follow, connect, and engage with them for the sole purpose of increasing your follower account.

3 - If you have plenty of followers, you don't need to use Instagram Ads.

Instagram has a huge audience growth and every day, someone is opening a new account or connecting their business page to their Instagram. A survey conducted by Instagram assessed over 400 campaigns worldwide on ad recall, Instagram's ad recall was 2.8 times higher than that of other online advertising channels. Just because you have a high follower count does not mean that they're all entirely engaged with your content and posts. Using ads is a great way to ensure you not only engage with your existing users but it also enables you to reach out to newer target audiences. Also, unless you are Kim Kardashian, use Instagram ads.

Idea #27- Facebook Marketing

What is it?

It's 2018 and by now, you know that everywhere you look on the internet; you will be bombarded with ads. One of the biggest ways the Internet knows what you like, what your last search was on your browser, who you are friends with, what articles you clicked on, and what was your last online purchase was through Facebook. One of the biggest ads popping up everywhere you look is Facebook ads. So what are they? We see them all the time, but do we know anything about them?

Who is it for?

If you're planning to reach a wider audience, you might want to rethink and focus your marketing efforts to include Facebook as well. Facebook is another great way to spread your ideas, create ads to increase leads and sales, and also, include it into your affiliate marketing. If you're a person who loves social media platforms, you prefer marketing online and most of your audience uses Facebook, then this platform is feasible for passive marketing.

How much money can you potentially earn?

Essentially, you make money through the ads that you create on Facebook. Facebook ads can be categorized according to i) Ads and ii) Sponsored stories. For example, you sell a product for $100 through your website. Each sale you make gives you a clear profit of $100. So long as you spend less than $100 on Facebook advertising your product, you make a positive ROI. Through Facebook Ads, you can increase your sales reach to a massive crowd if you target your ads to the right people, the right market, and with the right location.

How does Facebook marketing work?

To start advertising on Facebook, you'll be required to have a Business Manager account that enables you to manage at least one Facebook Page.

Step 1 - Setting Up Your Ad Account Info

Facebook will not allow you to start spending unless there is a value payment connected and some relevant business information shared. To set up your account, click on 'Ad Account Settings' on your Business Manager.

Step 2 - Identifying your Facebook Audiences

You need to use this convenient Facebook tool called 'Audience Manager Tool' to create niche audiences and manage these different categories. This tool is found in the Business Manager application at the Audiences Tab.

Step 3 - Location and Demographics Targeting

Facebook also allows you to target people in specific locations as well as through demographics. When you click on the Demographics tab, you find even more targeting topics to refine your audience based on age, gender, and location. Refine your audience using these filters.

Step 4- Creating your ads

Here are the different types of ads that you can create with Facebook ads. There are a total of 10 different types that fall into the ad category:

- Mobile App ad
- Page post photo ad
- App ad
- Domain ad
- Page Like ad
- Page Post video ad
- Event ad
- Page Post Ads
- Page Post Link ad
- Page Post Text ad
- Offer ad

Step 4 - Reviewing your campaign performance

The Facebook Ad Manager is the easiest way to review your campaign performance. By using the ad manager, you can filter your campaigns by the dates, its objectives, and also zooming in on any campaign to see its performance based on its ad set.

Myths about Facebook Marketing

- **Facebook's algorithms will always be the same** - The rules of social media are rapidly changing so making the assumption that you cannot embrace it is your own downfall. If you want to continue passively earning an income through actively using Facebook to push sales, then you must always keep abreast of its every changing algorithm, your ever-changing audience, the evolving industry, and how your business is adapting to it.

- **Facebook marketing is always going to be free** - Since Facebook is now public, the only way it can monetize from its platform is through ads. Facebook will continue looking for ways to create its continuous river of gold, which means if you want to continue your revenue stream, you need to start reaching into your pocket even more.

Idea #28- Create a Podcast

What it is?

Podcasts are commonly known as on-demand internet radio. You can listen to a podcast on any digital device so long as it's connected to the internet. The word "podcast" is a combination of the word 'pod' and 'broadcast.'

How much money can you potentially earn?

On an average basis, you can earn a minimum of $25 a month and up to even $820 a month based on what you're podcasting as well as the through programs that offer podcasting such as through Amazon Affiliate, Patreon as well as through Sponsors.

How it works - Step-by-Step

While the steps to do a podcast are a little bit more elaborate, here is the high-level outlook to how you can start a podcast:

1. Choose a topic you can commit to.
2. Define your show description and artwork.
3. Set up and thoroughly test your equipment.
4. Create a plan for your episodes.
5. Record your episodes.
6. Edit and publish your episodes.

7. Launch your podcast to your audience.

Myths about Podcasting

- Podcasting is a niche medium - many mainstream media keep spreading the fact that podcasting is niche and has a small audience. While there is some truth in it, that podcasts have a niche audience, with the internet, more and more people are turning to on-demand networks for their source of entertainment and information. Take Netflix, for example. If Netflix is extremely popular for TV content, then podcasts are the radio version.

- If your content is good, you'll attract listeners - Your listeners need more than just good content. For your podcasts to work, you need to ensure that content, style, and production all work in tandem so you can produce quality audio material. Content is key but delivering it in a quality way is also essential.

- Finding podcasts is hard - You've probably seen tabs on your favorite streaming channels that have 'Podcasts' shown. The truth is, it's now much easier to find and listen to podcasts than ever before especially with the majority of content available via mobile devices. Services such as Netflix, Spotify as well as iTunes, all have features where you can listen to podcasts.

Idea #29 - Buy an Existing Online Business

What it is?

Online business or e-commerce is a platform for buying and selling services and products over the Internet. An online business can encompass the following business models:

- Online shopping

- Business-to-business buying and selling

- Online financial exchanges for trading and forex

- Business-to-business (B2B) electronic data interchange

If you're interested in building a passive income via online businesses, it's best that you start with buying over existing sites than to start one on your own. Many successful individuals that are into online businesses generate a huge part of the revenue stream from purchasing and owning multiple businesses at one time. Not to discourage you from starting your own website, but like any business, it'll take time before it starts to generate cash and become profitable. As such, the next alternative is to buy an existing business that is for sale.

Who is it for?

It needs to be pointed out that buying an existing online business doesn't guarantee that you will make money right of the get-go. Just like an investment, it does take some effort and time to maintain and grow the business before you start seeing profits. As such, if you possess these criteria, then you should definitely consider dwelling into this type of passive income stream:

- Someone who is interested in developing and growing the business.

- Someone who has experience operating and growing online businesses and knows what it takes to keep them sustainable.

- Someone with a high-risk tolerance looking for a challenging project.

- Someone who has the money and energy to invest in buying and operating an existing online business.

- Someone who knows how to evaluate an existing business' strengths and weaknesses

How much money can you potentially earn?

In 2017, online businesses were reportedly just made up about 9% of the total retail sales in the U.S, but it is projected to reach about $414 billion by the end of 2018. In general, the best way to generate income from online business platforms is by the use of advertisements. Some businesses have been known to grow and generate revenue from $1,000 per month to $2,000 per months. Some have even gone up to $5,000 per month, but this will generally depend on the size of the community and traffic going into the said website.

How it works - Step-by-Step

If you're keen on purchasing an existing online business to diversify your income stream, you'll need to establish some key parameters on what you need to look out for and what would fit you and your goals. Here are some points that you should be exploring:

Product: Determine the type of product or service that you would be interested in and source for businesses that sell these kinds of items.

Market Niche: Going for a product that is a niche or serves a particular segment would definitely be a benefit to your business.

Be Industry Specific: Try to leverage your experience for a given market or industry. It could be something you have previously worked on or even a hobby you are passionate about.

Business Size: Try to source for a business that already has an existing customer base, employees, and distribution locations.

Profit and Income Generated: You may also want to seek businesses that are already generating healthy profits that are in line with your objectives and goals.

Healthy Customer Base: Always locate businesses that have a large and more importantly growing customer base.

Myths about online business

Before you dive into buying an online business, it's best to take a look at the most common myths or misconceptions associated with it:

- Work part-time to make a full-time income - Like any new business; the start usually will require a large amount of time and hard work to get it going and to generate revenue. It takes time to grow a business and create a sustainable income.

- It's easy with social media - The social media platforms have provided online businesses with an opportunity to reach out to a wider audience. But with any marketing strategy, it is important that any marketing campaign done to promote your business needs to target your intended market and demographics.

- Starting an online business is free - Unfortunately, this is only half-truth. While starting an online business or buying on is relatively easier than your traditional business, it still requires some capital investment to buy the business and maintain it.

Idea #30- Franchise a Business

What it is?

A franchise is, in simple terms, a licensing relationship. A company like Baskins or Starbucks usually operates this way by licensing its brand and operating systems to interested individuals. As such, the company gives you the rights to sell their products; in turn, you agree to pay certain a percentage of fees upfront and follow their conditions and guidelines. Examples of franchises are:

- Petrol kiosks

- Fast food restaurants

- Coffee houses

Who is it for?

A franchise business based on a passive income stream can suit most people, but it depends primarily on the individual on how long and often one wants to invest the time and effort into it. As such, one can balance his or her lifestyle and commitments to suit the needs of the franchise system. For example, one passive income franchise known as Xpresso Delight has over 150 franchisees and the operators are anywhere between 20 to 60 years of age.

How much money can you potentially earn?

The question of how much money can be potentially earned from a franchise business will roughly depend on the particular franchise's industry. As such, here is a list of various franchises to denote their required investment and their respective net-worth:

7-Eleven

Description: Convenience store

Type of Business: Brick and mortar

Minimum Investment Required: $34,550

Net-worth Requirement: $100,000

Franchise Fee: $10,000

Royalty Fee: none, profit sharing

Planet Fitness

Description: Gym and fitness facility focusing on occasional or first-time gym users

Type of Business: Brick and mortar

Minimum Investment Required: $728,000

Net-worth   Requirement: $3,000,000
Franchise Fee: $10,000

Royalty Fee: 5%

Two Men and a Truck

Description: Local packing and moving company

Type of Business: In-home service

Minimum Investment Required: $178,000

Net-worth Requirement: $350,000

Franchise Fee: $50,000

Royalty Fee: 6%

The Learning Experience

Description: Education-based childcare services

Type of Business: Brick and mortar

Minimum Investment Required: $495,299

Net-worth Requirement: $500,000

Franchise Fee: $60,000

Royalty Fee: 7%

How it works - Step-by-Step

Anyone looking to generate passive income via a franchise is definitely seeking a work-life balance as the main criteria. As such, there are two major prerequisites when deciding on what type of franchise you should enter.

You'll first need to identify a business that allows you to work from home, or in other words, use your home as an office space. This will allow you to spend more time with your family and doing the things you like instead of commuting from one place to another. Next, you would want to look out for a business that allows flexibility in terms of the hours that you put into it. This will enable you to balance time between other commitments and allow for greater efficiency into the schedule.

Myths

There are a number of misconceptions regarding owning a franchise. As such, here are some of the myths usually associated with it:

- You'll only be successful with the right business – Never limit yourself to what you're only good at. Explore various opportunities that require the same skill set or learn new ones to make your business successful.

- I need to quit my day job – Many current franchise systems provide flexibility in the work time arrangements. Also, many franchise owners are more passive than full-time investors.

- I'm unable to afford a franchise – Some franchises can be bought for anything less than $100,000 and some can go for as little as $10,000. You just need to conduct in-depth research and planning to find one that fits your commitments.

Idea #31- Rent out your clothes

What is it?

Apart from evening gowns and tuxedos, many people are now looking to even rent everyday wear instead of splashing money on clothes that they would otherwise wear only once in their lifetime. As such, if you have items in your closet just hanging around, you might want to consider renting them out instead of putting them in the trash. What used to be a taboo is currently becoming a trend, especially among women. Here are a few websites that allow you to rent out your clothes:

- StyleLend: They have specific brands they accept.
- RentezVous: Currently in beta, mostly available in London and Paris.

Who is it for?

Basically, if you have any pieces of clothing that you are not going to use or even those that have been in your closet for a number of years, you can start to rent them out. And it can also be extended to other accessories such as purses, heels, and any other types of attires.

How much money can you potentially earn?

There isn't much available data on the market about the profitability of clothes sharing platforms. But one popular site indicated how those who rent out their clothes and accessories cap the rental between 5-10% of the retail price for that item. So, your income stream will depend on two factors which are:

- How many items you have listed
- How often those items get rented

So, getting more items into your list will be a plus point to increase the rental likelihood. Also, having a wide array of outfits to fit many different sizes will also help.

How It Works - Step-by-Step

Stylelend.com is one website that provides a platform for online clothing rental to the general public. Once you're registered with them and it's approved, you can begin to list your items on there. Should anyone be interested in renting your piece of clothing, you will be notified of it, and then you'll need to prepare it for shipping. For Stylelend.com, it's vital to know that you can only list items of clothing under designer brands and not clothing from companies like Zara, H&M, and TopShop.

Myths

There are a number of misconceptions regarding clothing rental. As such, here are some of the myths usually associated with it:

- Options are usually out of season – Most platforms constantly update their collection to ensure it's within the season and not out of style.

- Dry-Cleaning – Most platforms ensure that the garments are dry-cleaned before they reach you, so you only need to ensure that there's no damage to the condition of the clothing upon return.

Idea #32- Develop WordPress Themes

What is it?

For WordPress, a theme is a group of templates that are used to enhance an appearance and general outlook of a WordPress website. It can be changed to suit the intended style of the user, whenever needed. WordPress.org has a huge database of these themes in their directory. Each theme has a specific layout, feature, and design. You can then select one that fits your website from these directories. Since there's a market for various types of WordPress themes, many developers have found a way to generate income by selling WordPress themes.

Who is it for?

You may think that since WordPress is a web-based platform that only expert web developers can create and market their unique themes; however, it may come as a surprise that creating WordPress themes aren't limited to those with web design knowledge. Creating a WordPress theme that suits your specific requirements is relatively straightforward. And it doesn't require a lot of technical knowledge or experience with web development.

How much money can you potentially earn?

ThemeForest is a platform designed for selling WordPress themes, and in 2008, they recorded around $280,000 worth of transactions just on WordPress themes alone. According to Vivek Nanda, a creator of PaySketch, developers are making around $200-300K per year on selling WordPress themes. But he also warned there are many who don't even make any income from the themes they have designed.

How it works - Step-by-Step

The amount of revenue you generate from your WordPress theme will depend based on the category of your theme, your competitors, and how effectively you market your themes. Therefore, here are some key essentials when starting on this venture:

- Have a good product – Always work towards having a theme that offers a feature that no one else or performs better than your competitor. Being unique and able to meet the requirements of the intended recipient is a sure-fire way to get ahead of the game.

- Affordable Pricing – Having a theme that's too expensive will drive away would-be buyers, as such; it is advisable that you begin by pricing your themes around $20-$30 as a start. This will, in turn, attract more customers to your themes.

- Marketing Plan – You need to spend a good amount of time to ensure that your product reaches its intended customer base. Get a blog running, advertise your product on your social media account, and also, it will be advantageous if you can start a website to promote your themes.

- Ensure continuous support and updates – Always ensure that you provide your customers with constant tech support and updates. This will provide repeat sales and make you stand out from your competition.

Myths

There are a number of misconceptions regarding WordPress. As such, here are some of the myths usually associated with it:

- WordPress isn't a blogging tool. It's a website builder that is used by more than 31% of websites on the Internet.

- WordPress is not secure. In contrary, it is very secure; hence, its popularity among developers.

- It doesn't support E-Commerce. WordPress has many plug-ins that provide E-Commerce functionality.

Idea #33- Launch a Webinar

What it is?

A webinar is online seminars that are crafted to teach or disseminate information around a specific topic. Most webinars are around 30 to 40 minutes and are viewed by those wanting to learn, see a demo about a product, see new feature or updates, gather tips and hacks as well as best practices. Webinars are also a perfect way to introduce yourself to your audience.

Who is it for?

Webinars are great for people who have something to share. Are you a lecturer and you want to share your content or your teaching materials to students not in your location? Are you a teacher with plenty of online content and you'd like to help students learn without coming to you physically?

Are you a mental coach or a business coach with a target audience wanting to hear your secrets of success? Or are you an industry expert who has plenty of business ideas to share? All of these make you a perfect candidate to launch a webinar. Basically, as long as you have information and content to share, you can use a webinar to launch yourself to your audience.

How much money can you potentially earn?

You can make money by getting people to pay before attending your webinar or if it's a free webinar, which is what most people offer, you have to offer a paid product or service at the end. Your audience can then purchase your product or service and also take back the lessons they have learned.

If you promote your webinar properly, disseminated your information to your audience in a proficient way, and your attendees have learned well from you, then they'll definitely purchase your product on the spot.

At the very least, you should be charging your audience $100 per person because it takes about $100 to produce a webinar and pay for other costs of set up.

How to launch a webinar?

There are several paid and free hosting sites available for you to consider and depending on what site you choose, there will be some form of technical assistance or step-by-step guide to help you create and launch your webinar. Below is a more synthesized version that can give you an idea of what it takes to launch a webinar:

1. Settle on a specific topic
2. Pick the right webinar format for your content
3. Plan your SEO and promotion strategies to inform your audience
4. Consider time zones
5. Create clear, persuasive, and directional slides
6. Test your signal, audio, and video equipment
7. Run a test webinar days ahead and few hours ahead
8. Write a strong script
9. Prep your recording area suitable with the topic
10. Don't forget to hit record!

11. Have an official hashtag

Myths about Launching a Webinar

- I just need to build a webinar and people will come!

  Attracting the relevant audience is by far the biggest challenge of your webinar. People will come to your webinar if your topic is genuine and it aims to educate and inform prospects or solve an issue or even help them to achieve better results in a specific topic. If your content is a 'nice to have,' chances are your prospective audience will ignore your email or even unsubscribe   from   it.

- I'm great at doing presentations, I'll just wing it!

  The virtual world is vastly different from that of the real, in-person one. And one of the major issues faced in webinars is connectivity issues with regards to internet connectivity, audio, and visual connectivity as well. When people find it hard to hear you, they'll tend to leave. If there are awkward silences or dead air, people will leave. You must use the tech tools efficiently and your slides need to be more directional than the ones you use in live presentations.

- Your audience is ready to buy

  Plenty of buyers do their research first before even attending a webinar. This is an unrealistic expectation and when it does not happen, there's a severe disappointment. Many of the people who register for your webinar are in various stages of buying, and most of them are looking for more information and just want to be educated. They're less likely to purchase a product from you by the end of your webinar. So, your main goal here is to ensure that the right information is given to your audience who came to find out more, not to buy more.

Idea #34- Give Fashion & Product Reviews

What it is?

With online platforms available to anyone who wants to create a profile, it's given people a new channel to voice out their opinions, give feedback, and seek answers. People are quick to channel their happiness as well as grievances with a brand on social media. Love a recent hotel you stayed in? Let's review them on TripAdvisor. Don't like the service at the Italian restaurant down your street? Let's review them on Yelp. Checking to see if a certain brand of vacuum cleaner works as advertised? Check Amazon reviews.

Reviews are a major source of information for plenty of people to judge whether a product or service does what it says or delivers its brands' promises which is why blogs and websites such as AliExpress, Amazon, and Ulta have a review section on their sites.

But what if you want more personal answers? Well, some people have turned to review fashion and beauty product on their own social media platforms and managed to amass a huge following of fans who want to hear and see what they have to say. Giving fashion and beauty product reviews are a lucrative passive income stream because there's a guaranteed following already.

Who is it for?

It's for anyone who is purveyors of fashion and beauty products who knows what works and what doesn't. If you love anything fashion and beauty and you see yourself purchasing a fair bit of products, you can definitely start giving your reviews as well. Users of today prefer hearing first-hand reviews of products to signify better credibility and greater transparency of a product or service.

How much money can you potentially earn?

On an average basis, you can sign up as testers and reviewers at places such as FameBit or CrowdTap or even Modern Mom where you can see yourself earning about $50 to $75 for the reviews you make. Some people have even gone to their own social media channels to make videos to inform their audience what they think of a product. As their audience grows, brands take notice and request for their own products to be reviewed. The reviewer can then charge them a certain sum for the number of views the video receives.

How it works - Step-by-Step

So, how do you get started on writing reviews? If you're not a fan of increasing your audience on social media, you can start creating your foundations as a reviewer on sites that pay you for writing reviews.

- Firstly, you can check out sites such as SwagBucks, Inbox Dollars, or Vindale Research.

- Next, you need to open an account with them. Follow the steps to sign up and provide the necessary verification information. Each site will have different verification as well as a rewards system. Swagbucks, for instance, provides its members with free gift cards and cash for daily things that they already do online.

- Depending on the reward criteria, you need to shop online or watch videos, or search the web, or answer surveys to redeem your points.

- When you've collected enough points, you can redeem these points as gift cards with online merchants such as Walmart or Amazon. You can also opt to get Cashback from PayPal.

Idea #35- Help Someone Learn a Language through Skype

What it is?

Skype is the latest communication tool that provides the ability to make video chats and voice calls between computers, tablets, and mobile devices over the Internet. Due to this technological advancement, there has been a huge growth in teaching language over the Internet. Plus, this opens up a limitless border as you can engage individuals from different continents and increase your revenue stream. Apart from that, Skype is also cheaper, more accessible, and it can be done from the comfort of your home.

Who is it for?

Well, if you're already proficient in a language or two, you're good to go. All you need now is a laptop and an Internet connection.

How much money can you potentially earn?

LiveLingua.com, a language tutoring website that uses Skype, charges $20 - $25 per hour based on the type of language course taken. Hence, the logic here will be to get as many students as you possibly can to generate higher revenue of income.

How does it work?

Here is a look at the various steps that you need to take in order to dwell into the teaching language online:

- Decide if you're going to teach in your mother tongue or another foreign language where you also possess proficiency.

- Know your purpose. Is it to make more money or connect with other language learners or to challenge yourself in new ventures? This will ensure that you are always motivated.

- You may want to begin your online tutoring journey by offering free classes as a start to build your base and confidence.

- Ensure that you use all avenues at your disposal to market yourself and your services. Use social media, blog, or websites to promote your language classes.

- Once you start getting more students, it's important that you build a lesson plan or syllabuses for your students. Have practice lessons that your students can work on in their free time.

Myths about Teaching through Skype

There are a number of misconceptions regarding online language tutoring. As such, here are some of the typical myths usually associated with it:

- Learning a language is difficult – Learning and teaching a new language isn't difficult. It just takes time.

- You have to live in the country that language is spoken – If you have a laptop and Internet connection, you can learn any language from the comfort of your home.

- Only children can learn a new language – Not true. Adults can also pick up a new language as long as the desire is there.

- Language can only be taught in a classroom environment – Once again, if this was true, then many courses that prestigious universities offer online will have to be closed down. As long as the course content is structured and organized, with well-planned tutorials and exercises, anyone can teach a language.

Conclusion

Based on the new economy, merged with the Internet, we have numerous ways to earn an income. Passive income is a great way to earn extra money to pay our bills, make ends meet, and even fund our travels with little input on our end. You also don't need to quit your day job to do so because most passive income stream explained in this book is ideal to be conducted on an online basis.

What's even better is that you can use whatever skills you already pose to kick-start a passive income stream or use the many different platforms that enable you to make money such as through self-publishing, affiliate marketing, and even Cashback rewards.

Although the premise of passive income is to contribute as little effort as possible to bring in your income, you still need to exert your time and a considerable amount of work to build up the foundations, so that you can reap your passive income later.

The business ideas listed in this book enable you to start generating passive income fairly quickly, but take note that none are get-rich-quick schemes.

With time, effort, and maybe a little bit of monetary investment, your passive income business will earn you a pretty good amount of money over time.

Thank you

Before you go, I just wanted to say thank you for purchasing my book.

You could have picked from dozens of other books on the same topic but you took a chance and chose this one.

So, a HUGE thanks to you for getting this book and for reading all the way to the end.

Now I wanted to ask you for a small favor. **Could you please consider posting a review on the platform? Reviews are one of the easiest ways to support the work of independent authors.**

This feedback will help me continue to write the type of books that will help you get the results you want. So if you enjoyed it, please let me know!

Lastly, don't forget to grab a copy of your Free Bonuses *"The Fastest Way to Make Money with Affiliate Marketing"* and *"Top 10 Affiliate Offers to Promote".*

Just go to the link below.

https://theartofmastery.com/chandler-free-gift

Printed in Great Britain
by Amazon